CLIMATE CHANGE AND CLIMATE FINANCE
CURRENT EXPERIENCE AND FUTURE DIRECTIONS

Edited by Fariborz Moshirian and Cyn-Young Park

SEPTEMBER 2023

ASIAN DEVELOPMENT BANK

ADB

© 2023 Asian Development Bank
6 ADB Avenue, Mandaluyong City, 1550 Metro Manila, Philippines
Tel +63 2 8632 4444; Fax +63 2 8636 2444
www.adb.org

Some rights reserved. Published in 2023.

ISBN 978-92-9270-308-0 (print); 978-92-9270-309-7 (electronic); 978-92-9270-310-3 (ebook)
Publication Stock No. TCS230333-2
DOI: http://dx.doi.org/10.22617/TCS230333-2

The views expressed in this publication are those of the authors and do not necessarily reflect the views and policies of the Asian Development Bank (ADB) or its Board of Governors or the governments they represent.

ADB does not guarantee the accuracy of the data included in this publication and accepts no responsibility for any consequence of their use. The mention of specific companies or products of manufacturers does not imply that they are endorsed or recommended by ADB in preference to others of a similar nature that are not mentioned.

By making any designation of or reference to a particular territory or geographic area, or by using the term "country" in this publication, ADB does not intend to make any judgments as to the legal or other status of any territory or area.

Please contact pubsmarketing@adb.org if you have questions or comments with respect to content, or if you wish to obtain copyright permission for your intended use that does not fall within these terms, or for permission to use the ADB logo.

Corrigenda to ADB publications may be found at http://www.adb.org/publications/corrigenda.

Notes:
In this publication, "$" refers to United States dollars.
ADB recognizes "America" as the United States; "China" as the People's Republic of China; and "Hongkong" and "Hong Kong" as Hong Kong, China.

Cover design by Francis Manio.

On the cover: A woman installing solar panels on the roof in Bhutan, Astana bridge over the Ishim River, and Khandke wind power project photos from ADB's Flickr account; mangrove seedlings and Shatin urban development (housing) project photos by Ariel Javellana; and a handshake photo by Mark Floro.

Contents

Tables and Figures

Figures

Foreword

Reaching ambitious global climate goals demands accelerated climate action through strong commitment and coordinated effort from the public and private sectors that will produce a clearer and more credible path forward.

As such, global climate leaders are *now* urging real world solutions to guide economies to a net zero future. This is obviously a tall order that requires deep analysis, stakeholder dialogue, and detailed planning at all levels of society—especially with policymakers, business leaders, and investors.

This volume scrutinizes issues related to the corporate sector's green investment that contributes to the knowledge base that enables us to maximize private sector engagement to mobilize resources, harness skills and technology, and deliver innovative climate solutions. To do so, businesses must consider environmental, social, and governance (ESG) impact to be an important factor that might influence corporate value.

Despite the catalytic role that businesses can play for the change we need, current corporate and market incentives may not be fully aligned with a corporate sector transformation across finance, industry, and technology for climate change mitigation and adaptation. Without significant top–down pressure from corporate leaders and investors, it may be difficult to scale up investment and innovative solutions.

Proliferating ESG investment, for example, may have raised the profile of climate change objectives in the corporate world and can accelerate the energy transition. But closer scrutiny may reveal unclear benefits to shareholders and raise allegations of "greenwashing" due to a lack of consistency and reliability.

Yet adroit handling of climate change issues—under the corporate social responsibility banner—can help expand shareholder value and ensure that company shareholders are on board. They in turn can help steer corporate actions more effectively and ensure corporate decisions are in fact socially responsible and not mere virtue signaling, or worse, socially *irresponsible*. The evidence suggests that shareholder "voice" is important in shaping effective firm response to climate change issues.

The book explores each of these issues—corporate responsibility, shareholder rights and values, greenwashing, and sustainable capital markets—through several detailed and informative chapters.

Meanwhile, the far-reaching economic impacts of climate change and environmental degradation have significant implications for financial stability and sustainable growth. The final chapters of the volume thus look at the important role that central banks, standard setters, policymakers, and regulators must play in safeguarding financial stability against climate risks and supporting green investment.

I am confident that this book—drawn from the insights and evidence of an impressive roster of experts from different fields—will shed important light on the issues that all business leaders, investors, and policymakers need to consider if we are to walk the talk and bring substance to our aspirations for a stable climate and sustainable economies.

Albert Park
Chief Economist and Director General
Economic Research and Development Impact Department
Asian Development Bank

Acknowledgments

This book was prepared by the Regional Cooperation and Integration Division (ERCI) of the Economic Research and Development Impact Department (ERDI) of the Asian Development Bank (ADB), in collaboration with the Institute of Global Finance (IGF), University of New South Wales. It was supported by the ADB technical assistance project, Building Financial Resilience and Stability to Reinvigorate Growth (TA 6592), financed by the Investment Climate Facilitation Fund under the Regional Cooperation and Integration Financing Partnership Facility, the People's Republic of China Poverty Reduction and Regional Cooperation Fund, the Republic of Korea e-Asia and Knowledge Partnership Fund, and ADB's technical assistance special fund.

Contributions from the authors who permitted the use of their material and also updated information are gratefully appreciated. They are Searat Ali, Serena Alim, John (Jianqiu) Bai, Suman Banerjee, Millicent Chang, Yongqiang Chu, Rebel Cole, Guanming He, Mark Humphery-Jenner, David Javakhadze, Jonathan Kearns, Vina Javed Khan, Sehoon Kim, Nitish Kumar, Jongsub Lee, Zhichao Li, Fariborz Moshirian, Vikram Nanda, Junho Oh, Anna Park, Cyn-Young Park, Ramkishen S. Rajan, Bethany Rodgers, Chen Shen, Yilin Shi, Richard Slack, Greg Tindall, Chi Wan, Jing Wu, Yu Zhang, and Zijun Zhao.

Rolando Avendano (economist, ERCI, ADB) and Paulo Rodelio Halili (senior economics officer, ERCI, ADB) coordinated the production of this book under the overall supervision and guidance of Jong Woo Kang (director, ERCI, ADB), with support from Marilyn Aure Parra (senior operations assistant, ERCI, ADB). Eric Van Zant edited the manuscript. Francis Manio created the cover design and Joe Mark Ganaban implemented the typesetting and layout. Tuesday Soriano proofread the report, while Joy Quitazol-Gonzalez handled the page proof checking with assistance from Carol Ongchangco (operations coordinator, ERCI, ADB) and Paulo Rodelio Halili. The Printing Services Unit of ADB's Corporate Services Department and the Publishing Team of the Department of Communications and Knowledge Management supported printing and publishing.

Editors

Fariborz Moshirian is director of the Institute of Global Finance (IGF) and an AGSM scholar at the UNSW Business School, Sydney, Australia. The IGF undertakes collaborative research on global governance, global financial stability, the role of innovation, climate change and climate finance. Fariborz was the Bertil Danielsson Professor of Finance at the Stockholm School of Economics.

Fariborz has published a number of influential research works in leading international journals, including the *Journal of Finance*, the *Journal of Financial Economics*, and the *Journal of Financial and Quantitative Analysis*.

He serves as an associate editor of a few major international journals. He has also been the editor of 15 special issues in leading journals published by Elsevier. The themes covered include global governance, global public goods, the global banking system, the global financial crisis, the global health crisis (COVID-19), globalization, global financial architectures, fintech and central bank digital currencies, Millennium Development Goals, sustainable economic growth, and global prosperity.

He has also been the coeditor of a number of policy works, in collaboration with senior researchers from the World Bank, the International Monetary Fund, the Bank for International Settlements, the Federal Reserve Bank of New York, the Bank of England, and the Reserve Bank of Australia on issues related to global financial stability, including the following publications: Globalization and Financial Services in Emerging Countries; Global Financial Crisis, Risk Analysis and Risk Management; Systemic Risk, Basel III, Global Governance and Financial Stability and Systemic Risk: Liquidity Risk, Governance and Global Financial Stability.

Cyn-Young Park is director of the Regional Cooperation and Integration (RCI) and Trade Division in the Climate Change and Sustainable Development Department of the Asian Development Bank (ADB). In her current capacity, she is responsible for managing ADB operations and knowledge on RCI and trade. She leads a team of experts to develop strategies and approaches to support RCI and to provide guidance in design and implementation of ADB RCI and trade projects. During her progressive career within ADB, she has been a main author and contributor to ADB's major publications including *Asian Development Outlook* (ADB's flagship publication), *Asian Economic Integration Report, Asia Capital Markets Monitor, Asia Economic Monitor, Asia Bond Monitor,* and *ADB Country Diagnostic Study Series.* She has also participated in various global and regional forums including the G20 Development Working Group, the Association of Southeast Asian Nations (ASEAN), ASEAN+3, Asia-Pacific Economic Cooperation (APEC), and the Asia-Europe Meeting (ASEM). She has written and lectured extensively about the Asian economy and financial markets. Her work has been published in peer reviewed academic journals including the *Journal of Banking and Finance,* the *Journal of Financial Stability,* the *Journal of Futures Markets,* the *Review of Income and Wealth,* and the *World Economy.*

Prior to joining ADB, she served as economist (1999–2002) at the Organisation for Economic Co-operation and Development (OECD), where she contributed to the OECD Economic Outlook. She received her PhD in economics from Columbia University. She holds a bachelor's degree in international economics from Seoul National University.

Authors

Searat Ali is a senior lecturer in finance at the University of Wollongong.

Serena Alim is senior manager, International Reserves at the Reserve Bank of Australia.

John (Jianqiu) Bai is an associate professor of finance at the D'Amore-McKim School of Business at Northeastern University.

Suman Banerjee is an associate professor at the School of Business, Stevens Institute of Technology.

Millicent Chang is a professor in the School of Business at the University of Wollongong.

Yongqiang Chu is director of the Childress Klein Center for Real Estate and Childress Klein, distinguished professor of real estate and urban economics and professor of finance at the University of North Carolina Charlotte Belk College of Business.

Rebel Cole is a Lynn Eminent Scholar Chaired Professor of Finance in the College of Business at Florida Atlantic University.

Guanming He is an associate professor at Durham University.

Mark Humphery-Jenner is an associate professor at the School of Banking and Finance, University of New South Wales.

David Javakhadze is a professor in the Finance Department at Florida Atlantic University.

Jonathan Kearns is chief economist and head of regulatory affairs at Challenger.

Vina Javed Khan is a PhD candidate at the University of Wollongong.

Sehoon Kim is an assistant professor of finance at the Warrington College of Business, University of Florida.

Nitish Kumar is an assistant professor of finance at the Warrington College of Business, University of Florida.

Jongsub Lee is an associate professor in the Department of Finance, SNU Business School, Seoul National University.

Zhichao Li is a lecturer (assistant professor) in finance and accounting at the University of Exeter.

Fariborz Moshirian is director of the Institute of Global Finance and an AGSM scholar at the University of New South Wales Business School.

Vikram Nanda is O.P. Jindal professor of finance at the Naveen Jindal School of Business, University of Texas at Dallas.

Junho Oh is an assistant professor of finance, Hankuk University of Foreign Studies.

Anna Park is a senior manager, Climate Analysis and Policy at the Reserve Bank of Australia.

Cyn-Young Park is director of the Regional Cooperation and Integration and Trade Division in the Climate Change and Sustainable Development Department of the Asian Development Bank.

Ramkishen S. Rajan is a Yong Pung How professor at the Lee Kuan Yew School of Public Policy, National University of Singapore.

Bethany Rodgers is a research associate at the Institute of Global Finance, University of New South Wales.

Chen Shen is an assistant professor in the Finance Department at Ontario Tech University.

Yilin Shi is a PhD student at the Chinese University of Hong Kong Business School.

Richard Slack is a professor of accounting at Durham University Business School.

Greg Tindall is an assistant professor of finance at Palm Beach Atlantic University.

Chi Wan is an assistant professor of finance at the College of Management, University of Massachusetts Boston.

Jing Wu is an associate professor in the Department of Decision Sciences and Managerial Economics, Chinese University of Hong Kong Business School.

Yu Zhang is an associate professor of finance at the Guanghua School of Management, Peking University.

Zijun Zhao is a PhD student in finance at the Wellington School of Business and Government.

Abbreviations

CEO	–	chief executive officer
CO$_2$	–	carbon dioxide
CSI	–	corporate social irresponsibility
CSR	–	corporate social responsibility
ECB	–	European Central Bank
ESG	–	environmental, social, and governance
GMI	–	green macroprudential index
IPCC	–	Intergovernmental Panel on Climate Change
OECD	–	Organisation for Economic Co-operation and Development
OLS	–	ordinary least squares
SEC	–	US Securities and Exchange Commission
SOX	–	Sarbanes-Oxley Act
US	–	United States

Introduction

Fariborz Moshirian and Cyn-Young Park

The urgency for action on climate change has captured the attention of international institutions, policymakers, regulators, and now the corporate world. Company directors, management, shareholders, and investors alike are calling for firms to do their part to shift to a carbon-neutral world economy—frequently under so-called environmental, social, and governance (ESG) frameworks.

Encouraged initially by decades of effort by climate and justice activists following the United Nations Framework Convention on Climate Change in 1992 and subsequent climate change conferences, corporate leaders were finally spurred into earnest action in the years following the Paris Agreement of 2015. More recently, authorities have called for *real* plans to reach "net zero" economies, including the Intergovernmental Panel on Climate Change (IPCC) Report in 2023, which highlighted the much greater increase in the pace of carbon emissions than they had reported earlier. The IPCC states that "we have options in all sectors to at least halve emissions by 2030." The report states that only such resolute global collective strategies and action will be able to limit global warming to 1.5°C by the early 2050s.

Some corporate leaders, however, are now calling with equal urgency for specifics on meeting global climate change goals—testament to the growing sense of commitment in the private sector—lest in the rush to achieve net zero economies, efforts and money are wasted or economies hobbled. At the same time, policymakers and regulators, including the central banks, have incorporated the impact and consequences of climate change into their overall policy mandates and operations. Policymakers and regulators are also consulting with various protagonists about the protection of the environment in their search for further clarity and more options for concrete and effective action, as firms seek ways to make real progress, while also protecting corporate interests.

In this context, this volume gathers the latest analysis on policymakers' and corporates' efforts on climate change, climate finance, and ESG. It identifies prominent areas of interest, of concern, and of success, to give firms and policymakers additional guidance as they look to build more effective and resilient strategies and action plans for the immediate years ahead. Opportunities abound, but so do potential pitfalls, meaning that greater transparency and information sharing will assist efforts to ensure that those opportunities are utilized effectively.

Climate Justice and Corporate Social Responsibility

Chapter 2 begins by laying down some historical context in which the corporate sector is now entering the picture. Bethany Rodgers examines the case for action that climate change activists have built up over decades of campaigning for the interests of the less powerful players in global economies. Rather than focusing on corporate interest, the climate justice movement views climate change from the perspective of justice, fairness, and equity. It holds that people in poverty and the otherwise less powerful have fewer financial and other resources to give them resilience when climate change disrupts their lives and livelihoods. While, effectively, they are excluded from decision-making about the environment and about national and global environmental policy, the way forward must consider the needs of everyone equitably.

Chapter 3 takes a hard look at ESG and the *real* responsibilities of corporate managers as they advance through the emerging and sometimes unclear lines unfolding around these new practices. Mark Humphery-Jenner asks a fundamental question for those responsible for corporate interests, which is whether and when directors should consider environmental impact. Indeed, do their duties allow it? Companies must comply with environmental planning laws, for example, but should they act when *not* legally compelled? Deviation from duties, even if deemed "moral" or "ethical," could see a director fined, sued, or fired.

With this corporate context in hand, in **Chapter 4**, Yilin Shi, Jing Wu, and Yu Zhang examine the true behavior of corporate disclosure about their social responsibility, as growing charges of "greenwashing" raise doubts about the sincerity of some actions so far. Assuming that corporations and other firms have in fact gone ahead with ESG efforts, public companies should forge strong relationships with environmentally responsible suppliers. However, evidence shows that public companies not only voluntarily disclose their relationships with environmentally responsible ("good") suppliers, but they also selectively choose not to disclose their relationships with "bad" suppliers. This chapter zooms in on corporate social responsibility in the "deep and complex" yet often overlooked supply chains of firms—a vital measure of performance.

Chapter 5 expounds on the coexistence of corporate social responsibility (CSR) and corporate social irresponsibility (CSI) by providing evidence from real cases and studies that demonstrate this relationship. Guanming He, Zhichao Li, and Richard Slack discuss the economic consequences of CSR and CSI and argue that their economic impacts differ, meaning that they should not be treated as opposite ends of the same continuum. Given that regulations and legislation relating to CSI (through "punishment") are better established than those of CSR (through "reward"), policymakers emphasize better regulations and legislation for CSR.

Environmental, Social, and Governance Performance and Corporate Decisions

The shareholder perspective is also an important one. In Chapter 6, Greg Tindall, Rebel Cole, and David Javakhadze note that shareholder proposals at company annual meetings have helped mitigate climate change by applying pressure on management to innovate. Shareholder proposal pressure "helps firms focus," argues the chapter, and innovation, not disclosure, should be the focus of firm policies to avoid the "best lighting" and "word-smithing" that characterizes greenwashing. The chapter takes up a suggestion from earlier research—that showed that climate-related proposals at meetings has spurred climate mitigating technologies—and explores the policy implications of its findings.

What are some of the ways in which firms deal with the long-term, severe, yet often unpredictable consequences of climate change? As John (Jianqiu) Bai, Yongqiang Chu, Chen Shen, and Chi Wan note in Chapter 7, some companies have demonstrated that firms can diversify away from one long-run climate risk—that of rising sea levels—through mergers and acquisitions. Businesses with commercial properties or operations in low-lying coastal areas might find it increasingly difficult to ensure their assets' safety as seas rise, yet it is a challenge to forecast such a rise. The chapter argues that firms exposed to significant sea level rise therefore diversify away from such risks by acquiring firms unlikely to be affected and that this action is rewarded by the market. The information environment in the acquiring firms improves as they diversify away from forecast uncertainty, that is, the risk of rising sea levels. The chapter also suggests that the combined firms' ESG scores should improve post-merger.

Chapter 8 takes up the issue of ESG performance from the perspective of corporate social responsibility beyond the interest of shareholders. In 2019, 222 CEOs of the largest companies in the United States (US) signed the "Statement on the Purpose of Corporation" and committed to lead their companies in the best interests of *all* stakeholders: employees, customers, suppliers, and shareholders, thus disregarding shareholder supremacy. This stakeholder view presumes to account for the "externalities" of company activities. Vina Javed Khan, Searat Ali, and Millicent Chang examine whether ESG activities do undermine investor interests in practice. It takes a contemporary risk-taking perspective on ESG to examine whether ESG activities affect downside and upside risk differently.

Environmental, Social, and Governance Considerations in Corporate Investment

Chapter 9 considers how investors should evaluate ESG in the context of their portfolios. Mark Humphery-Jenner, Suman Banerjee, and Vikram Nanda argue that facts about pollution issues can be unclear, competence in industry can be lacking, and a "cottage industry of courses" on the environmental subject are prone to hyperbolic language. This can leave CEOs and other interested parties with a general distrust of "ESG experts" which complicates investor choices. The chapter looks at ESG indexes and their problems and what investors must do about ESG factors within a portfolio. It also considers what officers and directors are obligated to do.

The investment side of ESG considerations is clearly important. Estimates suggest that "sustainable" investing has surged in the US, commanding about $15 trillion under management as of 2022, up nearly tenfold in 10 years, as Jongsub Lee, Sehoon Kim, Nitish Kumar, and Junho Oh note in Chapter 10. This has spurred inquiry into the forces driving the demand, with one fitting financial or economic explanation being that it reflects widespread concern among investors that a poor ESG profile may pose an important risk.

An alternative explanatory view is that investors derive nonfinancial utility when they reflect their environmental and social preferences in their investments, and extensive research in recent years has extensively studied these issues in *public capital markets*, such as publicly listed stocks or bonds. Yet, *private capital markets* represent a much larger segment of corporate financing, being as much as twice that of public capital markets in the amount of investments in 2020. The chapter examines sustainable investing from recent developments in private capital markets, what challenges may lie ahead, and how policymakers can help to overcome these challenges.

The Role and Contributions of Policymakers

The final three chapters examine climate policy by central banks and financial regulators. Chapters 11 and 12 analytically review climate change impact on economies, investors, shareholders, and the most vulnerable, and discuss how central banks should take up such risks in their monetary policy and financial regulations. Chapter 13 delves into the role of standard-setters, and regulators in this regard.

The far-reaching economic impacts of climate change and environmental degradation have significant implications for financial stability and the profitability of commercial enterprises. As such, central banks are increasingly stepping up efforts to account for climatic risks in their operations and analysis. Chapter 11 discusses the role of central banks in combating climate change and its associated effects on macrofinancial stability. Ramkishen S. Rajan and Cyn-Young Park argue that central banks and financial regulators should assume the role of mitigating the impact of climate-related financial risks on financial stability more prominently. The adoption of green prudential policies should aim at both nudging investors toward investing in green technologies and mitigating climate risks by steering investors away from brown investments.

Chapter 12 takes note of the broad and pervasive effects of climate change on economies, financial markets, and investor tolerance for risk. Jonathan Kearns, Anna Park, and Serena Alim point out that central banks are increasingly turning their attention to climate change as they chart the course of monetary policy. These effects occur through the impact of climate change on the economy and market participants' risk tolerance. Central banks have taken action by expanding analysis and their response to these developments.

Finally, in Chapter 13, Zijun Zhao argues that climate risk, policymakers, standard-setters, and regulators need to be more active in their efforts to combat climate change and stabilize the financial system. The chapter surveys the literature about green finance, environmental accounting, management of climate risk disclosure, and green technology innovation to provide more clarity about the policy implications of enhancing information transparency and facilitating green innovation. In so doing, she sheds light on the role that policymakers and regulators can play in these areas.

Fariborz Moshirian
Director, Institute of Global Finance
UNSW Business School
University of New South Wales
Sydney, Australia

Cyn-Young Park
Director
Regional Cooperation and Integration
and Trade Division
Climate Change and Sustainable
Development Department
Asian Development Bank

Climate Justice

Bethany Rodgers

2.1 Introduction

The climate justice movement views climate change through a lens of justice, fairness, and equity. It sees it as unfair that the negative impacts of rising global temperatures fall disproportionately on certain people and others less. This unfairness arises because of a purported divide between *responsibility* and *impact*: the people least responsible for the most severe effects of climate change are most negatively impacted by rising global temperatures.

These are often people who face existing social and political discrimination, like people in poverty, indigenous people, women, children, and people with disabilities. These people often have fewer financial and other resources; resources critical in developing the resilience necessary to cope with disasters triggered by natural hazards or adapt when rising sea temperatures change their food supply chains (Carbon Brief 2021). Key to climate justice is inclusivity in decision-making: including those hurt most by climate change in decision-making about the environment and helping to design environmental policy; a struggle to achieve with status quo approaches to date (Newell et al. 2021). In focusing on social justice, climate justice advocates seek to uphold the rights of marginalized groups of such people; improving their resilience to climate change-associated events like disasters, and ensuring the benefits of a clean environment, like access to safe drinking water, are equitably shared (Carbon Brief 2021).

Rising global temperatures

Climate change is among the most important issues of our generation. Without a safe environment, many other human rights and freedoms cannot be fulfilled, such as access to health care, education, housing, and to affordable and nutritious food. Greenhouse gas emissions have continued to rise over the past 3 decades (and in the century before then), despite clear evidence that greenhouse gas emissions are increasing global temperatures. Total net human-generated greenhouse gas emissions rose 12% from 2010 and 2019 and by 54% when compared to 1994, as per the Intergovernmental Panel on Climate Change 2022 report (IPCC 2022, 6) (Figure 2.1).

Figure 2.1: Major Anthropogenic Greenhouse Gas Emissions Continue to Rise Globally

Global net anthropogenic GHG emissions 1990–2019

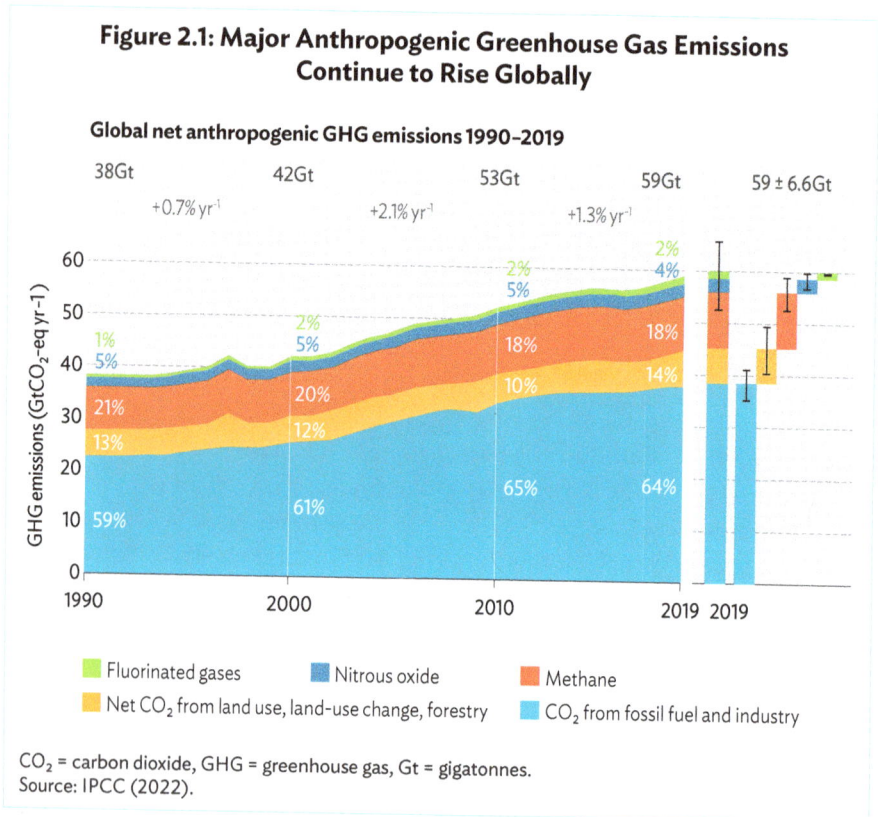

CO_2 = carbon dioxide, GHG = greenhouse gas, Gt = gigatonnes.
Source: IPCC (2022).

Certain regions will be particularly vulnerable to rising temperatures, including Australia, the Pacific, and Southeast Asia. Low-lying and small, economically developing nations in the Pacific are at particular risk. Tuvalu, an island of 12,000 people, is predicted to be fully submerged by the end of the 21st century. Already, 40% of the capital district lies underwater at high tide (Needham 2022). Wildfires are expected to increase significantly in frequency and intensity, a burgeoning issue in Australia, where fires have been catastrophic for human and animal populations, particularly in the summers of 2019 and 2020. Droughts, powerful storms, and heat waves each threaten people's health and safety further. An estimated 85% of the global population have already experienced extreme weather events (UNEP 2022). Some 3 billion to 3.6 billion people live in contexts highly vulnerable to climate change.[1] From 2010 to 2020, droughts, floods, and storms killed 15 times more people in highly vulnerable countries, such as in Africa, Asia, and small island states, than in the richest countries (IPCC 2022). By 2030, around 700 million people will be at risk of displacement by drought (footnote 1).

2.2 The Climate Justice Concept

Climate justice as a concept emerged following the strengths of the environmental justice movement of the 1980s (Dietz, Shwom, and Whitley 2020). Climate justice advocates in many ways are inspired by, and building upon, the principled success of the environmental justice movement. Environmental justice focused on fairly distributing environmental goods (such as safe food, water, and outdoor recreation areas) and ills (like landfill, radioactivity from nuclear testing, or from large-scale chemical manufacturing negatively affecting human health). Environmental justice advocates like Robert Bullard (1994) (the "father" of environmental justice) began drawing attention to the intersection between social and environmental issues. Bullard, for example, analyzed "environmental racism"; arguing environmental issues disproportionately harm racial minorities. His research pointed to examples like the fact that, in the 1970s, all garbage incinerators in Houston, Texas were in communities with majority African American or Latino residents.

---

[1] United Nations Sustainable Development Goals. Goal 13: Take Urgent Action to Combat Climate Change and Its Impacts. https://www.un.org/sustainabledevelopment/climate-change/ (accessed 8 February 2023).

The term climate justice was coined in 1989 (Newell et al. 2021, 3) and popularized in the 1990s (Carbon Brief 2021). It arose largely out of activism in the economically developing world, where climate injustices often amplify existing social inequalities (Carbon Brief 2021). The underlying themes of climate justice became a key issue in the last decade of the 20th century. Civil society groups began mobilizing around the issue of "climate debts," which they refer to as the debts or reparations that wealthier nations owe poorer nations for the environmental damage they had caused; in other words, an early iteration of the underlying themes of climate justice (Newell et al. 2021, 4–5).

Climate justice brings human rights and social inequality into the conversation surrounding climate action. Included within the remit of climate justice are a range of social justice issues: environmental protection, indigenous rights, human rights, and the rights of other living creatures. The negative effects of human activities on the natural environment are discussed through a social lens, focusing on how often those least powerful live in less safe and thriving natural environments. France's nuclear test explosions in the 20th century in remote Australia, the Marshall Islands, the central Pacific, and French Polynesia, for example, caused persistent radioactive contamination and community displacement (Ruff 2015).

Rather than simply a scientific or technical endeavor, advocates of climate justice focus on what is just or "right." They believe those large corporations and wealthier nations which have financially benefited from the burning of fossil fuels ought to redistribute wealth toward those who must now deal with the consequences of changing climates (Carbon Brief 2021). Climate change is described as a "triple injustice": the people least responsible for carbon emissions are most vulnerable to its impacts, but also most likely to be further disadvantaged by responses to climate change (Newell et al. 2021, 3).

Industrialized nations have historically faced minimal restrictions on burning of fossil fuels (Carbon Brief 2021), and have, historically and into the present day, burned the most. In Figure 2.2, one can see that North America and Europe rank highest in anthropogenic carbon dioxide emissions. Per capita, North America still ranks highest, but Australia, Japan, and New Zealand join the ranks in emissions, seen in Figure 2.3.

Figure 2.2: Cumulative Net Anthropogenic Carbon Dioxide Emissions per Region from 1850 to 2019

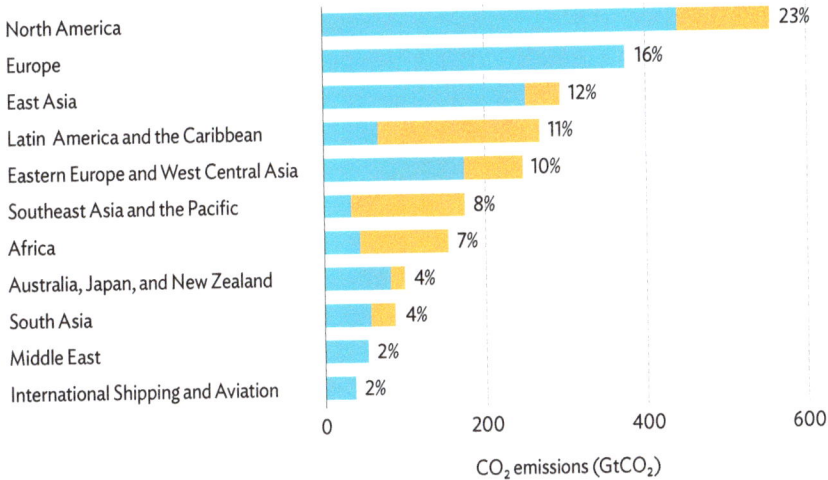

Region	Percentage
North America	23%
Europe	16%
East Asia	12%
Latin America and the Caribbean	11%
Eastern Europe and West Central Asia	10%
Southeast Asia and the Pacific	8%
Africa	7%
Australia, Japan, and New Zealand	4%
South Asia	4%
Middle East	2%
International Shipping and Aviation	2%

CO_2 emissions (GtCO$_2$): 0, 200, 400, 600

CO_2 = carbon dioxide, Gt = gigatonnes.
Source: Derived from IPCC (2022, 10).

Thus, arises a disconnect between who is most responsible for climate change and who is most impacted by climate change, with the most responsible, on average, being the least negatively impacted. The impacts of global warming are not equally felt throughout the world—"most affected people and areas" is a term used to describe this phenomenon (Carbon Brief 2021).

Climate justice centers on these people impacted most—now and into the future; those who are currently, and projected to be in future, most likely to experience extreme weather events, like floods, droughts, and typhoons (hurricanes). The approach links human rights and development, focusing on the differential consequences of climate change between the Global North (economically developed nations), and the Global South (economically developing nations), which continue to face huge difficulties with poverty-related issues, like famine and inadequate access to health care. Poorer nations are more often exposed to very high temperatures, have agriculturally reliant economies, and risk-management approaches like air-conditioning and insurance are less available (Levy and Patz 2015, 312).

Figure 2.3: Cumulative Net Anthropogenic Greenhouse Gas Emissions per Capita and for Total Population, per Region, 2019

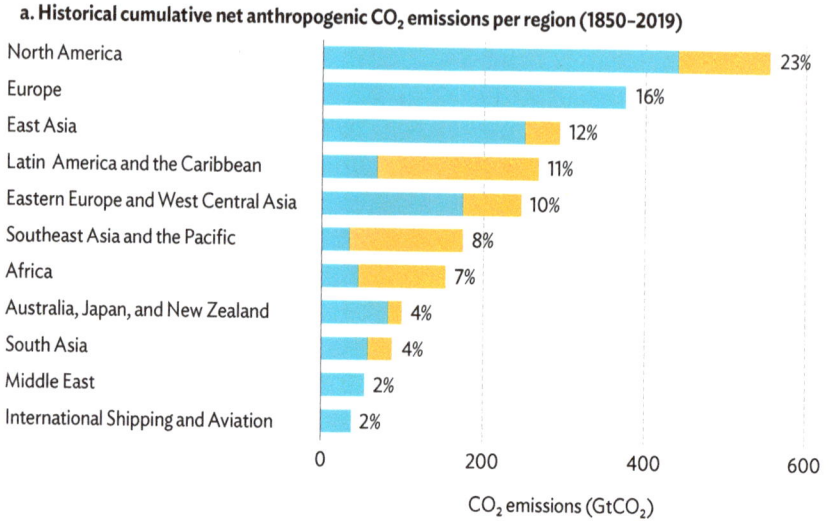

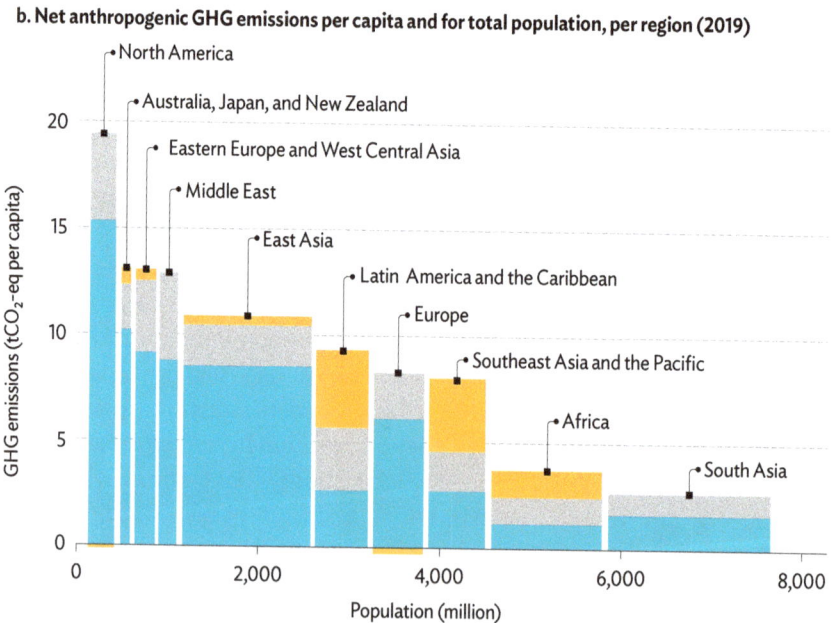

a. Historical cumulative net anthropogenic CO_2 emissions per region (1850–2019)

Region	%
North America	23%
Europe	16%
East Asia	12%
Latin America and the Caribbean	11%
Eastern Europe and West Central Asia	10%
Southeast Asia and the Pacific	8%
Africa	7%
Australia, Japan, and New Zealand	4%
South Asia	4%
Middle East	2%
International Shipping and Aviation	2%

CO_2 emissions (GtCO_2)

b. Net anthropogenic GHG emissions per capita and for total population, per region (2019)

GHG emissions (tCO_2-eq per capita)

Population (million)

Regions labeled: North America; Australia, Japan, and New Zealand; Eastern Europe and West Central Asia; Middle East; East Asia; Latin America and the Caribbean; Europe; Southeast Asia and the Pacific; Africa; South Asia

CO_2 = carbon dioxide, GHG = greenhouse gas, Gt = gigatonnes, tCO_2-eq = tons of CO_2 equivalent.
Source: Derived from IPCC (2022, 10).

Climate justice calls for industrialized countries—those its advocates say are most responsible for halting the warming of the planet—to help other countries adapt to climate change and develop economically with nonpolluting technologies. Stopping greenhouse gas emissions is not enough to repay the debt; addressing the consequences of these actions on vulnerable people is also a vital step in achieving justice (MIT Climate Portal n.d.). A related concept here is transformative justice. Transforming power is key to advancing climate justice; also crucial is equalizing social and institutional relations, which will help in designing sustainable, effective, and socially acceptable responses to climate change (Newell et al. 2021, 2).[2]

2.2.1   Four Pillars of Climate Justice

Newell et al. (2021) describe four pillars of climate justice: procedural, distributive, recognition, and intergenerational justice.

Procedural climate justice

Procedural climate justice relates to how authorities make decisions about the climate and climate change impacts—the process of decision-making. It promotes fair, accountable, and transparent decision-making through methods like allowing all parties access to relevant information when designing environmental policy and ensuring legal redress is available when environmental damage occurs and harms manifest (Newell et al. 2021, 4). Rather than tokenism, this pillar of climate justice promotes meaningful participation. One technique toward achieving procedural justice is ensuring free, prior, and informed consent from local communities affected by land acquisitions for plantation agriculture or communities participating in forestry projects. Informed consent is promoted as a response to injustices that can arise when large, powerful interests like multinational corporations have the authority to decide whether forests and forest lands should be exploited or protected. In such cases, motivated by profit, corporations generally win out over local communities and financially benefit from the exploitation. Such conflicts have manifested in many countries, as diverse as Uganda, Mexico, Bolivia, and multiple Southeast Asian nations (Newell et al. 2021, 4–5; Cariño and Colchester 2010).

---

2   Transforming power is at the heart of calls for "transformative climate justice." It is about disrupting dominant power relations and shifting institutional decision-making processes to address root causes of the climate crisis, helping ensure a just transition while allowing communities to adapt to climate change's existing impacts. For a useful explanation, see Newell et al. 2020.

Distributive climate justice

Distributive climate justice relates to the allocation of the costs and benefits of social goods on the one hand, and social ills on the other (Newell et al. 2021, 5). The distribution of these ills is discussed spatially, meaning throughout different geographic areas, and temporally, meaning into the past, present, and future.

A prime example of the unfair spatial distribution of social goods and ills was seen in the above discussion of how richer nations are historically (and to the present day) responsible for most greenhouse gas emissions, yet poorer nations disproportionately experience the most negative effects from rising global temperatures. Rising sea levels threatening small, low-lying nations in the Pacific or poor rural communities in low-lying areas of Bangladesh are examples. Record-breaking floods in June 2022 impacted about 7.2 million people in northeastern Bangladesh. The region faced the highest rainfall in decades (IFRC 2022). The country is already burdened by poverty-related issues, like inadequate access to clean and safe drinking water and food.

Solutions to climate change can also impact communities differently. When floods are dealt with by building flood defenses only in one or a few high-risk areas, for example, other high-risk communities downstream of the defenses face greater flood risk and are more impacted when floods manifest (Newell et al. 2021, 5; Eriksen et al. 2011, 11–13). It is vital that responses to flooding are multifaceted, effectively protecting people and communities from disparate geographic areas without worsening the risk for others.

Flooding is a significant future issue of distributive climate justice. Tellman et al. (2021) analyzed 12,719 Moderate Resolution Imaging Spectroradiometer, or MODIS images (a form of satellite imagery) from 2000 to 2018. They produced 913 flood maps, and found that, globally, 2.23 million square kilometers of land is at risk of flooding, putting an estimated 255 million to 290 million people at risk of direct impact by floods.

The uneven distribution of climate change's impacts on women is another burgeoning problem. Speaking at a population level, women have less access to financial and other resources than men and, as a result, have less capacity to navigate the negative consequences of climate change (Newell et al. 2021, 5), such as recovering and receiving adequate access to food, shelter, and health care after a disaster. This is particularly true of women with marginalized identities such as "lower" caste or social class (Newell et al. 2021, 5). Poorer women often have less ability to cope with and adapt to a changing environment (Terry 2009, 5–18).

Also crucial within distributive justice is considering those who have reaped the most financial, social, and cultural benefits from exploiting the natural environment, while others have not benefited from this wealth. A significant, but sometimes neglected factor causing climate change is companies, particularly those that extract fossil fuels for profit (Wright 2022). Richard Heede, the Director of the Climate Accountability Institute, collected data showing that just 90 companies were responsible for two-thirds of all greenhouse gases emitted between 1751 and 2016. Over half of those emissions occurred in the last 45 years, or since 1988 (Kenner and Heede 2021). The Great Barrier Reef, a 344,400 square kilometer World Heritage Area, has lost half its corals since 1995 (BBC News 2020), due to a combination of overfishing, farm pollution, and industrialization in the form of port expansion on nearby coastlines (WWF Australia n.d.). Profit-generating activities in the region have also had deleterious impacts on marine wildlife.

Recognition justice

Recognition justice, while encompassing procedural and distributional justice principles, focuses particularly on recognizing difference. Recognition justice seeks to acknowledge and inclusively address the way that people from marginalized groups who are socially or politically discriminated against, are included in conversations surrounding climate policy. The views of these groups, like the views of people in poverty or indigenous people, ought to be fairly and accurately represented, and reflected in designing climate policy and practice, without these people facing reprisal. Both the understanding of difference and the protection of equal rights is given emphasis in this aspect of climate justice (Newell et al. 2021, 6).

In many indigenous cultures, the environment is integral to cultural and spiritual practices. The climate justice movement seeks to include and advocate for the views and rights of indigenous people and the land they occupy (Newell 2021, 9). Rights for nature, for example, involve giving formal legal rights to the natural environment, in much the same way individual people have rights, and has taken hold all over the world, from North and

South America to Asia. These approaches accept the intrinsic value of nature. The rights of "mother nature" have been written into the Bolivian constitution (Newell et al. 2021, 10).

In a well-recognized example, Māori people, the indigenous people of Aotearoa (New Zealand), have been given ownership of parts of New Zealand's land and waterways. The Treaty of Waitangi, signed in 1840, is the country's founding document, entered by Māori chiefs and British officials wherein Māori ceded rights to land and the British were allowed to form government (New Zealand History n.d.).

In 1975, the Treaty of Waitangi Act was passed, formally implementing the principles under the treaty. Many of the policies passed since this date reflect principles associated with climate justice. The 290-kilometer-long Whanganui River, in New Zealand's North Island, which is of great significance in indigenous culture, became in 2017 the first river in the world to be recognized as a legal person after a long-running court case. The waterway has been significant for at least 880 years, relied on by indigenous people for travel and sustenance. That the Whanganui River is recognized as a legal person means that harm to the river generates legal rights. The river itself can litigate to address harms resulting from pollution or other unauthorized activities, providing a means to protect the river (The Guardian 2019; Evans 2020), and an innovative legal framework in which to implement climate justice (Newell et al. 2021, 10–11).

Intergenerational justice

In line with the concept of intergenerational justice, current generations should have a right to meet their needs, but this should occur without compromising the ability of future generations to do so. Intergenerational justice is central to the globally renowned Fridays for Future campaign, which drew significant international attention to the issue of climate justice. It is also crucial in many indigenous communities' views of environmental ethics. It is positioned as unfair that current generations of people are entitled to make decisions about the environment that lead to pollution and other environmental degradation, and benefit financially, socially, or practically from these actions.

The Fridays for the Future campaign evolved from the protest of 15-year-old Greta Thunberg, outside the Swedish Parliament every Friday with a sign saying *Skolstrejk för klimatet* (school strike for climate). From there, thanks in large part to social media, the one-person protest evolved into a global school climate strike movement, with people protesting on every continent. Over 100,000 people turned out in several cities, such as Berlin and New York City (The New York Times 2019). This movement focused on the unfairness of climate change's impact on children and future generations.

The World Bank has estimated that by the time these teenage climate activists are in their late 20s, climate change could put an additional 100 million people into extreme poverty (Carbon Brief 2021). Climate change is causing intergenerational inequity, with young and future generations bearing the brunt of individual and social harms arising from rising temperatures globally. The key unfairness here is that future generations will not be able to pollute in the same way and will instead be left with a damaged environment that they are not responsible for creating (Newell et al. 2021, 6). Implementing these values is an increasingly popular approach to decision-making by governments all over the world. For example, future generations have been represented in decision-making in parliaments in Finland, Chile, Hungary, and Wales. Another method of implementing the rights of future generations is using Ombudsmen that represent future generations to guide decision-making (Newell et al. 2021, 6).

Latest developments in achieving climate justice

Addressing climate change is a major issue internationally. The United Nations Sustainable Development Goals, a wide set of goals aiming to promote the basic rights of the world's most vulnerable, explicitly mention climate change as key to sustainable development. Goal 13, "Climate Action," seeks to "take urgent action to combat climate change and its impacts." Within this goal, there are targets related to strengthening "resilience and adaptative capacity to climate-related hazards," improving "human and institutional capacity" for climate change mitigation, adaptation, impact reduction and early warning, and raising capacity for "effective climate-change related planning and management in least developed countries and small island developing states, including focusing on women, youth, and local and marginalized communities" (footnote 1).

The primary international environmental agreement is the United Nations Framework Convention on Climate Change, in effect since June 1994. It is a joint cooperative of 197 nations, and thus an initiative of almost every nation. The signatory nations to the Framework Convention on Climate Change participate in the Conference of the Parties (COP), meetings of participating countries to discuss environmental issues and plan programs, policies, and agreements.

In 2015, the COP negotiated the Paris Agreement (UNFCCC 2015), a groundbreaking international agreement wherein countries, through article 2, aim to keep the increase in global temperatures to "well below" 2.0 degrees Celsius (°C) above pre-industrial levels, and "pursu[e] efforts" to limit the temperature increase to 1.5°C above pre-industrial levels (UNFCCC 2015, art. 2). This was a significant diplomatic achievement. Climate change is a hotly contested political issue, but all states present at COP signed the Agreement (Kenfack 2022).

Under the Paris Agreement, signatory countries pledge nationally determined contributions (UNFCCC 2015, art. 3). This is a more universal approach than previous international environmental agreements. The Kyoto Agreement, for example, involved top-down, legally binding requirements for countries to reduce emissions. the Paris Agreement involves bottom-up decisions by each nation, a more cooperative method of addressing climate change. Climate change and adaptation to the effects of climate change, as well as preventing the issue getting worse, are viewed as a globally shared challenge. The responsibility is not just with the policies of individual governments, but as an issue through which many stakeholders should cooperate and address together to improve outcomes for all.

Like the Sustainable Development Goals, the Paris Agreement makes special mention of "least developed countries and small island nations" (UNFCCC 2015, art. 4), in recognition of the significant challenges these nations already face, and will continue to face, because of climate change. In line with this focus on international equality, developed nations who signed the Paris Agreement agreed to mobilize $100 million annually, together, to fund climate action in developing nations (UNFCCC 2015). This is known as climate finance—international funding to support climate action in developing countries.[3] In 2018, the climate finance provided and mobilized by these

---

[3]   Oxfam Australia. Climate Justice. https://www.oxfam.org.au/what-we-do/climate-justice/.

developed countries totaled $78.3 billion, and $79.6 billion by 2019 (footnote 1). While a success, these figures are far below the estimated $1.6 trillion to $3.8 trillion needed each year through to 2050 for the world to transition to a low-carbon future and avoid warming the planet more than 1.5°C above pre-industrial levels (footnote 1).

Responsibility in the Paris Agreement lies with everyone, and a particular focus is on those who have been more responsible for climate change. Through the lens of distributive justice, this means investors and corporations are also responsible for achieving climate justice. Climate change is a reality that global financial markets are already grappling with.

One way this occurs is through investor awareness of climate litigation risks. Climate litigation can force financial institutions to abandon assets—if a judge orders a project halt due to risks to the natural environment, the project will have extremely limited returns (Pearce 2021). This has been a key theme in several court cases in Australia recently, a nation economically reliant on fossil fuel extraction (Wright et al. 2022). Reference has been made to Australia being a signatory to the Paris Agreement in domestic courts. Shareholders in the Commonwealth Bank of Australia, for example, sought disclosure from internal bank documents about whether certain projects complied with the goals of the Paris Agreement. Australia's Federal Court ordered shareholders be given access to documents on the basis that the projects may infringe the company's social and environmental policies.[4]

After COP21, the agreement shifted from a global aim to limit the rise in temperatures not to 2°C but rather to only 1.5°C. This was done considering increasingly strong scientific evidence that 1.5°C warmer was not a safe temperature for humanity to live at (Harvey 2022).

A range of developments have occurred at subsequent COP meetings. In 2016, at COP22, Germany presented its plan to reduce greenhouse gas emissions by 80% to 95% by 2050—the first nation to have an ambitious, long-term climate strategy. COP23, COP24, and COP25 each discussed the Paris Rulebook (World Resources Institute n.d.), which executes the Paris Agreement, dictating how countries measure and report on their greenhouse gas emissions. This Paris Rulebook was agreed-upon at COP26

---

4   Abrahams v Commonwealth Bank of Australia, No. NSD864/2021 (Federal Court of Australia 2021).

of November 2021, rescheduled from 2020 due to the COVID-19 pandemic. Nations at COP26 also agreed to end "inefficient" fossil fuel subsidies and move away from coal (Climate Partner 2022).

In late 2022, at the meeting of the parties to the UNFCCC in Sharm el-Sheikh, Egypt (COP27), the focus was on more substantial and speedier efforts toward mitigation and adaptation to the effects of climate change. Some nations wanted to remove the 1.5°C warming target, while others criticized "weak" language surrounding the obligations to phase out fossil fuels (Harvey 2022).

Climate finance and compensation for loss and damage were on the agenda (footnote 3). A significant focus was financial assistance for developing countries for loss and damage. Many argued for the need to help poorer nations rebuild physical and social infrastructure damaged by extreme weather events over the past 3 decades. At the summit's conclusion, attending nations agreed to create such a fund, but could not reach agreement on the means of creating such a fund, and exactly where such money will come from (Harvey 2022).

Tasks like these, and the implementation of climate justice policies like the fund to help developing nations cope with climate change are key issues of the next 12 months and beyond. Focus is expected to be on richer nations submitting more ambitious nationally determined contributions, pledging to take greater action to reduce their greenhouse gas emissions and to agree to offer more financial assistance to poorer nations (footnote 3). Some hope international agreements will become more binding in their language and thus impose greater legal obligations on countries to transition away from fossil fuels. A recognized limitation of the Paris Agreement is that to achieve consensus among nations, some of the language is nonbinding by nature (Sun et al. 2022).

The picture is not all grim—achieving climate justice and reducing the current and future impact of climate change are on the global agenda like never before. As a result of individual and collective action, momentum for change is building. A growing grassroots movement is pushing for the protection of the natural environment. It is not just the school strike for climate campaign, there is increasing consumer demand for goods that are environmentally sustainable and ethically produced (leading to increased supply of such products by many companies, including major multinational companies). Even large oil companies, like BP and Shell, are making commitments to reduce their environmental impact. Both these companies, in 2020, made similar commitments to become net zero by 2050, with market pressures forcing this decision, including national climate policy and public opinion (Kenner and Heede 2021).

Legal action like the disclosure orders against the Commonwealth Bank of Australia mentioned above are also becoming an increasingly popular method of climate action. Through the courts, individuals, nongovernment organizations, and other groups are increasingly asserting their rights to a safe and habitable environment, and sometimes having significant success doing so. In the United States, lawsuits in the 5 years since 2017 have been launched against Exxon Mobil, Royal Dutch Shell, BP, Chevron, Peabody Energy, and other major energy companies. These have sought compensation, with the aim of using that money to adapt to the impacts of climate change, like building seawalls in California to cope with rising sea levels, or combating wildfires, floods, agricultural losses, and heat waves in Colorado (Jarvis n.d.).

The involvement of affected communities in designing and implementing solutions to climate-related issues will be vital in achieving climate justice. Developing bottom-up policies in consultation with those who are affected by policies, like local communities, businesses, schools, and charities, will mean that these policies receive broad-based support into the future, increasing the legitimacy of climate justice responses. In designing a more environmentally sustainable future, just transitions will be important. A just transition seeks to ensure that the transition away from greenhouse gas emitting activities occurs fairly, without disproportionately harming those from poorer communities and worsening preexisting inequalities (Newell et al. 2021, 10). Inclusion of, and consideration toward those most affected by climate change, in the past, present, and into the future, in the global discussion on climate change, is critical for achieving climate justice.

2.3 Conclusion

Climate justice takes issues of environmental sustainability and raises important questions related to fairness and equity. The climate justice movement is seeking to ensure that climate change does not undo the immense progress toward improving people's well-being and basic living standards in recent decades.

The climate justice movement's four pillars—procedural, distributive, recognition, and intergenerational justice—seek to ensure those most impacted by extreme weather events are resilient enough to recover when their livelihoods are impacted by droughts, floods, heat waves, and other disasters.

Notable progress has been made on climate justice in recent years. The Paris Agreement was a significant diplomatic achievement, providing a foundation from which the world can cooperate to equitably address the existing consequences of climate change and try preventing this issue from escalating. Climate change will remain a complex policy issue for generations to come. Climate justice can help ensure solutions to climate change are targeted toward areas and populations where help is most needed, like ensuring adequate climate finance for those in developing countries.

References

BBC News. 2020. Great Barrier Reef Has Lost Half of Its Corals since 1995. 14 October. https://www.bbc.com/news/world-australia-54533971.

Bullard, R. 1994. Environmental Racism and Invisible Communities. *West Virginia Law Review*. 96 (4). pp. 1037–1050.

Carbon Brief. 2021. In-Depth Q&A: What Is 'Climate Justice'? 4 October. https://www.carbonbrief.org/in-depth-qa-what-is-climate-justice/.

Cariño, J. and M. Colchester. 2010. From Dams to Development Justice: Progress with 'Free, Prior and Informed Consent' Since the World Commission on Dams. *Water Alternatives*. 3 (2). pp. 423–437.

Climate Partner. 2022. From Pledges to Binding Commitments – A Review of Key Milestones in Previous COP Conferences. https://www.climatepartner.com/en/climate-action-insights/complete-review-of-key-milestones-from-previous-cop-conferences.

Dietz, T., R. L. Shwom, and C. T. Whitley. 2020. Climate Change and Society. *Annual Review of Sociology*. 46 (1). pp. 135–158.

Eriksen, S., P. Aldunce, C. S. Bahinipati, R. D'Almeida Martins, J. I. Molefe, C. Nhemachena, and K. O'Brien. 2011. When Not Every Response to Climate Change Is a Good One: Identifying Principles for Sustainable Adaptation. *Climate and Development*. 3 (1). pp. 7–20. https://doi.org/10.3763/cdev.2010.0060.

Evans, K. 2020. The New Zealand River That Became a Legal Person. *BBC Travel*. 21 March. https://www.bbc.com/travel/article/20200319-the-new-zealand-river-that-became-a-legal-person.

The Guardian. 2019. Saving the Whanganui: Can Personhood Rescue a River? 29 November. https://www.theguardian.com/world/2019/nov/30/saving-the-whanganui-can-personhood-rescue-a-river.

Harvey, F. 2022. What Are the Key Outcomes of Cop27 Climate Summit? *The Guardian*. 20 November. https://www.theguardian.com/environment/2022/nov/20/cop27-climate-summit-egypt-key-outcomes.

Intergovernmental Panel on Climate Change (IPCC). 2022. Summary for Policy Makers. https://www.ipcc.ch/report/ar6/wg3/downloads/report/IPCC_AR6_WGIII_SummaryForPolicymakers.pdf.

International Federation of Red Cross and Red Crescent Societies (IFRC). 2022. Millions in Bangladesh Impacted by One of the Worst Floodings Ever Seen. IFRC Press release. 28 June. https://www.ifrc.org/press-release/millions-bangladesh-impacted-one-worst-floodings-ever-seen.

Jarvis, B. n.d. Climate Change Could Destroy His Home in Peru. So He Sued an Energy Company in Germany. *The New York Times.* 9 April.

Kenfack, C. E. 2022. The Paris Agreement Revisited: Diplomatic Triumphalism or Denial of Climate Justice? *Journal of Environmental Protection.* 13 (2). pp. 183–203. https://doi.org/10.4236/jep.2022.132012.

Kenner, D. and R. Heede. 2021. White Knights, or Horsemen of the Apocalypse? Prospects for Big Oil to Align Emissions with a 1.5°C Pathway. *Energy Research & Social Science.* 79 (12). 102049. https://doi.org/10.1016/j.erss.2021.102049.

Levy, B. S. and J. A. Patz. 2015. Climate Change, Human Rights, and Social Justice. *Annals of Global Health.* 81 (3). pp. 310–322. http://dx.doi.org/10.1016/j.aogh.2015.08.008.

MIT Climate Portal. n.d. Climate Justice. https://climate.mit.edu/explainers/climate-justice.

Needham, K. 2022. Tuvalu, Sinking in the Pacific, Fears Becoming a Superpower 'Pawn.' *Reuters.* 13 May. https://www.reuters.com/world/asia-pacific/tuvalu-sinking-pacific-fears-becoming-superpower-pawn-2022-05-13/.

The New York Times. 2019. Protesting Climate Change, Young People Take to Streets in a Global Strike. 20 September.

New Zealand History. n.d. The Treaty in Brief: Treaty FAQs. https://nzhistory.govt.nz/politics/treaty/treaty-faqs.

Newell, P., S. Srivastava, L. O. Naess, G. A. Torres Contreras, and R. Price. 2020. Moving Towards Transformative Climate Justice: What Needs to Be Done?. *Global Dev Blog*. https://www.globaldev.blog/blog/moving-towards-transformative-climate-justice-what-needs-be-done (accessed 27 March 2023).

_____. 2021. Toward Transformative Climate Justice: An Emerging Research Agenda. *WIREs Climate Change*. 12 (6). e733. https://doi.org/10.1002/wcc.733.

Pearce, P. 2021. Duty to Address Climate Change Litigation Risks for Australian Energy Companies—Policy and Governance Issues. *Energies*. 14 (23). p. 7838. https://doi.org/10.3390/en14237838.

Ruff, T. A. 2015. The Humanitarian Impact and Implications of Nuclear Test Explosions in the Pacific Region. *International Review of the Red Cross*. 97 (899). pp. 775–813. https://doi.org/10.1017/S1816383116000163.

Sun, R., X. Gao, L. Deng, and C. Wang. 2022. Is the Paris Rulebook Sufficient for Effective Implementation of Paris Agreement? *Advances in Climate Change Research*. 13 (4). pp. 600–611. https://doi.org/10.1016/j.accre.2022.05.003.

Tellman, B., J. A. Sullivan, C. Kuhn, A. J. Kettner, C. S. Doyle, G. R. Brakenridge, T. A. Erickson, and D. A. Slayback. 2021. Satellite Imaging Reveals Increased Proportion of Population Exposed to Floods. *Nature*. 596 (7870). pp. 80–86. https://doi.org/10.1038/s41586-021-03695-w.

Terry, G. 2009. No Climate Justice without Gender Justice: An Overview of the Issues. *Gender & Development*. 17 (1). pp. 5–18. https://doi.org/10.1080/13552070802696839.

United Nations Environment Programme (UNEP). 2022. Australia: After the Bushfires Came the Floods. 17 March. http://www.unep.org/news-and-stories/story/australia-after-bushfires-came-floods.

United Nations Framework Convention on Climate Change (UNFCCC). 2015. Paris Agreement. https://unfccc.int/sites/default/files/english_paris_agreement.pdf.

World Resources Institute. n.d. Navigating the Paris Rulebook. https://www.wri.org/paris-rulebook.

Wright, C., R. Irwin, D. Nyberg, and V. Bowden. 2022. 'We're in the Coal Business': Maintaining Fossil Fuel Hegemony in the Face of Climate Change. *Journal of Industrial Relations*. 64 (2). pp. 544–563.

WWF Australia. n.d. Great Barrier Reef. https://www.wwf.org.au/what-we-do/oceans/great-barrier-reef/great-barrier-reef.

Do Directors Have a Duty to Consider Social and Environmental Impact?

Mark Humphery-Jenner

3.1 Introduction

Environmental, social, and governance (ESG) principles have proliferated in the investing world. Numerous indexes have emerged to capture whether firms sufficiently adhere to ESG doctrines.[1] The most controversial parts of ESG pertain to social and environmental impact. This has attracted significant investor attention, a high profile example being the campaign to prevent energy company AGL from demerging.[2]

But from a corporate governance perspective, the fundamental question is whether, and when, officers and directors should consider environmental impact: more specifically, whether—and when—directors, duties allow directors to consider impact.

Myriad "impact" funds and special interest groups have pushed for corporations to consider ESG factors. Likewise, myriad laws can influence whether, and when, officers and directors should consider environmental impact. Many of those laws are industry- or location-specific. These include environmental planning laws and laws governing pollution. Companies should comply with these lest they suffer legal consequences. However, the more pertinent question is whether officers and directors can, or should, consider environmental impact even when not legally compelled to do so.

---

1 See Berg, Kölbel, and Rigobon (2019).
2 For example, see Keep It Together Australia. Grok Ventures. Grok Investment Memo. https://www.keepittogetheraustralia.com.au/ (accessed 25 September 2022).

This chapter focuses on whether directors' duties allow those officers and directors to consider environmental impact. Notably, they must comply with directors' duties. These are not optional. Officers and directors cannot deviate from their duties even if they believe it is "moral" or "ethical." If they do, they could be fined, sued, or banned as a director.

There are three overarching types of duty here:[3] (i) the obligation to exercise care and diligence; (ii) the requirement to act in good faith, in the company's best interests, and for a proper purpose; and (iii) the prohibition on using one's position (or information gained from it) for improper personal benefit or in detriment to the corporation. These duties also interface with firms' and managers' disclosure requirements. The duties and legal obligations inform what officers and directors should do. The exact nature of these duties varies by jurisdiction.

The duties can permit and encourage directors to consider social and environmental impact, but only when it is relevant to the corporation. In this respect, social and environmental impact are much like any other consideration: officers and directors must consider how they influence the firm's cash flows, risk, and cost of capital. Reputational considerations are relevant if they influence the firm's operations. And compliance with legal obligations is always relevant and necessary.

This implies that officers and directors can pursue environmental or social impact only if its impact on shareholders is not negative. Officers and directors may not consider impact merely as the "right thing to do," as noted. They should resist outside pressure groups that promote specific causes to the detriment of shareholders. After all, their duties are to shareholders as a whole, not to a specific shareholder or group. Directors must also be honest with investors about the precise "impact" of initiatives and how those will influence cash flows, risks, and access to capital. They must focus on how impact investments influence shareholder wealth and therefore on financial metrics such as access to capital, cash flows, and the risk thereof. They should honestly present the risks, costs, and payoffs.

This chapter details how impact initiatives interface with directors, duties. It considers how directors owe a duty to act in the best interests of the corporation as a whole as well as improper use of position for a personal policy

---

[3]   Corporations Act 2001 (Cth) Section 180–183.

agenda, disclosure obligations, and the requirement for accurate disclosure of "impact" activities and the financial implications.

The next section discusses "duty of care," which requires directors to consider relevant risks.

3.2 "Best-Interests" Duty and Social and Environmental Impact

Directors must act "for a proper purpose" and in the "best interests of the corporation."[4] This is a fundamental duty and is common across jurisdictions, in general. However, it is well known that "agency conflicts" exist whereby agents (i.e., managers) prefer their own interests over those of the principals (i.e., the shareholders). This can manifest in self-interested, capricious, or value-destroying investments,[5] philanthropic pet causes,[6] and shirking.[7] Shareholders acknowledge that it is impossible to eliminate agency conflicts. But they aim to structure incentive contracts to ameliorate them and will tolerate some agency costs to secure a quality CEO who otherwise creates value. But the fundamental question is whether considering impact could violate the best-interests duty.

3.2.1 Does Best-Interests Duty Allow Environmental Considerations (and When)?

Officers and directors must evaluate the financial impact of all environmental initiatives. This is because officers and directors must act "in the best interests of the corporation."[8] In doing this, they must make informed decisions, rather than decisions on a whim or a mere feeling about what they regard as "right" or "moral."[9] Thus, they must consider the interests of existing

---

4   See Corporations Act 2001 (Cth) Section 180.
5   For example, there is evidence that CEOs make value-destroying acquisitions, especially when "entrenched" and protected from outside discipline: Masulis, Wang, and Xie (2007). This is partly attributable to CEOs exercising insufficient discipline when investing, and potentially prioritizing investments they prefer that might not otherwise create shareholder wealth: Harford, Humphery-Jenner, and Powell (2012).
6   See, for example, Masulis and Reza (2015).
7   "Shirking" especially appears to be the case when managers are entrenched; and thus, where agency conflicts can be especially pronounced: Bertrand and Mullainathan (2003).
8   Corporations Act 2001 (Cth) Section 181(1)(a).
9   This follows the comments in Australian Metropolitan Life Assurance Co Ltd v Ure (1923) 33 CLR 199 at 206 per Knox CJ.

shareholders.[10] The Australian Securities and Investments Commission (ASIC) (Australia's corporations regulator) has specifically stated that directors, "primary duty is to the company's shareholders."[11] Further, this is a duty to shareholders *as a whole*, rather than to specific shareholders or to the largest or loudest shareholder.[12]

The interests of other stakeholders are relevant if they involve maximizing shareholder value. For example, before Australia's Corporations Act was passed in 2001, there had been discussion about including duties to the wider community. The New Zealand *Companies Act 1993* Section 132 contemplates considering employees' interests. Australia's legislators have considered whether directors' duties should explicitly encompass environmental issues (Senate Standing Committee on Legal and Constitutional Affairs 1989). In 1989, the Standing Committee on Legal and Constitutional Affairs noted that directors' duties encompass environmental considerations if either they have a financial impact or (potentially) are relevant to other legislation. Despite this prior consideration, the Corporations Act 2001 does not include environmental matters in directors' duties. This suggests that the legislators intended financial considerations to drive whether and when directors consider environmental impact.[13]

The government in Australia also considered amending the Corporations Act to include broader stakeholder interests. However, it has declined to do so. The Corporations and Markets Advisory Committee considered whether to amend directors' duties to include myriad concepts surrounding social responsibility (CMAC 2006). It noted that doing so would create concerns about how directors balance competing interests and would hamper accountability by rendering duties vague. The Corporations Act was subsequently amended. The Bills Digest for that amendment specifically referenced the committee report. But the amendment did not alter directors' duties (Donaldson 2010). This further suggests that legislators considered expanding directors' duties but declined to do so.

---

[10]　Pilmer v Duke Group Ltd (in liq) (2001) 207 CLR 165; [2011] HCA 31 at [18]; Greenhalgh v Arderne Cinemas Ltd [1951] Ch 286 at [291].

[11]　Australian Securities and Investments Commission (ASIC). Insolvency for Directors: Information Sheet 42. https://asic.gov.au/regulatory-resources/insolvency/insolvency-for-directors/#directors-duties.

[12]　Percival v Wright [1902] 2 Ch 421; Brunninghausen v Glavanics (1999) 46 NSWLR 538.

[13]　See CIC Insurance Ltd v Bankstown Football Club Ltd [1997] HCA 2; 141 ALR 618 at 634–5 per Brennan, CJ, Dawson, Toohey and Gummow, JJ.

3.2.2 Is Impact Relevant Then?

Officers and directors can therefore consider environmental impact if it has a commercial impact. However, they may not consider environmental impact merely because it is moral or ethical itself. Nonetheless, environmental impact can influence a corporation's finances and its stock price. The firm's value is the present value of all future cash flows, discounted at the appropriate cost of capital. Thus, if cash flows fall, or the cost of capital increases, the firm's value will decrease. Therefore, officers and directors should consider sustainability much like any other investment.[14]

The precise impact depends on the company's circumstances. Strong ESG scores are not necessarily associated with higher stock returns (Cornell 2021), and are potentially negatively related to stock returns, on average (Avramov et al. 2022). Further, if the firm relies on external ratings agencies to certify its environmental impact, there can be significant disagreement between ratings agencies and methods (Berg, Kölbel, and Rigobon 2019). This can both reduce the trustworthiness of those ratings and their ability to improve performance. Interestingly, the more disagreement there is between ESG ratings, the *higher* the stock return (Brandon, Krueger, and Schmidt 2021). Thus, there is evidence that stock returns are lower for firms with "better" ESG ratings, especially when certainty about those ratings is greater.[15]

Environmental impact can influence firms' cash flows. Harming the environment can create negative publicity, potentially harming sales. It might also violate environmental laws, triggering fines and exclusion from government contracts or prohibitions on corporate activities. Additionally, some environmentally damaging activities might have a limited time horizon. For example, coal power generators have a finite life due to regulation. Thus, when maximizing shareholder value, it is important to analyze whether environmentally damaging actions are financially sustainable.

---

[14] This follows the analysis that ESG investing is similar to other investing in that it focuses on firms' cash flows and cost of capital and, thus, their share price and expected return (Edmans 2022).

[15] Avramov et al. (2022, 19). There are different interpretations of this result. On the one hand, it might suggest that stock returns are lower when ESG scores are stronger and more certain because investors demand a lower return from these companies. Therefore, greater certainty lowers the cost of capital. On the other hand, it can also simply suggest that firms that focus on ESG indexes underperform, even after controlling for other factors that can influence returns.

Sustainability-related factors might also reduce "tail risk": the risk of extreme negative events. This is distinct from the presence of extreme environmental events: an individual company's decision to prioritize sustainability is unlikely to significantly influence extreme events *by itself*. Rather, that requires economy-wide action. However, focusing on sustainability might enable companies to reduce regulatory risk, which could cause sudden and significant cash flow impacts. This reduces the risk of extreme cash flow events. In turn, this can benefit shareholders by reducing the firm's risk level, which can reduce stock price risk.[16]

Environmental impact can affect firms' cost of capital. MSCI asserts this to be the case (Lodh 2020); however, MSCI also produces and sells an ESG score. It can especially influence interest rates on debt and evidence exists of this (Hoque, Ahmed, and Richardson 2020), albeit mainly for firms in environmentally sensitive industries (Gerwanski 2020). This effect also appears to be stronger in more "stakeholder" oriented countries (Eliwa, Aboud, and Saleh 2021). This might occur because additional media scrutiny in the ESG space chills lending to environmentally damaging companies.[17] It could also be because environmentally damaging companies face greater regulatory and financial risks. This would cause lenders to be less willing to lend to damaging companies and to charge higher rates when doing so.

Environmental disclosures and sustainability performance might make it less costly to raise equity. This could be because investors perceive sustainability to reduce cash flow risk (Ng and Rezaee 2015). However, investors also appear to incorrectly value environmental initiatives. For example, while some investors might be willing to pay more for sustainable companies, they might not accurately distinguish between "low" and "high" impact initiatives (Heeb et al. 2023). Thus, companies should be precise about the specific way in which sustainability improves access to capital when making such assertions.

The foregoing suggests that officers and directors should consider sustainability. It can have a financial impact. However, it is important to be specific about precisely why initiatives would influence the firm's cash flows or its cost of capital.

---

[16]   Evidence exists that a higher ESG rating might be related to lower stock crash risk (Giese et al. 2019). However, this is not necessarily causal in nature and could be attributable to other characteristics.

[17]   This follows the analysis of the relationship between media ESG scrutiny and the cost of debt in Gao, He, and Li (2022).

3.3 Improper Use of Position

Officers and directors must not "improperly" use their position to either "gain an advantage for themselves or someone else" or "cause a detriment' to the corporation."[18] Managers can violate this duty by merely gaining an advantage, even if that does not harm the corporation.[19] This duty can create a significant barrier to prioritizing impact at the expense of shareholder wealth. This is the case even if a set of shareholders are willing to bear the cost of that impact: officers and directors act for *shareholders as a whole*, not merely one set of shareholders. This duty is common across jurisdictions and has several impacts.

This duty prohibits officers and directors from harming the corporation (i.e., using the corporation's money) to benefit themselves. This benefit can include nonpecuniary benefits (i.e., feeling morally good about what the corporation is doing). Thus, officers and directors should not support pet causes that have no clear corporate benefit. Indeed, supporting such pet interests could be an "in kind" benefit, which in turn could be akin to improperly obtaining fees.[20]

Unfortunately, such actions are commonplace.[21] However, the cost of policing such actions often outweighs the benefit of stopping them. And shareholders might regard tolerating small acts of personal philanthropy as a "cost of doing business" with a CEO that can otherwise perform well. In this case, this means that officers and directors cannot merely support impact because they believe it is morally right: this would involve gaining an advantage for themselves while causing a monetary cost to the company.

Directors would violate their duties if they merely supported the interests of a subset of investors or prioritized those investors' views over those of other investors. As indicated above, directors owe a duty to act for shareholders as a whole. This is not a duty to the loudest shareholder, the largest single shareholder, or the most media savvy shareholder. Further, even if specific investors supported and advocated for a director's appointment,

---

18 *Corporations Act 2001* (Cth) Section 182.
19 This follows from Chew v R (1992) 173 CLR 626, where the court found that it is not necessary to show that the actions did in fact cause a detriment, as could be the case if an injunction prevented them from doing so.
20 For example, see the situation in Australian Securities and Investments Commission v Lewski (2018) 362 ALR 286. Directors used their position to generate significant fees for a responsible entity, which would benefit themselves.
21 Empirical evidence exists that many managers do support pet causes via their companies: Masulis and Reza (2015, 6).

that director must still act for shareholders as a whole. Additionally, were the director to act for one set of shareholders—at the expense of the company— they would be using their position to "gain an advantage [...] for someone" while causing a detriment to the company.

An example is the situation that energy provider AGL must consider. AGL has looked at moving toward renewable energy. In 2022, the firm aimed to demerge into two entities. However, backlash from climate-focused investors subsequently halted this. A key voice in blocking the demerger was the largest investor: Mike Cannon-Brookes. Subsequent media reporting has focused on his specific views about AGL's renewables push,[22] and his personal views about board appointments.[23] There is no evidence that AGL, its officers, or its directors acted improperly. Similarly, Mike Cannon-Brookes—and his investment group—are acting within their rights as investors. However, this flags the risks that can arise: when interacting with activist investors, directors must show they are acting for shareholders as a whole—not merely a subset of investors. This is the case even if they are the largest shareholder or purport to be "doing good."

3.4   What about the Duty of Care?

The directors' duty of care might require directors to consider social and environmental impact, but only in economic terms. Here, the Corporations Act requires directors to "exercise their powers and discharge their duties with the degree of care and diligence that a reasonable person would." The duty begs the question of what a "reasonable person" would do when running a corporation. There are several key implications.

Directors must consider social and environmental impact like they would any other activity. Here, they must consider the effect of social and environmental factors on the firm's cash flows, cash flow risk, and the cost of capital. Officers and directors can also consider reputational harm, compliance with legal obligations, and the ability to continue operating.[24]

---

[22]   For example, see Thomson and Koob (2022) and Johnson (2022).
[23]   For example, see Hannam (2022).
[24]   Australian Securities and Investments Commission v Cassimatis (No 8) (2016) 336 ALR 209 at [480]-[483].

This impact will depend on the corporation's circumstances.[25] In this respect, impact considerations are no different to any other consideration. Failing to consider the financial implications of social and environmental impact could breach the duty. However, if, after evaluation, there is no corporate reason to act on social/environmental factors, then directors ought not do so. Further, if social and environmental impact will have a greater impact on a company's value, then they warrant greater consideration.

Climate risks could enliven this duty. Directors and officers should consider the impact of climate change and climate risks on their businesses.[26] Similarly, if the company's role in climate change could impose financial costs (i.e., through regulation, or worse access to debt), then the officers and directors would seemingly need to consider it. This can—and likely should—involve a proactive assessment to put in place systems to determine whether social and political factors have a genuine financial impact.[27] However, here, the focus is on the corporate impact, rather than on the alleged "moral" impact.

Prioritizing social and environmental factors over financial considerations would likely breach this duty. For example, engaging in a risky, or costly, transaction that has little chance of a financial payoff can breach this duty.[28] Rather, officers and directors should consider those factors in a broader risk analysis.[29] Thus, focusing on what managers deem "morally" or "ethically" justified, with only cursory consideration to the corporate or financial risks could breach the relevant duty of care.

Directors would also likely contravene this duty if they uncritically accepted, or dismissed, reports. Directors must consider reports about social and environmental impact. While directors would not necessarily be expected to be experts in all areas, they should ask relevant questions or obtain relevant

---

25 For example, see Australian Securities and Investments Commission v Maxwell (2006) 59 ACSR 373 at 397 per Brereton J.

26 This follows from Australian Securities and Investments Commission v Vines (2005) 55 ACSR 617. Here, the defendants failed to furnish relevant information about insurance costs associated with a hurricane. By parity of reasoning, failure to consider financial impacts of climate change could contravene the duty of care, depending on the circumstances.

27 This follows from DSHE Holdings Ltd (recs and grs. apptd) (in liq) v Abboud (No 3). Here, the defendant directors had failed to put in place systems to ensure proper inventory management. This implies that officers and directors should also have systems to consider whether—if at all—environmental or social factors might influence the corporation's financial position.

28 Australian Securities and Investments Commission v Sydney Investment House Equities Pty Ltd (2008) 69 ACSR 1; [2008] NSWSC 1224 at [28].

29 This follows the approach of Mason J in Wyong Shire Council v Shirt (1980) 146 CLR 40. Here, Mason J expressly referred to considering the risk and magnitude of an event when determining whether to act on it.

research-translations to ensure that they are adequately informed.[30] Further, officers and directors cannot merely delegate their decision-making, or analysis, to third parties. For example, directors cannot merely avoid their responsibility to ensure financials are accurate by hiring an auditor.[31] Thus, directors cannot simply delegate their decision-making to ESG consultants and must critically evaluate the financial impact of any social or environmental initiatives.

The overall implication of this duty is that directors must consider social and environmental impact much like they would consider any other corporate risk factor. If there is a financial risk, directors should act upon that risk. However, this must involve a genuine, and well informed, financial risk assessment. This should consider the risks and returns of acting.

3.5   Greenwashing and Misleading Statements

Greenwashing and misleading statements could also violate directors' duties. Most often, issuing false or misleading statements can violate the duty of care.[32] Therefore, if the directors make false or misleading statements about the firm's environmental or social impact they could violate both the relevant disclosure obligations and their duties of care. However, there is additional nuance.

These obligations come most commonly from two main groups. But the precise nature varies between countries. The duties are similar in Australia and the United States, for example. In Australia, the rules are similar to SEC Rule 10b-5 overall and derive from two areas. First, Corporations Act Sections 1041E and 1041H prohibit false and misleading statements. Section 1041E prohibits false statements that would encourage a person to "apply for" or dispose of a financial product, or would impact the price of a financial product. It is analogous to United States SEC Rule 10b-5. Section 1041H broadly prohibits conduct that is "misleading or deceptive" in relation to financial products and services. Second, the ASX continuous disclosure requirements have legal force via Corporations Act Section 674.

---

[30]   An extreme parallel is Australian Securities and Investments Commission v Sino Australia Oil and Gas Ltd (in liq) (2016) 115 ACSR 437. Here, the directors approved prospectuses but seemingly neither understood the English in the text nor sought translations to understand them.

[31]   For example, see ASIC v Healey & Ors [2011] FCA 717, discussed in Banerjee and Humphery-Jenner (2016).

[32]   For example, directors in Australian Securities and Investments Commission v Vocation Ltd (in liq) (2019) 371 ALR 155 violated their duty of care by providing false statements in a due diligence questionnaire. This enlivened Corporations Act Section 1041H and contravened the ASX listing rules, enlivening Corporations Act Section 674. Similarly, in Australian Securities and Investments Commission v Big Star Energy Ltd (No 3) (2020) 148 ACSR 334, the directors violated their ASX listing rules, which in turn violated the duty of care.

Issuing false and misleading statements can have corporate consequences, even if the statement is not per se material. That is, the decision to mislead the market sends a negative signal about the firm's corporate governance. This has implications for the firm. For example, after a class action or an enforcement action, firms often have worse access to debt and worse trade terms, suggesting a significant financial and reputational penalty (Karpoff, Lee, and Martin 2008a). Evidencing these negative effects, CEOs' job prospects often worsen after securities class actions and enforcement actions (Humphery-Jenner 2012; McTier and Wald 2011; Karpoff, Lee, and Martin 2008b).

The corollary is that officers and directors should not engage in greenwashing. Here, there are two main types of misleading conduct: (i) misleading people about how environmentally or socially friendly the company is, and (ii) misleading about the payoffs to such actions.

Greenwashing is typically seen as the practice of making the firm seem more environmentally (or socially) friendly than it really is. There is a spectrum of greenwashing, ranging from producing content-free puff pieces through to actively misleading investors about the firm's green (or social) credentials. Even if investors do not value those environmental and social statements, investors will likely penalize the firm if it lies about them. Thus, the fact of issuing a false or misleading statement could violate directors' duties.

Greenwashing can also involve misleading investors about the financial payoffs from (or costs of) social or environmental initiatives. Thus, directors must exercise reasonable care and skill to ensure that their payoff and cost estimates are accurate. If they inflate the benefits (or deflate the costs) of such actions, it would likely violate disclosure requirements in Corporations Act Sections 674, 1041E, and 1041H by (among other things) inflating the stock price. Further, this also means that directors cannot merely delegate this to an ESG consultant and uncritically accept ESG recommendations without undertaking their own independent assessment.[33]

---

[33]   This follows from ASIC v Healey & Ors [2011] FCA 717. Here, the court held that directors could not merely blindly defer to auditors to side step their duty to ensure that financial reports were accurate. By parity of reasoning, officers and directors cannot obviate their duty to provide accurate financial information by deferring to environmental and social impact reports.

This is a significant risk given that there is little evidence that merely having a higher ESG score improves company performance (indeed, it is often associated with negative returns)[34] and there is significant disagreement about what—if anything—matters for ESG scores.[35] Further, investors appear to have difficulty valuing the cost or benefit of environmental initiatives,[36] making them even more dependent on managers' disclosures.

The disclosure obligations have a clear implication: managers should consider environment and social impact in the same way they consider other corporate decisions. And they should be honest with investors about what specific initiatives they are undertaking and their financial benefit if any.

3.6   What about the Business Judgment Rule?

The foregoing raises the question whether the business judgment rule can help directors who might otherwise appear to breach their duties. The business judgment rule only protects directors against alleged breaches of their duty of care, not against other alleged breaches.[37] That is, it will not protect directors against allegations that they improperly used their position or acted against the company's best interests.

The scope of the business judgment rule varies across countries. In the United States, the rule is relatively generous, and could likely reduce the risk of being sued for such breaches. However, this is not the case in all jurisdictions. Australia, for example, has a relatively restrictive approach to the business judgment rule. There, the rule stipulates that officers or directors are deemed to have satisfied their duty of care if they take an action or judgment that (i) is done in good faith and for a proper purpose, (ii) does not involve a material personal interest, (iii) for which they have informed themselves to the extent they "reasonably believe" is appropriate, and (iv) they "rationally" believe is in the best interests of the corporation. This has several corollaries.

---

34   See Avramov et al. (2022, 19).
35   See Berg, Kölbel, and Rigobon (2019, 1).
36   For example, evidence exists that investors "care" about environmental impact, but they appear not to be able to value the cost/benefit of that impact: Heeb et al. (2023, 30). This makes it incumbent on managers to provide accurate statements given that a "reasonable" director in these circumstances would appreciate the difficulties that investors face in this context.
37   This is clear from the text in Corporations Act Section 180(2).

The directors will not be absolved from ignoring how environmental or social factors impact cash flows or risks. This is clear from Section 180(2)(c): the director must have informed themselves about a matter to involve the business judgment rule. If directors ignore a matter or pays only cursory attention to it, they cannot have informed themselves. Thus, on the one hand, if directors ignore environmental or social factors, they might still breach Section 180. Directors should therefore consider whether causing environmental or social damage will adversely impact the corporation. Conversely, if a director zealously pursues social causes while paying only lip service to how that might impact the corporation's "bottom line," they could also not involve the business judgment rule.

Directors must act "in good faith" and "for a proper purpose" and in a way that they rationally believe is in the "best interests" of the corporation. Thus, in this context, this involves acting in the interests of the company.[38] Altruistic purposes would generally not satisfy this. Thus, if the director acts for reasons other than maximizing shareholder wealth, the director would likely not be able to invoke the business judgment rule. This is the case even if one or more shareholders would like the director to act in a specific altruistic way.[39]

A complex issue is if a director erroneously believes that focusing on impact maximizes shareholder wealth when it does not. "Impact" initiatives may, but need not, maximize shareholder wealth. In this case, the directors will be attempting to act "in good faith" and "for a proper purpose." Here, whether the business judgment rule would focus on whether the directors could "rationally" believe they were acting in shareholders' best interests and whether they had informed themselves to the extent they "reasonably believed" was appropriate. At a minimum, this would likely require the directors to obtain credible and impartial financial modeling of how the impact initiatives would influence the firm's financial position, much as with any other major corporate decision.

This altogether suggests that well-meaning directors could use the business judgment rule if they make their best efforts to financially model impact initiatives properly. However, as indicated, this only helps in relation to the duty of care. And invoking the business judgment rule relies on the directors focusing on wealth maximization. However, as indicated, some jurisdictions— such as the United States—are more generous in their application of the business judgment rule.

---

38   Fitzsimmons v R (1997) 23 ACSR 355.
39   This follows from Glover v Willert (1996) 20 ACSR 182 at 188.

3.7 Conclusion

ESG investing has become popular. It has also recently come under scrutiny, with concerns about the arbitrariness of some ESG "analysis" and unclear benefits to shareholders. Allegations of greenwashing exacerbate the situation. This raises the question of whether—and to what extent—directors and officers are under a duty to consider environmental and social impact.

The clearest outcome is that directors and officers must consider environmental and social impact much like they must consider any factor that might influence corporate value. Indeed, failing to consider such impact—where relevant—could breach the directors' duties of care. However, when considering "impact," they must analyze it through the lens of shareholder wealth maximization. Thus, they must consider the costs and benefits of pursuing impact initiatives. These include how such factors will influence the firm's cost of capital, cash flows, and the riskiness thereof.

Directors and officers cannot pursue initiatives merely because they believe they are "right," or are passionate about them. This could violate both the duty of care, the obligation to act in the corporation's best interest, and the prohibition on benefiting themselves at the cost of shareholders. Directors' and officers' primary duty is to their shareholders.

Directors and officers must also be honest with investors about the costs and benefits of impact initiatives. Directors should not mislead investors about either the amount of impact activities they are doing or about the payoffs from such activities. Such misleading actions can ultimately harm the firm, violate disclosure obligations, and breach directors' duties.

The overall implication is that environmental and social considerations are not irrelevant per se. But their relevance is limited and officers and directors must consider these factors within a broader corporate framework. Directors should not treat corporations as a vehicle to pursue their own policy goals. Directors' duties are to their shareholders as a whole, not to specific shareholders that pressure for causes nor to outside interest groups.

References

Australian Securities and Investments Commission (ASIC). 2020. Insolvency for Directors: Information Sheet 42. https://asic.gov.au/regulatory-resources/insolvency/insolvency-for-directors/#directors-duties.

Avramov, D., S. Cheng, A. Lioui, and A. Terrelli. 2022. Sustainable Investing with ESG Rating Uncertainty. *Journal of Financial Economics*. 145 (2). pp. 642–664.

Banerjee, S. and M. Humphery-Jenner. 2016. Directors' Duties of Care and the Value of Auditing. *Finance Research Letters*. 19 (C). pp. 1–14.

Berg, F., J. Kölbel, and R. Rigobon. 2019. Aggregate Confusion: The Divergence of ESG Ratings. Forthcoming *Review of Finance*. https://ssrn.com/abstract=3438533 or http://dx.doi.org/10.2139/ssrn.3438533.

Bertrand, M. and S. Mullainathan. 2003. Enjoying the Quiet Life? *Corporate Governance and Managerial Preferences*. 111 (5). pp. 1043–1075.

Brandon, R. G., P. Krueger, and P. S. Schmidt. 2021. ESG Rating Disagreement and Stock Returns. *Financial Analysts Journal*. 77 (4). pp. 104–107.

Cornell, B. 2021. ESG Preferences, Risk and Return. *European Financial Management*. 27 (1). pp. 12–19.

Corporations and Markets Advisory Committee (CMAC). 2006. The Social Responsibility of Corporations. CMAC, Australian Government.

Donaldson, M. 2010. Bills Digest: Corporations Amendment (Corporate Reporting Reform) Bill 2010. *Bills Digest*. No. 185. https://parlinfo.aph.gov.au/parlInfo/download/legislation/billsdgs/0G2X6/upload_binary/0g2x60.pdf.

Edmans, A. 2022. The End of ESG. European Corporate Governance Institute. 847/2022. https://dx.doi.org/10.2139/ssrn.4221990.

Eliwa, Y., A. Aboud, and A. Saleh. 2021. ESG Practices and the Cost of Debt: Evidence from EU Countries. *Critical Perspectives on Accounting*. 79 (3). 102097.

Gao, H., J. He, and Y. Li. 2022. Media Spotlight, Corporate Sustainability and the Cost of Debt. 2022. *Applied Economics.* 54 (34). pp. 3989–4005.

Gerwanski, J. 2020. Does It Pay off? Integrated Reporting and Cost of Debt: European Evidence. *Corporate Social Responsibility and Environmental Management.* 27 (5). pp. 2299–2319.

Giese, G., L. Lee, D. Melas, Z. Nagy, and L. Nishikawa. 2019. Foundations of ESG Investing: How ESG Affects Equity Valuation, Risk, and Performance. *Journal of Portfolio Management.* 45 (5). pp. 69–83.

Hannam, P. 2022. Mike Cannon-Brookes to Back New AGL Board Members in Bid to Clean Up Climate Polluter. *The Guardian.* 28 September. https://www.theguardian.com/business/2022/sep/28/mike-cannon-brookes-to-back-new-agl-board-members-in-bid-to-clean-up-climate-polluter.

Harford, J., M. Humphery-Jenner, and R. G. Powell. 2012. The Sources of Value Destruction in Acquisitions by Entrenched Managers. *Journal of Financial Economics.* 106 (2). pp. 247–261.

Heeb, F., J. Kölbel, F. Paetzold, and S. Zeisberger. 2023. Do Investors Care About Impact? *The Review of Financial Studies.* 36 (5). pp. 1737–1787. https://doi.org/10.1093/rfs/hhac066.

Hoque, M. N., K. Ahmed, and G. Richardson. 2020. The Effect of Environmental, Social, and Governance Performance Factors on Firms' Cost of Debt: International Evidence. *International Journal of Accounting.* 55 (3). pp. 1–30.

Humphery-Jenner, M. 2012. Internal and External Discipline Following Securities Class Actions. *Journal of Financial Intermediation.* 21 (1). pp. 151–179.

Johnson, E. 2022. Tech Billionaire Mike Cannon-Brookes Sparks AGL Energy's Green Reboot. *The Australian.* 29 September.

Karpoff, J. M., D. S. Lee, and G. S. Martin. 2008a. The Consequences to Managers for Financial Misrepresentation. *Journal of Financial Economics.* 88 (2). pp. 193–215.

_____. 2008b. The Cost to Firms of Cooking the Books. *Journal of Financial and Quantitative Analysis.* 43 (3). pp. 581–611.

Lodh, A. 2020. ESG and the Cost of Capital. *MSCI*. 25 February. https://www.msci.com/www/blog-posts/esg-and-the-cost-of-capital/01726513589.

Masulis, R. W. and S. W. Reza. 2015. Agency Problems of Corporate Philanthropy. *Review of Financial Studies*. 28 (2). pp. 592–636.

Masulis, R. W., C. Wang, and F. Xie. 2007. Corporate Governance and Acquirer Returns. *Journal of Finance*. 62 (4). p. 1851–1889.

McTier, B. C. and J. K. Wald. 2011. The Causes and Consequences of Securities Class Action Litigation. *Journal of Corporate Finance*. 17 (3). pp. 649–665.

Ng, A. C. and Z. Rezaee. 2015. Business Sustainability Performance and Cost of Equity Capital. *Journal of Corporate Finance*. 34 (C). pp. 128–149.

Senate Standing Committee on Legal and Constitutional Affairs. 1989. Company Directors' Duties: Report on the Social and Fiduciary Duties and Obligations of Company Directors. Parliament of the Commonwealth of Australia. 395 of 1989. https://nla.gov.au:443/tarkine/nla.obj-1928589902.

Thomson, A. and S. F. Koob. 2022. Cannon-Brookes Pushes for Rapid Action as AGL Plots $20b Coal Exit. *Sydney Morning Herald*. 29 September. https://www.smh.com.au/business/companies/agl-puts-20bn-price-tag-on-early-coal-exit-20220929-p5blv7.html.

Chapter 4

Green or Green Image? Selective Disclosure of Corporate Suppliers

Yilin Shi, Jing Wu, and Yu Zhang

4.1 Examining Corporate Social Responsibility in Supply Chains

The average carbon emissions of a company's supply chain are more than 11 times greater than the company's direct emissions, according to a global supply chain report published by the Carbon Disclosure Project (CDP 2020). Clearly, the intermediate inputs manufactured by a company's supplier can be substantial. For example, 65% of airframe parts for Boeing's 787 Dreamliner are produced by upstream suppliers (Peterson 2011).

To be sure, most listed companies around the world strive to establish a clean image of how they make their products. Yet, the public usually pays little attention to the corporate social responsibility of their deep and complex supply chains—a vital measure of firm performance attracting interesting attention from consumers, business partners, and market investors.[1]

The literature certainly provides evidence that corporate social responsibility is favored by the financial market and consumers. Pastor, Stambaugh, and Taylor (2021a, 2021b) show that green assets yield higher returns with a shift in customers' preferences toward green products and a shift in investors' preferences toward green holdings. Servaes and Tamayo (2013) find that the benefits of market valuation are more pronounced for firms with greater customer awareness. Flammer (2015) shows that firms that pass corporate-social-responsibility-related shareholder proposals show superior financial performance.

---

[1] The content of this chapter is based on Shi, Y., J. Wu, Y. Zhang, and Y. Zhou. 2023. *Green Image Management in Supply Chains: Strategic Disclosure of Corporate Suppliers.* https://papers.ssrn.com/sol3/papers.cfm?abstract_id=3700310.

Corporate social responsibility is also related to the resilience of companies in withstanding shocks. Lins, Servaes, and Tamayo (2017) find that firms with higher corporate social responsibility scores experience higher stock returns during financial crises and show better operational performance afterward. In addition, Bardos, Ertugrul, and Gao (2020) provide direct evidence that corporate social responsibility scores are positively associated with product-market perceptions.

As corporate social responsibility is welcomed by both consumers and the financial market due to its multiple benefits, firms are incentivized to present an image of environmental responsibility.

Nonetheless, the disclosure of suppliers is mostly voluntary. Firms can determine what they want to disclose to the public after considering both the benefits and costs of disclosure. Therefore, it is possible for a focal firm to selectively disclose its suppliers to present specific corporate social responsibility images. Understanding whether listed companies truly care for environmentally responsible supply chains or simply want to portray an overtly "green" supply chain image is the key to accurately assessing the environmental responsibility of listed companies. However, no studies to date examine whether and to what degree listed firms selectively disclose green suppliers.

The analysis here provides the first examination of listed firms' selective disclosure of green suppliers and nondisclosure of less green ones, using large-scale datasets of listed firms and their respective suppliers worldwide. The key piece of information it uses from the supply chain dataset FactSet Revere is the disclosing party of the relationship, which indicates whether a supplier is voluntarily disclosed by the customer firm itself. Whether a supplier is voluntarily disclosed by the customer firm is significantly predicted by the supplier's environmental rating (measured by the environmental score in Thomson Reuters' ASSET4).

The empirical specification is a linear probability model in which the dependent variable is voluntary disclosure by the customer, and the explanatory variable of interest is the environmental rating of the supplier. The analysis adopts customer-by-year fixed effects and controls for known factors that influence voluntary disclosure. This ensures that the analysis compares the voluntary disclosure of suppliers that belong to the same customer in the same year and that are observationally equivalent, barring their environmental ratings.

The analysis identifies several firm-level factors that intensify the selective disclosure of green suppliers. First, although studies find that the positive financial effects of corporate social responsibility are stronger for companies that operate in a highly competitive industry (Bardos, Ertugrul, and Gao 2020; Ding et al. 2020), this analysis finds that firms that face more competitive pressure (as measured by firm market share) are more likely to selectively disclose green suppliers and present a positive corporate social responsibility image. Second, studies find that market value increases with corporate social responsibility for firms that have higher advertising expenditures (Servaes and Tamayo 2013).

Similarly, the analysis finds that firms that care more about customer awareness and reputation (as measured by their selling, general, and administrative expenses) are more likely to selectively disclose green suppliers. Third, the analysis shows that firms with larger holdings by institutional investors are more likely to greenwash their supply chains, which is consistent with the catering hypothesis (Desai and Jin 2011; Golubov, Lasfer, and Vitkova 2020). Finally, listed companies with lower environmental ratings tend to be more selective in disclosing suppliers with higher environmental ratings.

The analysis also finds that public awareness of climate change and government policies on corporate social responsibility disclosures influences supply chain greenwashing. It finds that listed firms in countries or regions with higher survey-reported awareness of climate change are more selective in their disclosure of suppliers based on the suppliers' environmental ratings. This pattern is not specific to cross-sectional variations in public awareness of climate change.

Consistently, the evidence here suggests that supply chain greenwashing increases when the state or the country in which the customer is located experiences a high frequency of wildfires, as wildfires are often a catalyst for climate change awareness.

If social awareness is not sufficient to deter supply chain greenwashing, then what is? The analysis finds that when regulations on corporate social responsibility disclosure are tightened, the extent of supply chain greenwashing is substantially reduced. This is consistent with theoretical findings in Wu, Zhang, and Xie (2020) that low information transparency environments in general incentivize profit-driven firms to engage in greenwashing.

The chapter's analysis contributes to the literature on several fronts, first as research on public firms' socially responsible supply chain practices. Studies in this cross-disciplinary field make significant effort to cover topics such as sustainable supply chain practices implemented by buyer firms (Plambeck and Taylor 2016; Agrawal and Lee 2019) and responsible supply chain regulations and policies (Sunar and Plambeck 2016). In particular, Schiller (2018) and Dai, Liang, and Ng (2021) show that customer firms exert influence on suppliers' corporate social responsibility through positive assortative matching and their decision-making process.

The prevalent behavior this analysis finds is that customer firms strategically display an ethical image by selectively disclosing "good" suppliers while concealing "bad" ones. This contrasts with—yet at the same time complements—the literature's prior focus on promoting suppliers to be "good" or establishing business relationships with "good" suppliers. Therefore, the focus on a different side of the customer's corporate social responsibility behavior offers a more holistic picture: once customers selected suppliers and exerted influence on supplies' environmental standards, the customer's disclosure practices can be biased in the suppliers' environmental performance.

Second, the analysis contributes to the corporate social responsibility literature on greenwashing (Kim and Lyon 2011; Lyon and Maxwell 2011; Lyon and Montgomery 2015; Marquis, Toffel, and Zhou 2016; Li and Wu 2020) from an innovative new angle, i.e., the voluntary disclosure of supply chains. Studies on greenwashing primarily focus on actions within the firms themselves. The analysis in this chapter showed that in addition to representing themselves as "good," firms representing their supply chains as "good" is a common method of greenwashing.

In addition, the analysis is the first empirical study to link research on corporate social responsibility to that on supply chain information disclosure, adding to the very limited number of empirical studies on voluntary supply chain disclosure. Ellis, Fee, and Thomas (2012) report that suppliers' disclosure of their customers comes at a proprietary disclosure cost, as their competitors may take advantage of such information. This analysis provides a contrasting perspective on the strategic disclosure of supply chains, which is that customers are likely to selectively disclose "good" suppliers that are environmentally responsible.

In the rest of the chapter, section 2 presents baseline empirical results on supplier environmental ratings and customer disclosure. Section 3 discusses moderating factors and section 4 concludes with discussion of implications.

4.2 Selective Disclosure of Green Suppliers

4.2.1 Empirical Specification and Baseline Result

The baseline regression analysis estimates a linear probability model in which the supplier is voluntarily disclosed by the customer. The linear probability model allows the analysis to control for an array of fixed effects, which ensures that it compares the likelihood of being voluntarily disclosed for two suppliers with different environmental ratings, with the customer, the year of the supply chain relationship, and other characteristics of the suppliers that can influence customer voluntary disclosure held constant. The model is as follows:

$$Disclose^c_{i,j,t} = \alpha + \beta * Envscore^s_{j,t,-1} + \phi^s * Z^s_{j,t} + FE + \epsilon_{i,j,t} \tag{1}$$

where $Disclose^c_{i,j,t}$ is a dummy that denotes whether the supply chain relationship is voluntarily disclosed by customer firm i in year t. The main explanatory variable focused on is $Envscore^s_{j,t,-1}$, which is the lagged value of environment score in ASSET4 for supplier j in year t–1. A vector of control variables $Z^s_{j,t}$ includes supplier characteristics that capture two channels that previous studies on supply chain voluntary disclosure find to be important: good news bias and proprietary costs (Ellis et al. 2012). Specifically, Zs comprise size (Sizes), profitability (ROAs), market valuation (Tobin's Qs), and proportion of institutional shareholding (InstOwns), all of which capture the good news bias channel. In addition, the supplier's research and development (R&D) expenditures and the industry disclosure ratio (DisRatios) can serve as proxies for the proprietary cost channel. To ensure the estimated influence of supplier environmental ratings on the customer's voluntary disclosure is held constant given the customer and the perios, the analysis controls for customer firm and year fixed effects.

Column (1) of Table 4.1 shows estimates of equation (1). It finds that the supplier's environment score is significantly positively associated with the probability of the customer voluntarily disclosing the supplier.

In other words, customers selectively disclose suppliers with higher ratings for environmental responsibility and do not disclose fewer green suppliers. To guard against the possibility that the industry, the country, or the customer itself experiences trends in the unconditional probability of voluntarily disclosing suppliers, the analysis progressively adds more fixed effects. Columns (2)–(4) consider the possibility that the time trends of customer disclosure behaviors differ in terms of country or industry or the pair, country and industry. Thus, the analysis adds country-year fixed effects in column (2), industry–year fixed effects in column (3), and country–industry–year fixed effects in column (4). In column (5), it further considers the possibility that a customer's trend for the unconditional probability of reporting any supplier may correlate with the supplier's environmental ratings and add customer-by-year fixed effects. That is, the analysis estimates the influence of the supplier's environmental ratings on the probability of the customer voluntarily disclosing the supplier, using only the comparison between suppliers that the analysis observes strictly within the same year for the same customer. The results in columns (2)–(5) of Table 4.1 are consistently the same as in column (1). The coefficients are almost the same in columns (1)–(4) and are only slightly smaller in column (5). The results in column (5) indicate that the effect of the supplier's environmental rating on the customer's voluntary disclosure is economically significant: a one-standard-deviation increase in a supplier's environment score corresponds to a 3.7% higher probability of being disclosed by the customer.

The direction of coefficients on the control variables is consistent with expectations. Higher values for the supplier's size, return on assets (ROA), institutional ownership, and Tobin's Q increases the likelihood of the customer disclosing the supplier, indicating that customers tend to disclose suppliers with better performance. Suppliers with higher R&D expenditure are less likely to be disclosed, indicating that customers are more inclined to conceal these suppliers as they may incur higher proprietary costs if the identities of these supply chain partners are made public. A supplier's industry disclosure ratio is positively associated with the likelihood of being disclosed by their respective customers. This suggests that peer influence plays a role in voluntary disclosure. Even after controlling for these nonenvironmental supplier characteristics, the analysis finds significant selective disclosures based on $Envscore^s$. This suggests that the selective disclosure of green suppliers cannot be explained by a preference for various observable characteristics of the supplier firm. Overall, the economic and statistical

Table 4.1: Main Results

Dependent Variable	Customer Voluntary Disclosure of Supplier ($Disclose^c$)				
	(1)	(2)	(3)	(4)	(5)
$Envscore^s$	0.133***	0.132***	0.133***	0.130***	0.118***
	(22.404)	(22.309)	(22.361)	(21.672)	(19.312)
$Size^s$	0.099***	0.099***	0.099***	0.097***	0.091***
	(37.128)	(37.130)	(37.049)	(36.064)	(32.884)
ROA^s	0.006***	0.005***	0.006***	0.005***	0.005***
	(3.679)	(3.190)	(3.649)	(3.452)	(2.796)
$InstOwn^s$	0.020***	0.021***	0.020***	0.021***	0.021***
	(9.854)	(10.423)	(10.067)	(10.536)	(10.121)
$R\&D^s$	−0.005***	−0.004***	−0.005***	−0.004**	−0.004**
	(−2.837)	(−2.602)	(−3.123)	(−2.264)	(−2.087)
Tobin's Q^s	0.015***	0.016***	0.016***	0.015***	0.016***
	(7.927)	(8.257)	(8.121)	(7.719)	(7.813)
$DisRatio^s$	0.055***	0.054***	0.054***	0.052***	0.048***
	(27.142)	(26.923)	(26.259)	(25.619)	(22.529)
Constant	0.365***	0.365***	0.365***	0.369***	0.374***
	(88.457)	(88.878)	(88.200)	(89.350)	(88.549)
Fixed effect	Customer Firm+ Year	Customer Firm+ Country* Year	Customer Firm+ Industry* Year	Customer Firm+ Country* Industry* Year	Customer Firm* Year
Observations	107,627	107,627	107,627	107,627	107,627
R-squared	0.699	0.703	0.703	0.719	0.748

c = customer, Envscore = environment score, InstOwn = proportion of institutional shareholding, DisRatio = industry disclosure ratio, R&D = research and development, ROA = return on assets, s = supplier, Tobin's Q = market valuation.
Note: Values in parentheses represent t-statistics, whereas values with *, **, and *** denote significance at the 10%, 5%, and 1% levels, respectively.
Source: Shi et al. (2023).

significance of the relationship between $Envscore^s$ and whether the customer voluntarily discloses the supplier is stable after controlling for other potential considerations in voluntary supply chain disclosure.

In sum, the estimates of equation (1) suggest that the environmental performance of suppliers is indeed an important independent consideration in the customer disclosure of supply chains.

4.3 Factors Driving the Selective Disclosure of Green Suppliers

4.3.1 Customer Firm Characteristics as Moderating Channels

The analysis first inspects the customer firm's internal aspects, i.e., firm-specific characteristics. It finds that customers that face more competitive pressure, care more about brand image and reputation, and are owned more by institutional investors are more likely to selectively disclose their suppliers depending on the supplier's environmental rating.

Column (1) shows that customer firms with low environment scores are more likely to selectively disclose suppliers based on their environmental ratings. This is because firms that are already lagging behind in environmental performance may have fewer resources to invest in corporate social responsibility improvements to their product life cycles than in greenwashing. Therefore, they prefer to "talk the walk" as opposed to actually making changes to become more environmentally friendly. Column (2) in Table 4.2 shows that firms with a lower market share are more likely to selectively disclose suppliers

Table 4.2: Moderator—Customer Firm Characteristics

| Dependent Variable | Customer Voluntary Disclosure of Supplier ($Disclose^c$) | | | |
	(1)	(2)	(3)	(4)
$Envscore^s \times Envscore^c$	−0.054*** (−7.260)			
$Envscore^s \times MS^c$		−0.012** (−2.203)		
$Envscore^s \times SG\&A^c$			0.018*** (2.899)	
$Envscore^s \times InstOwn^c$				0.047*** (7.617)
$Envscore^s$	0.135*** (18.488)	0.118*** (19.329)	0.120*** (18.451)	0.113*** (18.813)
Control	Yes	Yes	Yes	Yes
Fixed effect	Customer Firm* Year	Customer Firm* Year	Customer Firm* Year	Customer Firm* Year
Observations	73,919	107,627	95,921	107,627
R-squared	0.659	0.748	0.746	0.749

c = customer, Envscore = environment score, InstOwn = proportion of institutional shareholding, MS = industry market share, s = supplier, SG&A = selling, general, and administrative expenses.
Note: Values in parentheses represent t-statistics, whereas values with *, **, and *** denote significance at the 10%, 5%, and 1% levels, respectively.
Source: Shi et al. (2023).

based on their environmental ratings. Therefore, firms that face more fierce competition in the product market may also "talk the walk" more, i.e., compared with firms with larger market shares, those with smaller market shares display a stronger pattern of selectively disclosing green suppliers. Flammer (2015) and Aghion et al. (2020) suggest that product market competition increases a firm's engagement in corporate social responsibility. However, the greenwashing findings here reconcile conflicting evidence in the corporate social responsibility literature, such as Duanmu, Bu, and Pittman (2018), who find that market competition negatively affects a firm's environmental performance. Other than demonstrating a real corporate social responsibility impact, greenwashing serves as a visible strategy by which to present an image of being green, especially for firms that face fierce competition.

Servaes and Tamayo (2013) find that corporate social responsibility affects firm value only through its interaction with advertising intensity. Harjoto and Jo (2011) find that high corporate social responsibility firms on average spend more on advertising and have a larger share of institutional holding. Bardos et al. (2020) find that corporate social responsibility positively impacts product market perception. Column (3) examines a firm's spending on advertising, as proxied by selling, general, and administrative expenses. It is found that firms with more advertising spending conduct more supply chain greenwashing. These firms care more about reputation and consumer awareness (Servaes and Tamayo 2013) and thus, have more incentive to create a better corporate social responsibility image through the strategic disclosure of green suppliers.

In addition, the analysis finds that firms with more institutional ownership perform more supply chain greenwashing, as shown in column (4) in Table 4.2. It argues that institutional investors care more about portfolio firms' corporate social responsibility, due to pecuniary and nonpecuniary motivations (Flammer 2015; Amiraslani et al. 2017; Hartzmark and Sussman 2019; Kim et al. 2019). However, an information asymmetry may exist between firms and institutional investors. Once the low-corporate social responsibility suppliers are disclosed, the news spreads quickly to investors, and firms with higher institutional ownership receive more severe punishments from their institutional investors. An alternative explanation is that, in reality, not all institutional investors mandate sincere corporate social responsibility efforts. Some institutional investors are profit-mongers and support greenwashing strategies.

Dyck et al. (2019) and Choi, Gao, and Jiang (2020) find that the presence of institutional investors increases a firm's corporate social responsibility performance, but that performance is lower when the institutional investors are distracted and pay little attention to its operations. In particular, Choi, Gao, and Jiang (2020) review the literature on corporate social responsibility performance and institutions' portfolio choices, and propose two hypotheses: (i) real effort (has an effect), and (ii) catering (no real effect). They find evidence for (i) but not for (ii). In contrast, the results in this chapter add evidence for (ii); it shows that institutional investors partially cater to investors by holding stocks that are more likely to selectively disclose green suppliers.

4.3.2 Public Awareness of Climate Change

This analysis next inspects the role of external attributes of customer firms. It finds that customers in countries with higher public environmental awareness may intensify their selective disclosure of green suppliers and selective nondisclosure of less green suppliers.

The mechanism proposed here is that increased general public awareness of climate change attracts more stakeholder attention to corporate environmental management. However, this greater awareness may also increase incentive for a customer to manage its environmental image through the selective disclosure and nondisclosure of suppliers.

The analysis first directly measures the public's environmental awareness based on responses in the World Value Survey. The survey includes nationally representative surveys conducted in almost 100 countries, which account for nearly 90% of the world's population. Seven waves of the survey were conducted from 1981 to 2020, with each cross-sectional wave taking 4–5 years to complete on a global scale. The analysis here uses the answers for the item "taking care of the environment/caring for nature is important" from wave 5 (2005–2009) and wave 6 (2010–2014). The analysis here assigns 1–6 points for the answer to measure the degree to which respondents agree with this statement, with 1 point representing maximum disagreement and 6 points representing maximum agreement. It then averages the score of each respondent to the country level, which represents the country-level public awareness of environmental issues. The results are reported in column (1) in Table 4.3. The positive coefficient of the interaction term between $SurveyAwareness^c$ and $Envscore^s$ indicates that greater public attention to the environment corresponds to a higher likelihood of a firm greenwashing its image.

To ensure that results using the survey-based measure of public environmental awareness are not influenced by the (in) frequency with which the surveys are conducted, this analysis further employs wildfires as a shock to public awareness of climate change. The exogenous shock approach designates the occurrence of wildfires as external to the firms and not directly related to other potential drivers of supply chain disclosures. However, the occurrence of wildfires is related to the strength of the environmental awareness of the market and the public faced by customers.

Wildfires have caused particularly severe damage in recent decades. Wildfires are driven by climate change and help propel it. Public awareness of climate change increases when people abandon their houses due to wildfires and see the burned forests and scorched animals. The analysis here constructs a dummy $WildFire^c$, which equals 1 if at least one wildfire occurs in the country/state in which the customer is located in a given year.[2] Data on wildfire events are obtained from the EM-DAT database, which records core disasters across the world from 1990 to the present day. Column (2) of Table 4.3 reports the results. The positive coefficients of the interaction terms between $Envscore^s$ and $WildFire^c$ indicate that customers are more likely to greenwash their images if wildfires occur around the firms.

Table 4.3: Moderator—Public Awareness and Regulation

Dependent Variable	Customer Voluntary Disclosure of Supplier ($Disclose^c$)		
	(1)	(2)	(3)
$Envscores \times SurveyAwareness^c$	0.014**		
	(2.207)		
$Envscore^s \times WildFire^c$		0.037**	
		(2.509)	
$Envscore^s \times Regulation^c$			-0.029**
			(-2.071)
$Envscore^s$	0.122***	0.113***	0.142***
	(16.992)	(17.897)	(10.488)
Controls	Yes	Yes	Yes
Fixed effect	Customer Firm * Year	Customer Firm * Year	Customer Firm * Year
Observations	83,572	107,627	107,627
R-squared	0.744	0.748	0.748

c = customer, Envscore = environment score, s = supplier.
Note: Values in parentheses represent t-statistics, whereas values with *, **, and *** denote significance at the 10%, 5%, and 1% levels, respectively.
Source: Shi et al. 2023.

[2]   For US firms, $WildFire^c$ equals 1 if a wildfire occurs in the state in which the customer firm is located; for non-US firms, $WildFire^c$ equals 1 if a wildfire occurs in the country in which the customer firm is located.

4.3.3 Government Regulation and Supply Chain Greenwashing

Thus far, all of the moderators analyzed complement the main results. How can supply chain greenwashing be stopped? This section identifies one factor that mitigates greenwashing behavior.

Using country-level government regulatory policy implementation, the analysis finds that information transparency reduces greenwashing behavior, as such corporate social responsibility mimicking behavior gains fewer rewards when the market is more transparent in terms of information.

The analysis collects a comprehensive sample of significant changes to mandatory environment reporting requirements around the world. The main data source for environmental reporting regulations is the Carrots & Sticks, a website that collects sustainability regulations worldwide. Although none of the reporting regulations clearly demand that firms must disclose their supplier lists, it is reasonable to believe that information transparency regarding corporate social responsibility increased to some extent after the regulations were implemented.

The analysis constructs a dummy that equals 1 if mandatory reporting requirements are in effect and then interacts the dummy variable with the supplier environment score. The results are shown in column (3) of Table 4.3. It again uses the most stringent customer-by-year fixed effects. The negative coefficients of the interaction term in Table 4.3 indicate that supply chain greenwashing reduces after the implementation of mandatory disclosure and reporting policies. Countries with tight corporate social responsibility enforcements have less room for greenwashing, which agrees with the theoretical predictions made by Wu, Zhang, and Xie (2020).

4.4 Conclusion

Although corporate social responsibility has become a high priority for companies, with increasing recognition of its business-related benefits, the prevalence of greenwashing has skyrocketed in recent years. This study investigates corporate social responsibility in the setting of voluntary supply chain disclosure. It uncovers robust empirical evidence showing that listed firms selectively disclose environmentally friendly suppliers while selectively not disclosing suppliers with poor environmental performance. That is, they conduct supply chain greenwashing. This is a prevalent behavior in the sample of countries studied in this analysis.

Factors are identified that can moderate selective disclosure of suppliers by the supplier's environmental rating. In firm-specific attributes, it is found that customer firms that face more competitive pressure, care more about brand image and reputation, and have larger shares of institutional holdings are more likely to conduct such selective disclosure. The analysis adopts variations in the public awareness of climate change from worldwide surveys and the occurrence of wildfires to show that public concerns about climate change do in fact induce listed firms to selectively disclose more aggressively. Using country-level regulatory policy implementations, the analysis finds that information transparency reduces such behavior.

The findings have implications for financial markets and social welfare in understanding the green practices of listed firms. Consumers and investors should become more knowledgeable and pay attention to listed firms' strategic disclosures in their corporate social responsibility image. Suppose consumers and investors do not become savvy enough to detect greenwashing. In that case, companies that actually have superior environmental performance in the supply chain may not receive fair recognition.

The findings here are also relevant to government regulators and nongovernment organizations. Countries around the world have implemented various regulations on environmental responsibility, which usually focus directly on focal firms' behaviors, but pay less attention to their suppliers. Therefore, from the perspective of firms' environmental footprint, regulations that aim to increase transparency in the firm's supply chain network should be strengthened.

References

Aghion, P., R. Bénabou, R. Martin, and A. Roulet. 2020. Environmental Preferences and Technological Choices: Is Market Competition Clean or Dirty? *National Bureau of Economic Research Working Paper*. No. 26921. Cambridge, MA.

Agrawal, V. and D. Lee. 2019. The Effect of Sourcing Policies on Suppliers' Sustainable Practices. *Production and Operations Management*. 28 (4). pp. 767–787.

Amiraslani, H., K. V. Lins, H. Servaes, and A. Tamayo. 2017. The Bond Market Benefits of Corporate Social Capital. *European Corporate Governance Institute Finance Working Paper*.

Bardos, K. S., M. Ertugrul, and L. S. Gao. 2020. Corporate Social Responsibility, Product Market Perception, and Firm Value. *Journal of Corporate Finance*. 62 (C). 101588.

Carbon Disclosure Project (CDP). 2020. Global Supply Chain Report 2020. https://cdn.cdp.net/cdp-production/cms/ reports/documents/000/005/554/original/CDP_SC_Report_2020.pdf?1614160765.

Carrots & Sticks. https://www.carrotsandsticks.net/.

Choi, D., Z. Gao, and W. Jiang. 2020. Attention to Global Warming. *The Review of Financial Studies* . 33 (3). pp. 1112–1145.

Dai, R., H. Liang, and L. Ng. 2021. Socially Responsible Corporate Customers. *Journal of Financial Economics*. 142 (2). pp. 598–626.

Desai, M. A. and L. Jin. 2011. Institutional Tax Clienteles and Payout Policy. *Journal of Financial Economics*. 100 (1). pp. 68–84.

Ding, W., R. Levine, C. Lin, and W. Xie. 2020. Competition Laws, Norms and Corporate Social Responsibility. *National Bureau of Economic Research Working Paper*. No. 27493. Cambridge, MA.

Duanmu, J.-L., M. Bu, and R. Pittman. 2018. Does Market Competition Dampen Environmental Performance? Evidence from China. *Strategic Management Journal*. 39 (11). pp. 3006–3030.

Dyck, A., K. V. Lins, L. Roth, and H. F. Wagner. 2019. Do Institutional Investors Drive Corporate Social Responsibility? International Evidence. *Journal of Financial Economics*. 131 (3). pp. 693–714.

Ellis, J. A., C. E. Fee, and S. E. Thomas. 2012. Proprietary Costs and the Disclosure of Information About Customers. *Journal of Accounting Research*. 50 (3). pp. 685–727.

Flammer, C. 2015. Does Corporate Social Responsibility Lead To Superior Financial Performance? A Regression Discontinuity Approach. *Management Science*. 61 (11). pp. 2549–2568.

Golubov, A., M. Lasfer, and V. Vitkova. 2020. Active Catering to Dividend Clienteles: Evidence from Takeovers. *Journal of Financial Economics*. 137 (3). pp. 815–836.

Harjoto, M. and H. Jo. 2011. Corporate Governance and CSR Nexus. *Journal of Business Ethics*. 100 (1). pp. 45–67.

Hartzmark, S. M. and A. B. Sussman. 2019. Do Investors Value Sustainability? A Natural Experiment Examining Ranking and Fund Flows. *The Journal of Finance*. 74 (6). pp. 2789–2837.

Kim, E.-H. and T. P. Lyon. 2011. Strategic Environmental Disclosure: Evidence from the DOE's Voluntary Greenhouse Gas Registry. *Journal of Environmental Economics and Management*. 61 (3). pp. 311–326.

Kim, I., H. Wan, B. Wang, and T. Yang. 2019. Institutional Investors and Corporate Environmental, Social, and Governance Policies: Evidence from Toxics Release Data. *Management Science*. 65 (10). pp. 4901–4926.

Li, J. and D. Wu. 2020. Do Corporate Social Responsibility Engagements Lead to Real Environmental, Social, and Governance Impact? *Management Science*. 66 (6). pp. 2564–2588.

Lins, K. V., H. Servaes, and A. Tamayo. 2017. Social Capital, Trust, and Firm Performance: The Value of Corporate Social Responsibility During the Financial Crisis. *The Journal of Finance*. 72 (4). pp. 1785–1824.

Lyon, T. P. and J. W. Maxwell. 2011. Greenwash: Corporate Environmental Disclosure Under Threat of Audit. *Journal of Economics & Management Strategy*. 20 (1). pp. 3–41.

Lyon, T. P. and A. W. Montgomery. 2015. The Means and End of Greenwash. *Organization & Environment*. 28 (1). pp. 223–249.

Marquis, C., M. W. Toffel, and Y. Zhou. 2016. Scrutiny, Norms, and Selective Disclosure: A Global Study of Greenwashing. *Organization Science*. 27 (2). pp. 483–504.

Pastor, L., R. F. Stambaugh, and L. A. Taylor. 2021a. Dissecting Green Returns. *Journal of Financial Economics*. 146 (2). pp. 403–424.

_____. 2021b. Sustainable Investing in Equilibrium. *Journal of Financial Economics*. 142 (2). pp. 550–571.

Peterson, K. 2011. Special Report: A Wing and a Prayer: Outsourcing at Boeing. *Reuters*. 20 January. https://www.reuters.com/article/us-boeing-dreamliner/special-report-a-wing-and-a-prayer-outsourcing-at-boeing-idUSTRE70J2UX20110120.

Plambeck, E. L. and T. A. Taylor. 2016. Supplier Evasion of a Buyer's Audit: Implications for Motivating Supplier Social and Environmental Responsibility. *Manufacturing & Service Operations Management*. 18 (2). pp. 184–197.

Schiller, C. 2018. Global Supply-Chain Networks and Corporate Social Responsibility. In *13th Annual Mid-Atlantic Research Conference in Finance (MARC) Paper*.

Servaes, H. and A. Tamayo. 2013. The Impact of Corporate Social Responsibility on Firm Value: The Role of Customer Awareness. *Management Science*. 59 (5). pp. 1045–1061.

Shi, Y., J. Wu, Y. Zhang, and Y. Zhou. 2023. *Green Image Management in Supply Chains: Strategic Disclosure of Corporate Suppliers*. https://papers.ssrn.com/sol3/papers.cfm?abstract_id=3700310.

Sunar, N. and E. Plambeck. 2016. Allocating Emissions among Co-Products: Implications for Procurement and Climate Policy. *Manufacturing & Service Operations Management*. 18 (3). pp. 414–428.

Wu, Y., K. Zhang, and J. Xie. 2020. Bad Greenwashing, Good Greenwashing: Corporate Social Responsibility and Information Transparency. *Management Science*. 66 (7). pp. 3095–3112.

Chapter 5

The Economic Consequences of Corporate Social Irresponsibility and Policy Implications

Guanming He, Zhichao Li, and Richard Slack

5.1 Introduction

Although extensive research has explored topics related to corporate social responsibility (CSR)—particularly within the context of the Sustainable Development Goals—including its impact on firms' performance, the evidence is mixed and inconclusive.[1] Further, even as the research focusing on CSR has increased, a relatively small number of studies have investigated "corporate social irresponsibility" (CSI). Yet, CSR and CSI may exist simultaneously and have distinct economic consequences on firms.

This chapter first discusses the coexistence of CSR and CSI then expounds on their different economic consequences. It analyzes factors that affect the economic consequences of CSR and CSI, summarizes relevant regulations and legislation, and details the policy implications of CSR and CSI.

As governments and wider civil society have grown more aware of environmental and social issues, the public too has started to emphasize and expect companies to play a role as social citizens. This has fueled interest in CSR in academia, in practice, and from policymakers.

---

[1] Achieving sustainable development is a primary goal of the United Nations. In September 2015, UN member states adopted the 2030 Agenda for Sustainable Development, with its 17 goals. The agenda recognizes the critical importance of environmental and social issues, such as ending poverty, improving health and education, reducing inequality, and tackling climate change.

5.2 Coexistence of Corporate Social Responsibility and Corporate Social Irresponsibility

CSR and CSI coexist, according to considerable evidence. For instance, Siemens, a German multinational conglomerate corporation, operated with high social and environmental standards but was found guilty of bribery by the United States (US) Corrupt Foreign Practices Act in December 2008. Another German company, the automaker Volkswagen Group, claimed to be a "corporate citizen," and held a leading position in various international CSR indexes (Riera and Iborra 2017). Despite this outstanding performance in CSR, the US Environmental Protection Agency in September 2015 accused the company of cheating on the emissions test by installing a "defeat device" in diesel engines to deflate the reported level of excessive carbon dioxide emissions. These two scandals resulted in significant reputational losses and, relatedly, severe unfavorable economic consequences for the firms. Extant studies further suggest that a firm can have a strong CSR performance in one dimension of CSR or one geographic location but commit social misconduct in another dimension or geographic location (Strike, Gao, and Bansal 2006; Herzig and Moon 2013; Keig, Brouthers, and Marshall 2015).

Researchers further explore these seemingly contradictory behaviors of firms and propose a causal relationship between CSR and CSI. CSR engagement can be used as a vehicle to offset a firm's *past* socially irresponsible behaviors.[2] In this regard, firms that behave more socially irresponsibly will invest more in CSR to rebuild their reputation or conceal unethical behavior. CSR can also act as insurance against *future* CSI and alleviate the potential losses stemming from CSI (Godfrey, Merrill, and Hansen 2009; Minor and Morgan 2011). Klein and Dawar (2004) find that good CSR performance will mitigate the negative brand evaluation of consumers in the case of a product-harm crisis. Flammer (2013) demonstrates that firms that enjoy higher environmental CSR will experience lighter adverse stock market reaction to ecologically harmful events.

---

[2] For example, see Muller and Kräussl 2011; Kotchen and Moon 2012; Kang, Germann, and Grewal (2016); Lenz, Wetzel, and Hammerschmidt (2017); Raghunandan and Rajgopal (2022); Chen, He, and Krishnan (2023).

5.3 Economic Consequences of Corporate Social Responsibility and Corporate Social Irresponsibility

5.3.1   Corporate Social Responsibility

From political, economic, and societal expectations, there is little doubt that firms should take responsibility for their impact on society and the environment. However, there has been considerable debate whether CSR behaviors violate maximization of shareholder wealth (Karnani 2011). Conventional wisdom argues that the priority of a firm is to generate profits for its shareholders. Using limited corporate resources to perform CSR activities will generate unnecessary costs and siphon off the resources that can be invested in value-enhancing investment or operation activities (Friedman 1970; Brammer and Millington 2008). In the same vein, even if a firm has the resources, it should distribute more dividends to shareholders rather than devote itself to CSR activities. This is because involvement in CSR implies a transfer of wealth from the company's owners to a third party without rightful claims. Further, involvement in CSR activities can be time-consuming. Managers emphasizing CSR performance too much may overlook their primary management responsibilities and profitable-investment opportunities. This inefficient resource allocation is more evident when managers use CSR engagement to burnish their reputation[3] or to conceal corporate wrongdoing (Hemingway and Maclagan 2004; Kotchen and Moon 2012).

However, although enacting CSR activities is costly, substantial evidence has found that CSR activities can bring myriad benefits to a firm in various facets. First, good CSR performance can enhance corporate reputation and strengthen the relationship with stakeholders (Sen, Bhattacharya, and Korschun 2006). Corporate reputation is an essential intangible asset conducive to a firm's competitive advantages. A good reputation due to CSR signals firm ability and commitment to work in the interest of stakeholders and increases its creditworthiness, contributing to its societal legitimacy and a solid contractual relationship or tacit agreement with its stakeholders (Choi and Wang 2009; Cao et al. 2015). Stakeholders, in turn, will have more favorable attitudes toward the firm and be more inclined to supply their resources (Frooman 1999; Backhaus, Stone, and Heiner 2002).

---

[3]   For example, see Haley (1991); Galaskiewicz (1997); Cennamo, Berrone, and Gomez-Mejia (2009); and Barnea and Rubin (2010).

Employees are the most critical internal stakeholders for a firm, and their attitudes toward CSR engagement would significantly affect their work performance and even employee retention. Extant research reveals that a strong commitment to CSR showcases a prosocial firm culture (Collier and Esteban 2007; Linnenluecke and Griffiths 2010) and produces a sense of meaningfulness (Bauman and Skitka 2012; Grant 2012) that increases employees' commitment,[4] job satisfaction (Valentine and Fleischman 2008), and identification with the firm (Berger, Cunningham, and Drumwright 2006; Rodrigo and Arenas 2008; Kim et al. 2010). These positive employee work attitudes will improve productivity and create positive word-of-mouth for a firm as a good employer. This will, in turn, attract and retain more talented employees.[5]

Customers and suppliers are two external stakeholders that significantly impact corporate performance. Prior studies indicate that firms with higher CSR performance can reap economic benefits from customers and suppliers. CSR initiatives portray a positive corporate image among customers, fostering loyalty to the products/services of a firm and increasing their willingness to pay a higher price and resist other negative news about the firm.[6] These increased brand value and customer satisfaction further provoke positive word-of-mouth among customers, raise their active advocacy behavior, and enable the firm to differentiate itself from its competitors. In the long run, firm sales and profitability will increase (Bloom et al. 2006; Lev, Petrovits, and Radhakrishnan 2010). Further, good CSR performance helps a firm maintain a solid relationship with its suppliers and thereby attract more trade credit from them (Zhang et al. 2014; Xu, Wu, and Dao 2020).

Second, good relationships with broad stakeholders facilitate information communication between a firm and its stakeholders and enable the firm to derive more external knowledge (Jansen, Van Den Bosch, and Volberda 2006), spurring its innovation potential (Luo and Du 2015). From another perspective, better communication between insiders and outsiders reduces information asymmetry, mitigating conflict of interest between managers and stakeholders (Jo and Harjoto 2011, 2012; Cui, Jo, and Na 2018).

---

4   See Peterson (2004); Rupp et al. (2006); Brammer, Millington, and Rayton (2007); and Collier and Esteban (2007).
5   See Greening and Turban (2000); Bhattacharya, Sen, and Korschun (2008); Hansen et al. (2011); and Carnahan, Kryscynski, and Olson (2017).
6   See Luo and Bhattacharya (2006); Du, Bhattacharya, and Sen (2007); Lev, Petrovits, and Radhakrishnan (2010); and Iglesias et al. (2020).

Third, firms behaving socially responsibly are more likely to realize capital market benefits, including lower cost of capital and better debt covenants with creditors. The cost of capital is the required rate of return based on capital providers' perception of a firm's financial performance and risks. A better (lower) financial performance (risk) is instrumental in lowering the cost of capital. Numerous studies document a positive association between CSR and financial performance that is proxied by accounting ratios such as return on assets and return on equity (Wang and Qian 2011). Meanwhile, researchers demonstrate that CSR activities will reduce firms' risk including investment, operational, financial, and information risks.[7] Investors who perceive better financial performance and lower risk as a result of CSR participation will charge lower costs for providing capital to the firm.[8]

Overall, contributing to CSR involves both economic costs and benefits for a firm. On this account, whether and to what extent CSR will ultimately influence firm value rests on the trade-off between the costs and benefits of pursuing CSR. Existing literature provides conflicting evidence on the impact of CSR engagement on firm value. On the one hand, some studies show that firms executing CSR initiatives will have higher firm value.[9] On the other hand, some research argues that CSR activities have negative or no influence on corporate financial performance and firm value (Brammer, Brooks, and Pavelin 2006; Nelling and Webb 2009; Crisóstomo, de Souza Freire, and de Vasconcellos 2011). Some evidence indicates that the positive impact of CSR on firm value only exists in some conditions, without which there is no, or even a negative, relationship between CSR and firm value. For example, Servaes and Tamayo (2013) find that the value-enhancing role of CSR only exists for firms with high customer awareness (i.e., brand or firm visibility), whereas the relationship between CSR and firm value is either negative or insignificant for firms with low customer awareness. Arouri and Pijourlet (2017) find that a high CSR rating results in a higher value of cash holdings only for firms operating in countries where shareholders are well protected from expropriation by managers and in countries where the institutional and regulatory quality is high. Buchanan, Cao, and Chen (2018) find that

---

[7]   See Boutin-Dufresne and Savaria (2004); Lee and Faff (2009); Hong and Andersen (2011); Kim, Park, and Wier (2012); Oikonomou, Brooks, and Pavelin (2012); Mishra and Modi (2013); Kim, Li, and Li (2014); Sun and Cui (2014); Bozzolan et al. (2015); Shahrour, Girerd-Potin, and Taramasco (2021); and Shih et al. (2021).

[8]   See Sharfman and Fernando (2008); El Ghoul et al. (2011); Goss and Roberts (2011); Ye and Zhang (2011); Chava (2014); Oikonomou, Brooks, and Pavelin (2014); Ge and Liu (2015); Shi and Sun (2015); and Lin, Servaes, and Tamayo (2017).

[9]   See Guenster et al. (2011); Jo and Harjoto (2011); Kim and Statman (2012); Gregory and Whittaker (2013); Gregory, Tharyan, and Whittaker (2014); and Lin, Servaes, and Tamayo (2017).

firms with high CSR-investment intensity experience more loss in firm value during financial crisis, while these firms have higher value before a crisis. This conflicting evidence may be attributed to the fact that CSR does not always bring benefits that outstrip the associated costs to all firms. Section 4 details country-, industry-, and firm-level characteristics that affect the benefits as compared with the costs of CSR.

5.3.2 Economic Consequences of Corporate Social Irresponsibility

CSI activities refer to either intentional or unintentional activities of a firm. In most scenarios, firms socially misbehaving, such as pollution, child labor, and bribery, have objectives to reduce costs and increase profits. Notwithstanding the potential of intentional CSI to create positive ramifications for the firm, it may be more detrimental for the firm once the CSI is discovered by stakeholders.

When regulators uncover corporate misbehavior in relation to environmental, social, and governance aspects, this may result in lawsuits that may take years to settle and would pose substantial litigation costs, regulatory fines, reputational harm, and other expenses on the firm. For instance, Siemens paid around $1.6 billion by December 2008 to resolve corruption-related charges;[10] British Petroleum paid about $65 billion by January 2018 to cover environmental cleanup, compensation, and penalties for the Deepwater Horizon oil spill in 2010 (Vaughan 2022). This pending litigation and associated expenses brings huge reputational losses and uncertainty to the firm's future performance.

Besides the preceding costs, CSI destroys firm value and diminishes the competitive advantages of a firm by eroding its relationship with stakeholders. Ample research evidence reveals stakeholders' negative attitudes toward, and strong intents to punish, unethical and socially irresponsible firms.[11] Consumers are inclined to stop buying products or services from a firm that behaves in a socially irresponsible manner and to spread negative word-of-mouth to a range of acquaintances to boycott the firm's products or services (Braunsberger and Buckler 2011). In addition, CSI behaviors also elicit employee anger, resulting

---

[10]   Information obtained from the US Securities and Exchange Commission. https://www.sec.gov/news/press/2008/2008–294.htm (accessed 20 December 2022).

[11]   For example, see Lindenmeier, Schleer, and Pricl (2012); Grappi, Romani, and Bagozzi (2013); Sweetin et al. (2013); Xie, Bagozzi, and Gronhaug (2015); Antonetti and Maklan (2016); and Xie and Bagozzi (2019).

in negative word-of-mouth among them (Hericher and Bridoux 2022). These potential stakeholder sanctions or boycotts significantly limit the ability of a firm to achieve satisfactory financial outcomes. In line with this argument, prior research provides empirical evidence that CSI is negatively (positively) related to financial performance (risk).[12]

5.3.3 Comparing the Economic Consequences of Corporate Social Responsibility and Corporate Social Irresponsibility

The impact of CSR and CSI varies in direction, magnitude, and duration. Stakeholders may not require all firms to participate in CSR activities proactively, but they are more sensitive to any CSI issue that harms their interests (Foreman 2011; Barnett 2014; Kölbel, Busch, and Jancso 2017). So an asymmetry exists of stakeholders' reactions to good versus bad news associated with CSR versus CSI behavior. In particular, given that some firms— such as financially constrained and start-up companies—cannot afford to be socially responsible. This is based on their capacities and available resources and stakeholder expectations, and the attention to the CSR performance of these firms may be relatively low. However, all firms are expected to avoid taking socially irresponsible actions. This difference in the emphases on CSI as compared with CSR by stakeholders may result in stronger stakeholders' negative reactions to CSI scandals, including more severe punishment for CSI, compared with the positive rewards for CSR.

Indeed, some studies corroborate that CSI has a greater effect on corporate performance and risk than CSR.[13] Hawn (2021) finds that media coverage of CSR has no impact on the firms' cross-border acquisitions, while media coverage of CSI impedes the completion of such acquisitions. Li et al. (2021) show that providing CSR disclosures in the management discussion and analysis section of annual reports does not increase the value of firms with good CSR performance but does decrease the value of firms with high ESG concerns.

CSR and CSI affect corporate reputation and the firm's relationship with its stakeholders and thereby influence firm performance and firm value. Nevertheless, it often takes a long period for a firm to establish a good reputation via CSR activities. In contrast, corporate reputation could be quickly ruined by CSI scandals once discovered in the public arena.

---

[12] See Gupta and Goldar (2005); Karpoff, Lott, and Wehrly (2005); Oikonomou, Brooks, and Pavelin (2012); Mishra and Modi (2013); Kölbel, Busch, and Jancso (2017); and Harjoto, Hoepner, and Lie (2021).

[13] For example, see Chava (2014); Goss and Roberts (2011); Jayachandran, Kalaignanam, and Eilert (2013); and Oikonomou, Brooks, and Pavelin (2014).

5.4 Characteristics That Affect the Benefits versus the Costs of Corporate Social Responsibility and Corporate Social Irresponsibility

As the economic ramifications of CSR and CSI are inconclusive, it is of great importance to understand the major factors that would affect the benefits in relation to the costs of CSR and CSI.

5.4.1 Country-Level Characteristics

Firms in countries with diverse cultures, economic conditions, institutional environments, etc. may have distinct levels of benefits and costs of CSR and CSI (Doh and Guay 2006; Wang and Qian 2011; Wang, Dou, and Jia 2016). The rationales behind this notion are multifaceted. First is related to stakeholders' differential perceptions of CSR in relation to CSI, which play a crucial role in shaping their economic consequences on firms. Stakeholders with high levels of social concerns will expect firms to take more responsibility in society. Consequently, they will value (punish) the firm with better CSR performance (worse CSI behaviors) to a larger extent. Stakeholders' attitudes toward CSR and CSI are rooted in the culture of a country and thereby vary significantly across countries (Husted 2005; Williams and Zinkin 2008). Compared with people living in developed countries, citizens of developing countries are generally less sensitive to CSR behaviors (Xu and Yang 2010). Customers in developing economies, as an illustration, care more about the price and quality of a product and are more unaware of CSR (Chou and Chen 2004; Arli and Lasmono 2010).

Apart from the divergence of stakeholders' views, the institutional variations in the cross-national context can also explain the different economic consequences of CSR and CSI in different countries. Developed markets usually have well-established "reward and punishment" policies, as exemplified by tax relief to encourage firms to pursue CSR and by huge penalties to deter CSI. In such a scenario, firms may gain benefits from CSR that outweigh the associated costs and would suffer substantial reputational and legal losses due to CSI. Conversely, in a loose and ineffective institutional system, both the degree of regulatory sanctions caused by CSI and the economic benefits linked to CSR are lower. Hence, socially conscious firms under this institutional system may find the costs of CSR outweigh the benefits, while firms acting in a socially irresponsible way will not experience negative economic consequences. Furthermore, developed countries with mature capital markets have more professional institutional investors. Existing studies show that institutional investors are more positive toward social capital and thus are inclined to invest in firms pursuing CSR.[14] Therefore, CSR activities are likely to be better recognized by investors in developed countries, so it is more likely to see the value-enhancing (value-destroying) role of CSR (CSI) in developed economies.

The economic consequences of CSR or CSI are also contingent on how well stakeholders are aware of the CSR and CSI activities and performance of firms.[15] Only the informed stakeholders can respond appropriately to CSR and CSI. In other words, a high level of stakeholder awareness gives rise to greater economic benefits (sanctions) toward CSR (CSI). Developed markets provide diverse information channels and effective market supervision. Hence, firms operating in developed countries are more visible and transparent to stakeholders than those in developing countries, facilitating the greater flow of information among stock market participants. In this sense, the positive (negative) association between CSR (CSI) and corporate financial performance is more evident for firms in developed markets (Wang, Dou, and Jia 2016).

Some other studies also provide evidence of how different country-level characteristics affect the economic consequences of CSR and CSI. Breuer et al. (2018) show that the level of investor protection in a country will determine how CSR affects the cost of equity of a firm. In countries with a higher (lower) level of investor protection that safeguards the shareholders against expropriation by insiders, CSR reduces (increases) the cost of equity. Chang, Shim, and Yi (2019) illuminate the role of country-level media freedom in the relationship between CSR and firm value, and specifically that CSR is positively associated with the financial performance of firms in countries with full media freedom but is negatively or insignificantly associated with the corporate performance in countries with partial or no media freedom. Sampath, Gardberg, and Rahman (2018) elucidate that firms engaging in bribery in a less corrupt country have greater market penalties. Harjoto, Hoepner, and Lie (2021) find that the negative impact of CSI on firms is larger for civil law countries and for nations with higher institutional trust and higher confidence in corporations.

---

[14]   See Graves and Waddock (1994); Wang, Choi, and Li (2008); Petersen and Vredenburg (2009); and Zhang, Xie, and Xu (2016).

[15]   See McWilliams and Siegel (2001); Schuler and Cording (2006); Du, Bhattacharya, and Sen (2010); Servaes and Tamayo (2013); and Dyck et al. (2019).

5.4.2 Industry-Level Characteristics

Stakeholders have different expectations of CSR engagement for firms in different industries, so industry-level characteristics may affect the economic consequences of CSR or CSI. For instance, firms in "sin" industries, which relate to tobacco, alcohol, gambling, firearms, military, and nuclear power, among others, are considered "harmful" to society and receive negative attitudes from stakeholders because these firms provide products/services that do not conform to social norms. Socially conscious investors or investors under high regulatory and public scrutiny tend to avoid investing in firms operating in such industries (Hong and Kacperczyk 2009; Fu, Lin, and Zhang 2020). It is thus of greater importance for firms in sin industries, relative to those in other industries, to strengthen their reputation among stakeholders. CSR engagement is a good means to achieve so. Prior studies find that engagement in CSR reduces firm risk and increases firm value in sin industries (Cai, Jo, and Pan 2012; Jo and Na 2012), and the risk-reduction effect is more pronounced, both economically and statistically, for firms in sin industries compared to those in other industries (Jo and Na 2012).

Some other studies also provide evidence that industry-level characteristics shape the economic consequences of CSR and CSI. For example, Lenz, Wetzel, and Hammerschmidt (2017) propose that a firm with CSR records in a domain where it also performs socially irresponsibly will be perceived as insincere, significantly damaging firm value. Yet, for firms in industries with a high level of CSI, this value-destroying effect is attenuated, as stakeholders may interpret this inconsistent behavior of firms (i.e., engaging in CSR and CSI simultaneously in one domain) as active corporate responses to the negative impact of the industrially unavoidable CSI rather than a lack of morality. Sun and Ding (2021) document that the negative impact of CSI on firm value persists longer and is stronger for firms in industries with high levels of business uncertainty or competition.

5.4.3 Firm-Level Characteristics

Firm characteristics reflect the capabilities and resources of a firm, so stakeholders' expectations of CSR or CSI also vary from firm to firm. As such, firms operating in the same industry and in the same country may be subject to different economic consequences of CSR and CSI. Research on the moderating effect of firm-level characteristics on the association between CSR/CSI and firm performance seems limited. The opinion in this chapter is that there are three main firm-level determinants of CSR/CSI.

Visibility. Corporate visibility is the prerequisite for firms to benefit from CSR endeavors and receive punishments as a result of CSI. A higher level of corporate visibility will heighten stakeholders' awareness of CSR/CSI and prompt their reactions to this corporate behavior to a larger extent. Therefore, visibility should increase the benefits or penalties to a firm for pursuing CSR or CSI activities. Firms with considerable investments in advertising are more likely to be seen and followed by various stakeholders. A great deal of literature has proved that firms with higher advertising intensity will attract more attention from stakeholders, and consequently, CSR/CSI, if any, will induce more pronounced economic benefits or penalties for these firms (e.g., Wang and Qian 2011).

Firm size. Larger firms tend to have more resources (Gupta, Raj, and Wilemon 1986). Hence, they are able to invest more in projects with uncertain future returns and long payback periods, such as CSR-related projects which strengthen firm performance in the long run (van Beurden and Gössling 2008; Aguinis and Glavas 2012). On the other hand, larger firms are more visible to the market, and thus more likely to attract stakeholders' attention and reaction to their behaviors. In this regard, the economic consequences of CSR and CSI are more pronounced for larger firms.

Financial health. Financial constraints will restrict managers' discretionary investment in CSR. In this circumstance, stakeholders may understand that the firm's limited resources should be primarily applied to the core business activities rather than the pursuit of CSR. As such, stakeholders may not expect financially constrained firms to perform in a socially responsible way and will be less interested in their CSR performance. Conversely, financially healthy firms not constrained in their financial ability to pursue CSR will enjoy more benefits from their CSR investment, as it will likely be more recognized and expected by stakeholders (Wang and Qian 2011).

5.5 Regulations and Legislation of Corporate Social Responsibility and Corporate Social Irresponsibility and Its Policy Implications

Corporate social responsibility is generally a voluntary initiative rather than a legal mandate in most countries worldwide (Lin 2021). Yet, with the increasing importance and expectations attached to firms' role in serving society, a growing number of countries have enforced legislation that explicitly requires firms to carry out CSR. Against this backdrop, Mauritius is a pioneer in legally mandating firms to devote a specific amount to CSR. Since independence in 1968, Mauritius has long been plagued by poverty and inequality. Therefore, it is imperative to appeal to corporate contribution in CSR activities for Mauritius. In 2009, the Government of Mauritius amended "The Income Tax Act of 1995" and released "The Finance (Miscellaneous Provisions) Bill (No. XVI of 2009)," which compels all profitable firms to set up a CSR fund that accounts for 2% of their preceding year's book profits.[16] According to the current regulation, at least 75% of this CSR fund should be remitted to the Ministry of Finance. Then the National Social Inclusion Foundation will allocate this remitted money to CSR-related national schemes, such as poverty reduction, educational support, and environmental protection. The company can use the remaining CSR fund to implement a CSR program or lend financial support to a nongovernmental organization implementing a CSR program in the priority areas of governmental intervention as specified in the 10th Schedule of Income Tax Act (Mauritius Revenue Authority 2021).[17]

In August 2013, India passed a mandatory CSR law, Section 135 of the Companies Act formulated by the Ministry of Corporate Affairs. This act requires firms, which have a net worth of over ₹50 billion (about $616 million), a sales turnover of over ₹100 billion (about $1.2 billion), or a net profit of over ₹50 billion (about $616 million) in the previous financial year, to establish a CSR board committee. This board committee should ensure that the firm annually allocates at least 2% of the average of its net profits, which are made in the three immediately preceding financial years, to its qualified CSR programs. If a firm fails to invest the required amount, the board should expound the reasons for the noncompliance in its annual report.[18]

Following Mauritius and India, corporate philanthropy became compulsory in Nepal. Under the "Industrial Enterprise Act (IEA) 2076 (2020)," a firm in industries with an annual sales turnover of more than NRs150 million (about $1.2 million) must deposit at least 1% of its annual profits in the CSR fund. Besides, in 2017, Nepal Rastra Bank, the central bank of Nepal, issued the Circular No. 11/073/74 that forces all Nepalese banks and financial institutions

---

16 See The Finance (Miscellaneous Provisions) Bill (No. XVI of 2009): Explanatory Memorandum at https://mauritiusassembly.govmu.org/Documents/Bills/intro/2009/bill1609.pdf.

17 See Mauritius Revenue Authority (2022). Specific priority areas of governmental intervention can be gained from the same report.

18 The clause of the Section 135 of the Companies Act was acquired from the Ministry of Corporate Affairs at https://www.mca.gov.in/Ministry/pdf/InvitationOfPublicCommentsHLC_18012019.pdf.

to spend at least 1% of their net profits in specific CSR sectors—social projects, direct donation, Sustainable Development Goals (SDGs), and/or childcare centers for employees.[19]

Except for the foregoing three countries that have enacted mandatory CSR laws and created quantifiable legal standards to measure corporate endeavors in CSR, other countries have also made CSR a legal obligation in relevant laws, although they do not have quantitative criteria. For instance, in the United Kingdom (UK), Section 172 of the Companies Act (2006), says that it is a statutory and fiduciary duty of directors to consider the interests of firms' stakeholders, including employees, suppliers, customers, communities, environments, etc., when promoting the success of the firm.[20] Article 5 of the China Companies Law, revised in 2018, stipulates that firms should bear social responsibility.[21] Likewise, Article 74 of the Indonesian Law No. 40 of 2007 on Limited Liability Companies specifies that "the company having its business activities in the field of, and/or related to, natural resources shall be obliged to perform its social and environmental responsibility."[22] Unlike the foregoing laws, the French Duty of Vigilance Law 2017 interprets CSR as a management process, and requires business groups, which employ above 5,000 employees in France or 10,000 worldwide, to identify social and environmental hazards related to their operations and implement practical plans to mitigate the hazard risks.[23]

Although only a few countries have executed mandatory CSR laws/regulations, most countries have relevant laws/regulations focusing on social issues (i.e., human rights and labor) and environmental issues. Any violation of these laws/regulations, such as corporate social and environmental misconduct, will engender legal punishments, including fines and imprisonments.[24]

---

[19] Articles of the law in English can be found in Chapters 9–54 of the Industrial Enterprise Act 2076 from https://moics.gov.np/uploads/shares/laws/Industrial%20Enterprises%20Act%20%202020.pdf. The relevant information in English about Circular No. 11/073/74 was obtained from https://pioneerlaw.com/existing-laws-on-corporate-social-responsibility/.

[20] Legal provision retrieved from https://www.legislation.gov.uk/ukpga/2006/46/section/172.

[21] "Company Law of the People's Republic of China" (Chinese version) from http://www.gov.cn/ziliao/flfg/2005–10/28/content_85478.htm. English translation: http://zyxy.zuel.edu.cn/_upload/article/files/e1/f1/78afb97f426d88d621c8a14e725d/774ca606–4d62–4729–8009–9f6c816441ec.pdf.

[22] The Indonesian Law No. 40 of 2007 on Limited Liability Companies (in English) from https://www.indonesia-investments.com/business/foreign-investment/company-law-indonesia/item8311.

[23] The English version of French Duty of Vigilance Law 2017 could be checked via https://vigilance-plan.org/wp-content/uploads//2019/06/2019-VPRG-English.pdf#page=80.

[24] Since specific regulations and laws focusing on environmental and social issues differ from country to country, and that the number of these laws is large even for one country, this chapter does not discuss detailed provisions of these laws for any country.

5.6 Conclusion

Researchers have widely explored topics relating to CSR and CSI, as emphasis on the role that firms play in society has increased. More and more research distinguishes between CSI and CSR, and studies these two distinct concepts separately.

This chapter expounds on the coexistence of CSR and CSI by providing evidence from real cases and studies that show the relationship between CSR and CSI. It discusses the economic consequences of CSR and CSI and identifies the country-, industry-, and firm-level characteristics that shape the economic outcomes of CSR and CSI.

In general, given the coexistence of CSR and CSI and their different economic impacts on firms, CSI should be regarded as a construct separate from CSR rather than the opposite end of the same continuum of CSR. Given that regulations and legislation relating to CSI (through "punishment") are better established than those of CSR (through "reward"), policymakers should put more emphasis on improving the regulations and legislation of CSR. Finally, when founding the relevant regulations that encourage firms to contribute to CSR, it is essential to consider the associated costs and benefits for different firms in various industries in the context of a specific country.

References

Aguinis, H. and A. Glavas. 2012. What We Know and Don't Know about Corporate Social Responsibility: A Review and Research Agenda. *Journal of Management*. 38 (4). pp. 932–968.

Antonetti, P. and S. Maklan. 2016. An Extended Moral of Moral Outrage at Corporate Social Irresponsibility. *Journal of Business Ethics*. 135 (3). pp. 429–444.

Arli, D. I. and H. K. Lasmono. 2010. Consumers' Perception of Corporate Social Responsibility in a Developing Country. *International Journal of Consumer Studies*. 34 (1). pp. 46–51.

Arouri, M. and G. Pijourlet. 2017. CSR Performance and the Value of Cash Holdings: International Evidence. *Journal of Business Ethics*. 140 (2). pp. 263–284.

Backhaus, K. B., B. A. Stone, and K. Heiner. 2002. Exploring the Relationship between Corporate Social Performance and Employer Attractiveness. *Business and Society*. 41 (3). pp. 292–318.

Barnea, A. and A. Rubin. 2010. Corporate Social Responsibility as a Conflict between Shareholders. *Journal of Business Ethics*. 97 (1). pp. 71–86.

Barnett, M. L. 2014. Why Stakeholders Ignore Firm Misconduct: A Cognitive View. *Journal of Management*. 40 (3). pp. 676–702.

Bauman, C. W. and L. J. Skitka. 2012. Corporate Social Responsibility as a Source of Employee Satisfaction. *Research in Organizational Behavior*. 32. pp. 63–86.

Berger, I. E., P. H. Cunningham, and M. E. Drumwright. 2006. Identity, Identification, and Relationship through Social Alliances. *Journal of the Academy of Marketing Science*. 34 (2). pp. 128–137.

Bhattacharya, C. B., S. Sen, and D. Korschun. 2008. Using Corporate Social Responsibility to Win the War for Talent. *MIT Sloan Management Review*. 49 (2). pp. 37–44.

Bloom, P. N., S. Hoeffler, K. L. Keller, and C. E. B. Meza. 2006. How Social-Cause Marketing Affects Consumer. *MIT Sloan Management Review*. 47 (2). pp. 49–55.

Boutin-Dufresne, F. and P. Savaria. 2004. Corporate Social Responsibility and Financial Risk. *Journal of Portfolio Management*. 13 (1). pp. 57–66.

Bozzolan, S., M. Fabrizi, C. A. Mallin, and G. Michelon. 2015. Corporate Social Responsibility and Earnings Quality: International Evidence. *The International Journal of Accounting*. 50 (4). pp. 361–396.

Brammer, S., C. Brooks, and S. Pavelin. 2006. Corporate Social Performance and Stock Returns: UK Evidence from Disaggregate Measures. *Financial Management*. 35 (3). pp. 97–116.

Brammer, S. and A. Millington. 2008. Does It Pay to Be Different? An Analysis of the Relationship between Corporate Social and Financial Performance. *Strategic Management Journal*. 29 (12). pp. 1325–1343.

Brammer, S., A. Millington, and B. Rayton. 2007. The Contribution of Corporate Social Responsibility to Organizational Commitment. *International Journal of Human Resource Management*. 18 (10). pp. 1701–1719.

Braunsberger, K. and B. Buckler. 2011. What Motivates Consumers to Participate in Boycotts: Lessons from the Ongoing Canadian Seafood Boycott. *Journal of Business Research*. 64 (1). pp. 96–102.

Breuer, W., T. Müller, D. Rosenbach, and A. Salzmann. 2018. Corporate Social Responsibility, Investor Protection, and Cost of Equity: A Cross-Country Comparison. *Journal of Banking and Finance*. 96 (C). pp. 34–55.

Buchanan, B., C. X. Cao, and C. Chen. 2018. Corporate Social Responsibility, Firm Value, and Influential Institutional Ownership. *Journal of Corporate Finance*. 52 (C). pp. 73–95.

Cai, Y., H. Jo, and C. Pan. 2012. Doing Well While Doing Bad? CSR in Controversial Industry Sectors. *Journal of Business Ethics*. 108 (4). pp. 467–480.

Cao, Y., J. N. Myers, L. A. Linda, and T. C. Omer. 2015. Company Reputation and the Cost of Equity Capital. *Review of Accounting Studies*. 20 (1). pp. 42–81.

Carnahan, S., D. Kryscynski, and D. Olson. 2017. When Does Corporate Social Responsibility Reduce Employee Turnover? Evidence from Attorneys Before and After 9/11. *Academy of Management Journal.* 60 (5). pp. 1932–1962.

Cennamo, C., P. Berrone, and L. R. Gomez-Mejia. 2009. Does Stakeholder Management Have a Dark Side? *Journal of Business Ethics.* 89 (4). pp. 491–507.

Chang, K., H. Shim, and T. D. Yi. 2019. Corporate Social Responsibility, Media Freedom, and Firm Value. *Finance Research Letters.* 30 (C). pp. 1–7.

Chava, S. 2014. Environmental Externalities and Cost of Capital. *Management Science.* 60 (9). pp. 2223–2247.

Chen, L., G. He, and G. Krishnan. Forthcoming. Does CEO Debt-Like Compensation Mitigate Corporate Social Irresponsibility? *Accounting Forum.*

Choi, J. and H. Wang. 2009. Stakeholder Relations and the Persistence of Corporate Financial Performance. *Strategic Management Journal.* 30 (8). pp. 895–907.

Chou, T. and F. Chen. 2004. Retail Pricing Strategies in Recession Economies. *Journal of International Marketing.* 12 (1). pp. 82–102.

Collier, J. and R. Esteban. 2007. Corporate Social Responsibility and Employee Commitment. *Business Ethics: A European Review.* 16 (1). pp. 19–33.

Crisóstomo, V., F. de Souza Freire, and F. C. de Vasconcellos. 2011. Corporate Social Responsibility, Firm Value and Financial Performance in Brazil. *Social Responsibility Journal.* 7 (2). pp. 295–309.

Cui, J., H. Jo, and H. Na. 2018. Does Corporate Social Responsibility Affect Information Asymmetry? *Journal of Business Ethics.* 148 (3). pp. 549–572.

Doh, J. P. and T. R. Guay. 2006. Corporate Social Responsibility, Public Policy, and NGO Activism in Europe and the United States: An Institutional-Stakeholder Perspective. *Journal of Management Studies.* 43 (1). pp. 47–73.

Du, S., C. B. Bhattacharya, and S. Sen. 2007. Reaping Relationship Rewards from Corporate Social Responsibility: The Role of Competitive Positioning. *International Journal of Research in Marketing*. 24 (3). pp. 224–241.

——. 2010. Maximizing Business Returns to Corporate Social Responsibility (CSR): The Role of CSR Communication. *International Journal of Management Review*. 12 (1). pp. 8–19.

Dyck, A., K. V. Lins, L. Roth, and H. F. Wagner. 2019. Do Institutional Investors Drive Corporate Social Responsibility? International Evidence. *Journal of Financial Economics*. 131 (3). pp. 693–714.

El Ghoul, S., O. Guedhami, C. C. Y. Kwok, and D. R. Mishra. 2011. Does Corporate Social Responsibility Affect the Cost of Capital? *Journal of Banking and Finance*. 35 (9). pp. 2388–2406.

Flammer, C. 2013. Corporate Social Responsibility and Shareholder Reaction: The Environmental Awareness of Investors. *Academy of Management Journal*. 56 (3). pp. 758–81.

Foreman, J. 2011. Corporate Social Responsibility (CSR) in Buyer-Supplier Relationships: US Firms and Foreign Suppliers. *International Journal of Business, Marketing, and Decision Science*. 4 (1). pp. 33–45.

Friedman, M. 1970. The Social Responsibility of a Business Is to Increase Its Profits. *The New York Times Magazine*. 13 September.

Frooman, J. 1999. Stakeholder Influence Strategies. *Academy of Management Review*. 24 (2). pp. 191–205.

Fu, X., Y. Lin, and Y. Zhang. 2020. Responsible Investing in the Gaming Industry. *Journal of Corporate Finance*. 64 (C). 101657.

Galaskiewicz, J. 1997. An Urban Grants Economy Revisited: Corporate Charitable Contributions in the Twin Cities, 1979–81, 1987–89. *Administrative Science Quarterly*. 42 (3). pp. 445–471.

Ge, W. and M. Liu. 2015. Corporate Social Responsibility and the Cost of Corporate Bonds. *Journal of Accounting and Public Policy*. 34 (6). pp. 597–624.

Godfrey, P. C., C. B. Merrill, and J. M. Hansen. 2009. The Relationship between Corporate Social Responsibility and Shareholder Value: An Empirical Test of the Risk Management Hypothesis. *Strategic Management Journal*. 30 (4). pp. 425–45.

Goss, A. and G. S. Roberts. 2011. The Impact of Corporate Social Responsibility on the Cost of Bank Loans. *Journal of Banking and Finance*. 35 (7). pp. 1794–1810.

Grant, A. M. 2012. Giving Time, Time After Time: Work Design and Sustained Employee Participation in Corporate Volunteering. *Academy of Management Review*. 37 (4). pp. 589–615.

Grappi, S., S. Romani, and R. P. Bagozzi. 2013. Consumer Response to Corporate Irresponsible Behavior: Moral Emotions and Virtues. *Journal of Business Research*. 66 (10). pp. 1814–1821.

Graves, S. B. and S. A. Waddock. 1994. Institutional Owners and Corporate Social Performance. *Academy of Management Journal*. 37 (4). pp. 1034–1046.

Greening, D. W. and D. B. Turban. 2000. Corporate Social Performance as a Competitive Advantage in Attracting a Quality Workforce. *Business and Society*. 39 (3). pp. 254–280.

Gregory, A., R. Tharyan, and J. Whittaker. 2014. Corporate Social Responsibility and Firm Value: Disaggregating the Effects on Cash Flow, Risk and Growth. *Journal of Business Ethics*. 124 (4). pp. 633–657.

Gregory, A. and J. Whittaker. 2013. Exploring the Valuation of Corporate Social Performance – A Comparison of Research Methods. *Journal of Business Ethics*. 16 (1). pp. 1–20.

Guenster, N., R. Bauer, J. Derwall, and K. Koedijk. 2011. The Economic Value of Corporate Eco-Efficiency. *European Financial Management*. 17 (4). pp. 679–704.

Gupta, A. K., S. P. Raj, and D. Wilemon. 1986. A Model for Studying R&D—Marketing Interface in the Product Innovation Success. *Journal of Marketing*. 50 (2). pp. 7–17.

Gupta, S. and B. Goldar. 2005. Do Stock Markets Penalize Environment-Unfriendly Behaviour? Evidence from India. *Ecological Economics*. 52 (1). pp. 81–95.

Haley, U. C. 1991. Corporate Contributions As Managerial Masques: Reframing Corporate Contributions as Strategies to Influence Society. *Journal of Management Studies*. 28 (5). pp. 485–510.

Hansen, S. D., B. B. Dunford, A. D. Boss, R. W. Boss, and I. Angermeier. 2011. Corporate Social Responsibility and the Benefits of Employee Trust: A Cross-Disciplinary Perspective. *Journal of Business Ethics*. 102 (1). pp. 29–45.

Harjoto, M. A., A. G. F. Hoepner, and Q. Lie. 2021. Corporate Social Irresponsibility and Portfolio Performance: A Cross-National Study. *Journal of International Financial Markets, Institutions and Money*. 70 (3). 101274.

Hawn, O. 2021. How Media Coverage of Corporate Social Responsibility and Irresponsibility Influences Cross-Border Acquisitions. *Strategic Management Journal*. 42 (1). pp. 58–83.

Hemingway, C. A. and P. W. Maclagan. 2004. Managers' Personal Values As Drivers of Corporate Social Responsibility. *Journal of Business Ethics*. 50 (1). pp. 33–44.

Hericher, C. and F. Bridoux. 2022. Employees' Emotional and Behavioral Reactions to Corporate Social Irresponsibility. *Journal of Management*. 49 (5). pp. 1–37.

Herzig, C. and J. Moon. 2013. Discourses on Corporate Social Ir/Responsibility in the Financial Sector. *Journal of Business Research*. 66 (10). pp. 1870–1880.

Hong, H. and M. Kacperczyk. 2009. The Price of Sin: The Effects of Social Norms on Markets. *Journal of Financial Economics*. 93 (1). pp. 15–36.

Hong, Y. and M. L. Andersen. 2011. The Relationship between Corporate Social Responsibility and Earnings Management: An Exploratory Study. *Journal of Business Ethics*. 104 (4). pp. 461–471.

Husted, B. W. 2005. Culture and Ecology: A Cross-National Study of the Determinants of Environmental Sustainability. *Management International Review*. 45 (3). pp. 349–371.

Iglesias, O., S. Markovic, M. Bagherzadeh, and J. J. Singh. 2020. Co-Creation: A Key Link Between Corporate Social Responsibility, Customer Trust, and Customer Loyalty. *Journal of Business Ethics*. 163 (2). pp. 151–166.

Jansen, J. J. P., F. A. J. Van Den Bosch, and H. W. Volberda. 2006. Exploratory Innovation, Exploitative Innovation, and Performance: Effects of Organizational Antecedents and Environmental Moderators. *Management Science*. 52 (11). pp. 1661–1674.

Jayachandran, S., K. Kalaignanam, and M. Eilert. 2013. Product and Environmental Social Performance: Varying Effect on Firm Performance. *Strategic Management Journal*. 34 (10). pp. 1255–1264.

Jo, H. and M. A. Harjoto. 2011. Corporate Governance and Firm Value: The Impact of Corporate Social Responsibility. *Journal of Business Ethics*. 103 (3). pp. 351–383.

Jo, H. and M. A. Harjoto. 2012. The Causal Effect of Corporate Governance on Corporate Social Responsibility. *Journal of Business Ethics*. 106 (1). pp. 53–72.

Jo, H. and H. Na. 2012. Does CSR Reduce Firm Risk? Evidence from Controversial Industry Sectors. *Journal of Business Ethics*. 110 (4). pp. 441–456.

Kang, C., F. Germann, and R. Grewal. 2016. Washing Away Your Sins? Corporate Social Responsibility, Corporate Social Irresponsibility, and Firm Performance. *Journal of Marketing*. 80 (2). pp. 59–79.

Karnani, A. 2011. Doing Well by Doing Good: The Grand Illusion. *California Management Review*. 53 (2). pp. 69–86.

Karpoff, J. M., J. R. Lott, and E. W. Wehrly. 2005. The Reputational Penalties for Environmental Violations: Empirical Evidence. *Journal of Law and Economics*. 48 (2). pp. 635–675.

Keig, D. L., L. E. Brouthers, and V. B. Marshall. 2015. Formal and Informal Corruption Environments CSIR: Review and Multinational Enterprise Social Irresponsibility. *Journal of Management Studies*. 52 (1). pp. 89–116.

Kim, H., M. Lee, H. Lee, and N. Kim. 2010. Corporate Social Responsibility and Employee–Company Identification. Journal of Business Ethics. 95 (4).pp. 557–569.

Kim, Y., H. Li, and S. Li. 2014. Corporate Social Responsibility and Stock Price Crash Risk. Journal of Banking and Finance. 43 (1). pp. 1–13.

Kim, Y., M. S. Park, and B. Wier. 2012. Is Earnings Quality Associated with Corporate Social Responsibility? The Accounting Review. 87 (3). pp. 761–796.

Kim, Y. and M. Statman. 2012. Do Companies Invest Enough in Environmental Responsibility? Journal of Business Ethics. 105 (1). pp. 115–129.

Klein, J. and N. Dawar. 2004. Corporate Social Responsibility and Consumers' Attributions and Brand Evaluations in a Product-Harm Crisis. International Journal of Research in Marketing. 21 (3). pp. 203–217.

Kölbel, J. F., T. Busch, and L. M. Jancso. 2017. How Media Coverage of Corporate Social Irresponsibility Increases Financial Risk. Strategic Management Journal. 38 (11). pp. 2266–2284.

Kotchen, M. and J. J. Moon. 2012. Corporate Social Responsibility for Irresponsibility. The B. E. Journal of Economic Analysis and Policy. 12 (1). pp. 1–23.

Lee, D. D. and R. W. Faff. 2009. Corporate Sustainability Performance and Idiosyncratic Risk: A Global Perspective. Financial Review. 44 (2). pp. 213–237.

Lenz, I., H. A. Wetzel, and M. Hammerschmidt. 2017. Can Doing Good Lead to Doing Poorly? Firm Value Implications of CSR in the Face of CSI. Journal of the Academy of Marketing Science. 45 (5). pp. 677–697.

Lev, B., C. Petrovits, and S. Radhakrishnan. 2010. Is Doing Good Good for You? How Corporate Charitable Contributions Enhance Revenue Growth. Strategic Management Journal. 31 (2). pp. 182–200.

Li, X., A. Tsang, S. Zeng, and G. Zhou. 2021. CSR Reporting and Firm Value: International Evidence on Management Discussion and Analysis. China Accounting and Finance Review. 23 (2). pp. 102–145.

Lin, K. V., H. Servaes, and A. Tamayo. 2017. Social Capital, Trust, and Firm Performance: The Value of Corporate Social Responsibility during the Financial Crisis. *The Journal of Finance.* 72 (4). pp. 1785–1824.

Lin, L. 2021. Mandatory Corporate Social Responsibility Legislation around the World: Emergent Varieties and National Experiences. *University of Pennsylvania Journal of Business Law.* 23 (2). pp. 429–469.

Lindenmeier, J., C. Schleer, and D. Pricl. 2012. Consumer Outrage: Emotional Reactions to Unethical Corporate Behavior. *Journal of Business Research.* 65 (9). pp. 1364–1373.

Linnenluecke, M. K. and A. Griffiths. 2010. Corporate Sustainability and Organizational Culture. *Journal of World Business.* 45 (4). pp. 357–366.

Luo, X. and C. B. Bhattacharya. 2006. Corporate Social Responsibility, Customer Satisfaction, and Market Value. *Journal of Marketing.* 70 (4). pp. 1–18.

Luo, X. and S. Du. 2015. Exploring the Relationship Between Corporate Social Responsibility and Firm Innovation. *Marketing Letters.* 26 (4). pp. 703–714.

Mauritius Revenue Authority. 2021. CSR. https://www.mra.mu/download/CSRGuide.pdf.

McWilliams, A. and D. Siegel. 2001. Corporate Social Responsibility: A Theory of the Firm Perspective. *Academy of Management Review.* 26 (1). pp. 117–127.

Minor, D. and J. Morgan. 2011. CSR as Reputation Insurance: Primum Non Nocere. *California Management Review.* 53 (3). pp. 40–59.

Mishra, S. and S. B. Modi. 2013. Positive and Negative Corporate Social Responsibility, Financial Leverage, and Idiosyncratic Risk. *Journal of Business Ethics.* 117 (2). pp. 431–448.

Muller, A. and R. Kräussl. 2011. Doing Good Deeds in Times of Need: A Strategic Perspective on Corporate Disaster Donations. *Strategic Management Journal.* 32 (9). pp. 911–929.

Nelling, E. and E. Webb. 2009. Corporate Social Responsibility and Financial Performance: The 'Virtuous Circle' Revisited. *Review of Quantitative Finance and Accounting.* 32 (2). pp. 197–209.

Oikonomou, I., C. Brooks, and S. Pavelin. 2012. The Impact of Corporate Social Performance on Financial Risk and Utility: A Longitudinal Analysis. *Financial Management*. 41 (2). pp. 483–515.

_____. 2014. The Effects of Corporate Social Performance on the Cost of Corporate Debt and Credit Ratings. *The Financial Review*. 49 (1). pp. 49–75.

Petersen, H. L. and H. Vredenburg. 2009. Morals or Economics? Institutional Investor Preferences for Corporate Social Responsibility. *Journal of Business Ethics*. 90 (1). pp. 1–14.

Peterson, D. K. 2004. The Relationship Between Perceptions of Corporate Citizenship and Organizational Commitment. *Business and Society*. 43 (3). pp. 296–319.

Raghunandan, A. and S. Rajgopal. 2022. Do Socially Responsible Firms Walk the Talk? *Social Science Research Network Working Paper*.

Richardson, A. and M. Welker. 2001. Social Disclosure, Financial Disclosure and the Cost of Equity Capital. *Accounting, Organizations and Society*. 26 (7–8). pp. 597–616.

Riera, M. and M. Iborra. 2017. Corporate Social Irresponsibility: Review and Conceptual Boundaries. *European Journal of Management and Business Economics*. 26 (2). pp. 146–162.

Rodrigo, P. and D. Arenas. 2008. Do Employees Care about CSR Programs? A Typology of Employees According to Their Attitudes. *Journal of Business Ethics*. 83 (2). pp. 265–283.

Rupp, D. E., J. Ganapathi, R. V. Aguilera, and C. A. Williams. 2006. Employee Reactions to Corporate Social Responsibility: An Organizational Justice Framework. *Journal of Organizational Behavior*. 27 (4). pp. 537–543.

Sampath, V. S., N. A. Gardberg, and N. Rahman. 2018. Corporate Reputation's Invisible Hand: Bribery, Rational Choice, and Market Penalties. *Journal of Business Ethics*. 151 (3). pp. 743–760.

Schuler, D. and M. Cording. 2006. A Corporate Social Performance-Corporate Financial Performance Behavioral Model for Consumers. *Academy of Management Review*. 31 (3). pp. 540–558.

Sen, S., C. B. Bhattacharya, and D. Korschun. 2006. The Role of Corporate Social Responsibility in Strengthening Multiple Stakeholder Relationships: A Field Experiment. *Journal of the Academy of Marketing Science.* 34 (2). pp. 158–166.

Servaes, H. and H. Tamayo. 2013. The Impact of Corporate Social Responsibility on Firm Value: The Role of Customer Awareness. *Management Science.* 59 (5). pp. 1045–1061.

Shahrour, M. H., I. Girerd-Potin, and O. Taramasco. 2021. Corporate Social Responsibility and Firm Default Risk in the Eurozone: A Market-Based Approach. *Managerial Finance.* 47 (7). pp. 975–997.

Sharfman, M. P. and C. S. Fernando. 2008. Environmental Risk Management and the Cost of Capital. *Strategic Management Journal.* 29 (6). pp. 569–592.

Shi, G. and J. Sun. 2015. Corporate Bond Covenants and Social Responsibility Investment. *Journal of Business Ethics.* 131 (2). pp. 285–303.

Shih, Y. C., Y. Wang, R. Zhong, and Y. M. Ma. 2021. Corporate Environmental Responsibility and Default Risk: Evidence from China. *Pacific-Basin Finance Journal.* 68 (1). 101596.

Strike, V. M., J. Gao, and P. Bansal. 2006. Being Good While Being Bad: Social Responsibility and the International Diversification of US Firms. *Journal of International Business Studies.* 37 (6). pp. 850–862.

Sun, W. and K. Cui. 2014. Linking Corporate Social Responsibility to Firm Default Risk. *European Management Journal.* 32 (2). pp. 275–287.

Sun, W. and Z. Ding. 2021. Is Doing Bad Always Punished? A Moderated Longitudinal Analysis on Corporate Social Irresponsibility and Firm Value. *Business and Society.* 60 (7). pp. 1811–1848.

Sweetin, V. H., L. L. Knowles, J. H. Summey, and K. S. McQueen. 2013. Willingness-to-Punish the Corporate Brand for Corporate Social Irresponsibility. *Journal of Business Research.* 66 (10). pp. 1822–1830.

Valentine, S. and G. Fleischman. 2008. Ethics Programs, Perceived Corporate Social Responsibility and Job Satisfaction. *Journal of Business Ethics.* 77 (2). pp. 159–172.

van Beurden, P. and T. Gössling. 2008. The Worth of Values—A Literature Review on the Relation Between Corporate Social and Financial Performance. *Journal of Business Ethics*. 82 (2). pp. 407–424.

Vaughan, A. 2022. BP's Deepwater Horizon Bill Tops $65bn. *The Guardian*. 16 January. https://www.theguardian.com/business/2018/jan/16/bps-deepwater-horizon-bill-tops-65bn#:~:text=BP%20is%20nearing%20the%20end,final%20few%20hundred%20outstanding%20claims.

Wang, H., J. Choi, and J. Li. 2008. Too Little or Too Much? Untangling the Relationship between Corporate Philanthropy and Firm Financial Performance. *Organization Science*. 19 (1). pp. 143–159.

Wang, H. and C. Qian. 2011. Corporate Philanthropy and Corporate Financial Performance: The Roles of Stakeholder Response and Political Access. *Academy of Management Journal*. 54 (6). pp. 1159–1181.

Wang, Q., J. Dou, and S. Jia. 2016. A Meta-Analytic Review of Corporate Social Responsibility and Corporate Financial Performance: The Moderating Effect of Contextual Factors. *Business and Society*. 55 (8). pp. 1083–1121.

Williams, G. and J. Zinkin. 2008. The Effect of Culture on Consumer Willingness to Punish Irresponsible Corporate Behaviour: Applying Hofstede Typology to the Punishment Aspect of Corporate Social Irresponsibility. *Business Ethics: A European Review*. 17 (2). pp. 210–226.

Xie, C. and R. P. Bagozzi. 2019. Consumer Responses to Corporate Social Irresponsibility: The Role of Moral Emotions, Evaluations, and Social Cognitions. *Psychology and Marketing*. 36 (6). pp. 565–586.

Xie, C., R. P. Bagozzi, and K. Grønhaug. 2015. The Role of Moral Emotions and Individual Differences in Consumer Responses to Corporate Green and Non-Green Actions. *Journal of the Academy of Marketing Science*. 43 (3). pp. 333–356.

Xu, H., J. Wu, and M. Dao. 2020. Corporate Social Responsibility and Trade Credit. *Review of Quantitative Finance and Accounting*. 54 (4). pp. 1389–1416.

Xu, S. and R. Yang. 2010. Indigenous Characteristics of Chinese Corporate Social Responsibility Conceptual Paradigm. *Journal of Business Ethics*. 93 (2). pp. 321–333.

Ye, K. and R. Zhang. 2011. Do Lenders Value Corporate Social Responsibility? Evidence from China. *Journal of Business Ethics*. 104 (2). pp. 197–206.

Zhang, M., L. Ma, J. Su, and W. Zhang. 2014. Do Suppliers Applaud Corporate Social Performance? *Journal of Business Ethics*. 121 (4). pp. 543–557.

Zhang, M., L. Xie, and H. Xu. 2016. Corporate Philanthropy and Stock Price Crash Risk: Evidence from China. *Journal of Business Ethics*. 139 (3). pp. 595–617.

Climate Change: Policy, Innovation, and Proposals

Greg Tindall, Rebel Cole, and David Javakhadze

6.1 Introduction

Shareholder voice at company annual meetings has played a valuable, efficient role in mitigating climate change by applying pressure on management to innovate, without allowing shareholders to micromanage agents. Indeed, shareholder proposal pressure, monitored closely by the United States (US) Securities and Exchange Commission (SEC) each year, has persuaded management to confront the low-carbon energy transition through technological advancement. Figure 6.1 illustrates the shareholder feedback loop.

In short, proposals help firms focus. As with any change, climate or otherwise, innovation should be the primary focus of firm policies, as opposed to disclosure, which all too often becomes a game of best lighting and word-smithing. Substance first, form second.

This argument emerges out of an earlier study by the authors—Tindall, Cole, and Javakhadze (2023), the original research to the follow up policy implications in this chapter—showing that climate patent counts and citations increase and become more efficient and valuable in response to shareholders' climate proposals at annual meetings. The authors demonstrate the climate mitigating technologies spurred by these climate-related proposals.

This chapter takes up the paper's suggestion to explore the policy implications of its findings. The main policies involve the SEC's recent and contemplated changes to the proposal process, itself, in the Federal Code of Regulation (14a-8), and to other US securities regulations involving climate change disclosure.

Figure 6.1: Shareholder Proposal Feedback Loop

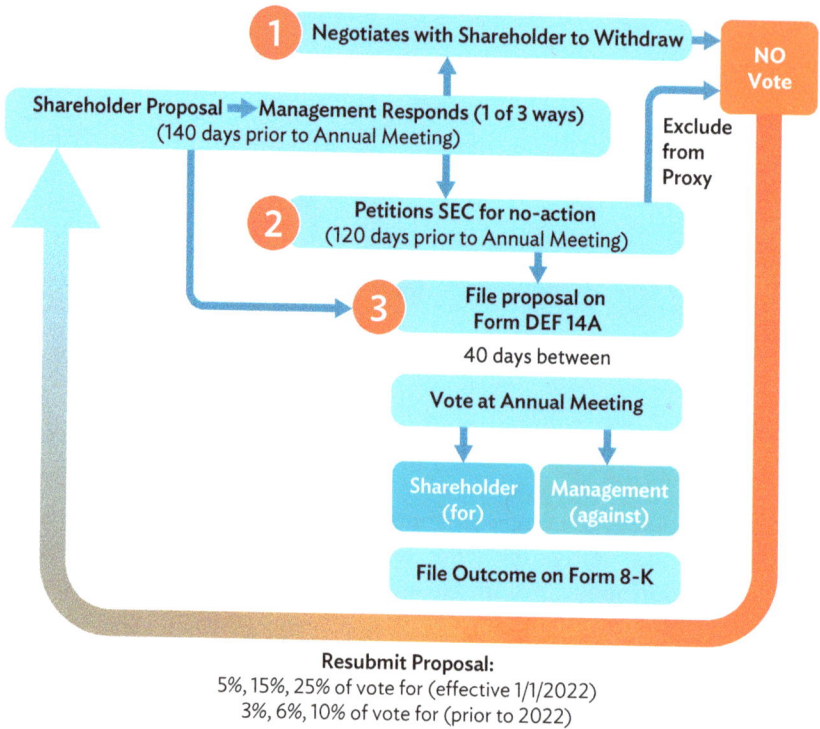

1 Negotiates with Shareholder to Withdraw

NO Vote

Shareholder Proposal ➔ Management Responds (1 of 3 ways)
(140 days prior to Annual Meeting)

Exclude from Proxy

2 Petitions SEC for no-action
(120 days prior to Annual Meeting)

3 File proposal on Form DEF 14A

40 days between

Vote at Annual Meeting

Shareholder (for)   Management (against)

File Outcome on Form 8-K

Resubmit Proposal:
5%, 15%, 25% of vote for (effective 1/1/2022)
3%, 6%, 10% of vote for (prior to 2022)

SEC = Securities and Exchange Commission, DEF 14A = Definitive Proxy Statement.
Note: This figure demonstrates the submission, processing, filing, voting, and resubmission requirements, and the timing of shareholder proposals in the United States.
Source: Authors.

The chapter aims mainly to synthesize the two policies being contemplated: first, to weigh shareholder "voice" through the proposal process against firm resources that provide the surrounding acoustics for voice to be heard; and second, to assist with firm focus on the actual mitigation of climate change through innovation, instead of relegating the issue to an endless, rancorous debate.

To make such a case, the chapter contends that the evolution of shareholder proposals about climate change sheds light on investor concerns over the subject and how they have shaped firm innovation policies. The chapter thus begins with the first mentions of "climate change" at annual meetings, in 1994.

6.1.1   Proposal Sponsors: Don't Mess with the Sisters of San Antonio, Texas

Much of the policy debate over shareholder proposals lies between giving small investors a voice and them abusing their voice by squandering firm resources dedicated to putting together enough information for other shareholders to make an informed decision when votes are cast at annual meetings. As is obvious to anyone who has been to a public meeting of any sort, invariably someone in the audience speaks up with nothing to discuss other than how much he loves to hear his own voice. Of course, the 13 explicit provisions laid out in 14a-8 limit shareholders from veering tangentially to "proper subject matter." Besides the 13 explicit provisions—which range from prohibiting shareholders from declaring dividends to interfering with ordinary business—the implicit spirit of 14a-8 aims to reconcile owner-agent conflicts, not provide an opportunity for micromanagement. Much of the spirit of 14a-8 lies in the ample amount of time for management and sponsoring shareholder(s) to work out their differences and negotiate a withdraw of the proposal.[1] Carleton, Nelson, and Weisbach (1998) discover that even an institutional investor like Teachers Insurance and Annuity Association of America–College Retirement Equities Fund prefers to negotiate with management (and in their study, shareholder and management found common ground 95% of the time with 70% of the proposals withdrawn). Such was the intention of 14a-8. Yet, gadflies earn their negative connotation and draw the ire of corporate lawyers across the US precisely because there is no room for negotiation. Gadflies often refuse to meet even with the fourth highest ranking member of public firms—the corporate secretaries. Such stubborn behavior clearly contradicts the intent of 14a-8. Despite the many persuasive elements of 14a, gadflies might need a bit of coercing.

As Gillan and Starks (2007) explain, these "gadflies" continue to be a concern: the benefit of providing shareholders with a voice comes at the expense of firm resources dedicated to compiling information. According to Gibson Dunn (2018, 4), one gadfly submitted or co-filed 187 shareholder proposals during the 2018 proxy season—an astounding 24% of all proposals that year.

---

[1]   When a shareholder makes a proposal, management can respond one of three ways: negotiate to withdraw, petition the SEC to exclude the proposal from an annual meeting, or allow the proposal to be filed on DEF 14A, the definitive proxy statement. See Figure 6.1 for a general overview of the submission and resubmission dynamics of proposals and their time frames.

In response to this and other concerns, the SEC conducted a 2018 roundtable discussion entitled "Statement Announcing SEC Staff Roundtable on the Proxy Process." This roundtable resulted in new legislation passed during 2020 and effective as of 1 January 2022, intended to balance shareholder voice with firm resources (SEC 2020). The 2020 amendment contains three main provisions: (i) increased thresholds for resubmission;[2] (ii) lengthened periods of stock ownership; and (iii) increased minimum amounts of stock ownership, where these last two provisions tradeoff between each other. Ownership amount gives way to length of time for a shareholder to resubmit the same proposal. For example, prior to the 2020 change, the minimum stock holding amounted to $2,000 held for 1 year. Effective 1 January 2022, a stockholder could submit a proposal by owning only $2,000 worth of stock but only if she had held it for 3 years, or a stockholder could make a proposal having only owned a stock for 1 year, but she would have to own at least $25,000 worth of stock (the midpoint on the sliding scale being $15,000 and 2 years). Again, one of the SEC's intents being a balance between voice for small shareholders that does not invite gadflies to dominate annual meetings and firm resources required in preparation of annual meetings. Yet, climate change proposals are different than most proposals, at least with respect to sponsor type. Panel A in Figure 6.2 shows that "individuals"[3] comprise the largest percentage of sponsoring shareholders (38%, shown in gray) for all proposal types. Climate change proposals, on the other hand, are dominated by religious groups, not gadflies. In 1994, the Benedictine Sisters of San Antonio, Texas, first set in motion one of the most contentious issues raised at annual meetings.

"Don't Mess with Texas," is a slogan and source of pride for Texas that New York habitually ignores, whether in popular politics or those at the firm level. The two states often lock horns, mostly notably when New York Attorney General Eric Schneiderman sued Exxon for what he suspected the firm knew but failed to disclose about climate change. Suspicions, however, held no sway with the New York Supreme Court, as Schneiderman "produced no testimony from any investor who claimed to have been misled by any disclosure," (Paul Weiss 2019) resulting in a "complete defense verdict" for Exxon, i.e., Schneiderman failed on all claims.

---

[2]   To resubmit a proposal in subsequent years, a shareholder must gather sufficient voter support. Prior to the 2020 change, the first time a proposal is voted on at the annual meeting, it needs at least 3% in favor to be resubmitted at the next meeting. The next time the same proposal is submitted, it needs 6% support or greater to be resubmitted again. For the same proposal to be submitted three or more times, it must gather at least 10% support. These thresholds increased in 2020 to 5%, 15%, and 25%, respectively, for subsequent resubmissions.

[3]   The term "gadfly"—according to Merriam Webster, a person who stimulates or annoys other people especially by persistent criticism—applies to an individual, but, of course, not all individuals are gadflies.

Figure 6.2: Proposals by Sponsor

Panel A: All Proposal Sponsors (%)

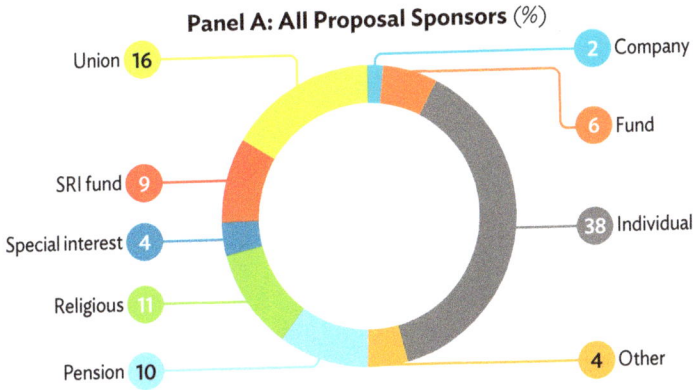

Union 16
Company 2
Fund 6
SRI fund 9
Individual 38
Special interest 4
Religious 11
Pension 10
Other 4

Panel B: Climate Change Proposal Sponsors (%)

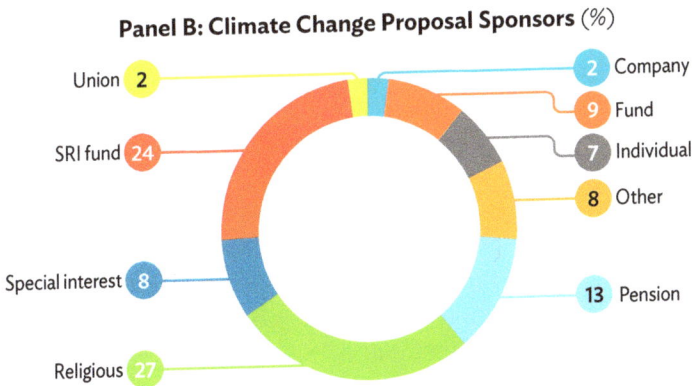

Union 2
Company 2
Fund 9
Individual 7
Other 8
SRI fund 24
Special interest 8
Pension 13
Religious 27

Panel C: Number of Climate Change Proposals by Top Two Sponsors

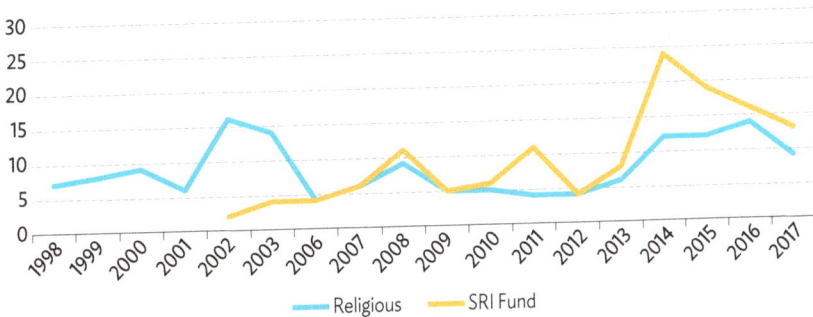

Religious   SRI Fund

SRI = socially responsible investor.
Source: Institutional Shareholder Services.

Yet, in juxtaposed role play, the Sisters of San Antonio, Texas, articulated their climate concerns to Mohawk Power Corporation located in Niagara Falls, New York, at the 1994 annual meeting: the first appearance of "climate change" on a shareholder proposal. Despite Mohawk's contention that it went to great lengths to mitigate its climate risk (with an endorsement from Al Gore, no less), the Sisters set in motion what became a proposal crusade dominated by faith-based investors. Also in 1994, the Texan Sisters were joined by the Immaculate Heart Missions from Arlington, Virginia, who sponsored a proposal to General Public Utilities Corporation of New Jersey, and by the Sisters of St. Dominic of Caldwell, New Jersey, who sponsored a proposal to Allegheny Power Systems of New York. These origins and early composition of shareholders sponsoring climate proposals provide a basis for us to suspect that firm level politics might be different than popular politics, and that climate change might not be a frivolous issue that gives rise to gadfly voices.

The Exxon experience with climate-related proposals sheds light on what comprises "proper subject matter" as defined by the Federal Code of Regulation, which the SEC tries to balance when either side of the owner-agent divide gains disproportionate weight. Exxon's first climate change proposal in 1998 strikes much deeper than investor protection, shareholder voice, or conservation of firm resources in responding to proposal resolutions. This proposal cuts to the core of what it means to book a liability. For decades, accountants have struggled in determining *when* firms must recognize liabilities on their balance sheets and subsequently charged against income, especially in connection with anticipated litigation. Is the recognition itself an admission of guilt or at least a public invitation to be sued, for an amount specified on the financial statement no less? That is the question weighed at length by the US Financial Accounting Standards Board (FASB) in issuing Statement No. 5: Accounting for Contingencies. To be clear, the FASB states: "Accruals for general or unspecified business risks ("reserves for general contingencies") are no longer permitted" (FASB n.d.). Nonetheless, based on the popular press in a Business Week article, the Province of St. Joseph of the Capuchin Order in Milwaukee, Wisconsin, requested that Exxon's board "included… any anticipated liabilities [Exxon] may incur from its possible contribution to"[4] (Exxon Mobil 1998) climate change. While it is difficult to extrapolate precisely what the Capuchin Order meant by "any anticipated liabilities" from their proposal, the request certainly fell short of FASB's standard for booking a liability. Exxon's management based its response to this shareholder

---

4   See page 19 for the proposal entitled "Additional report on climate change" on Exxon's DEF 14A filing in 1998, at https://www.sec.gov/Archives/edgar/data/34088/000119312517122538/d182248ddef14a.htm.

proposal on Massachusetts Institute of Technology's (MIT) Joint Program on the Science and Policy of Global Change (Jacoby, Prinn, and Schmalensee 1997), which expressed skepticism about climate change that was gaining momentum, at least in 1997. Business Week or MIT sources should always be considered when forming an opinion, but especially when complying with FASB No. 5 standard "that it is probable that ... a liability had been incurred" and "an amount of loss can be reasonably estimated" (FASB n.d.).

To appreciate the ability of shareholder proposals to flesh out firm interests, fast-forward to 2017 and again focus on Exxon. By this time, religious groups were not issuing the most climate proposals by sponsor type; SRI funds had become the dominant force for sponsoring climate proposals from 2013 onward (Figure 6.2, panel C). In 2017, the New York Common Retirement Fund took the lead of a proposal requesting that Exxon provide an "assessment of the long-term portfolio impacts of technological advances and global climate change policies"[5] (Exxon Mobil 2017). This proposal was covered in the Wall Street Journal in a story highlighting the 62.3% support it gathered and the critical role that institutional investors such as Vanguard, State Street, Fidelity, and BlackRock play in sending emphatical messages when opposing management at annual meetings (Olson 2017). From 1998 to 2017, in the Exxon experience alone, the delicate balance the SEC weighs as moderator can be appreciated. When the Capuchin Order sponsored Exxon's first climate proposals, they may have been vastly misguided in what it means to book a liability but their sentiment went on to express what some of the world's most diligent monitors (the New York Common Retirement Fund) would eventually articulate. It just took a decade to get there. Whether shareholder proposals play a definitively causal role in the technological advances that the New York Retirement Fund alluded to, might be as difficult to prove as the "smoking gun" that the Business Week article claimed to have found.

6.2 Climate Change as "Proper Subject for Action"

Climate change is nothing new.[6] In 1859, John Tyndall discovered the heat trapping properties of greenhouse gases. In 1896, Nobel laureate Svante Arrhenius concluded that fossil fuel combustion could raise global

---

5   For the full proposal, see Item 12 – Report on Impacts of Climate Change Policies at https://www.sec.gov/Archives/edgar/data/34088/000119312517122538/d182248ddef14a. htm#toc182248_23.

6   The content for the following paragraph has been adapted from Nathaniel Rich's New York Times article of 2018 "Losing Earth: The Decade We Almost Stopped Climate Change" (Rich 2018).

temperatures. In 1957, Roger Revelle helped Charles Keeling measure carbon dioxide concentrations 11,500 feet atop Hawaii's Mauna Loa to create the Keeling Curve. That same year, Humble Oil, which was acquired by Standard Oil and would later become Exxon, issued a report concluding that fossil fuels were releasing an "enormous quantity of carbon dioxide" into the atmosphere (Brannon et al. 1957). By 1968, the Stanford Research Institute explained the ramifications of fossil fuel contributions to a warming atmosphere: melting ice caps and rising sea levels. Even then, the scientists found it odd how politicians seem to perseverate on individual events, instead of focusing on the broad warming trends. In 2022, the fourth most disastrous hurricane on record devastated southwest Florida. Afterwards, the Governor of Florida Ron DeSantis and President Joe Biden met to survey the damage, prompting Biden to claim that Hurricane Ian "ended" the debate on climate change. Yet, as of 29 December 2022, Tom Knutson, a senior scientist at National Oceanic and Atmospheric Administration, stated

> "In summary, it is premature to conclude with high confidence that human-caused increases in greenhouse gases have caused a change in past Atlantic basin hurricane activity that is outside the range of natural variability, although greenhouse gases are strongly linked to global warming."[7]

Possibly the best indication of how firm-level policy implications may unfold also took place on the west coast of Florida in 1981. Forty years earlier, Congress summoned the nation's top experts under the Energy Security Act of 1980 and requested that they propose legislation for how to handle global warming. Despite largely agreeing on the science behind climate change and the contributions to it, the experts failed to craft any policy recommendation, even after a week of discussions. The science was fairly clear. The paragraph or two that the experts wrote on policy was so vague that they essentially gave up in frustration, not due to personality differences or political stances but what to report back to Congress. Indeed, the discussion over climate change ended long before Hurricane Ian revisited the first attempt to legislate it.

---

[7]   See Geophysical Fluid Dynamics Laboratory. Global Warming and Hurricanes: An Overview of Current Research Results. As updated 9 February 2023. https://www.gfdl.noaa.gov/global-warming-and-hurricanes/.

6.3   The Instigation and Lessons from 2008

The global financial crisis that began during 2008 was not the best chapter in the SEC's history. As the gatekeeper between Wall Street and Main Street, many looked to the SEC for explanations about the $65 billion ponzi scheme perpetrated by Bernie Madoff and how it went undetected for so long, as well as the more cryptic repackaging of toxic debt and its conversion to the highest AAA ratings. Just keeping track of anacronyms and jargon involved—CDO, FDIC, RMBS, NINJA loans, securities tranches, etc.—might be difficult for the average person. Most Americans do not know the difference between AAA and AA bond ratings. But a ponzi scheme? Most people get that. The SEC did not.

On the heels of the 2008 global meltdown, many investors were speculating about what might be the next big surprise of hidden risk, something all too obvious when seen in hindsight. Climate change and global warming appeared to be a good candidate. Outcry for more disclosure on potential hidden risk caused then-SEC Commissioner Mary Shapiro to issue a press release in January 2010 entitled, "SEC Issues Interpretive Guidance on Disclosure Related to Business or Legal Developments Regarding Climate Change" (SEC 2010). Given the sensitive nature of the subject, she clarified the SEC's position regarding what the commission could and could not address.

> "We are not opining on whether the world's climate is changing, at what pace it might be changing, or due to what causes. Nothing that the Commission does today should be construed as weighing in on those topics."

Essentially, the SEC deferred to existing regulation on disclosure where materiality is a threshold no firm policy can escape. If material, it must be disclosed. The SEC's position on climate disclosures began to shift somewhat during 2021, when it sent out letters to specific firms but remained focused on material risks (Kiernan 2021). During 2022, the SEC began gathering input on standardizing disclosure for all firms, including audited climate-related financial metrics.

The SEC's Proposed Rule for "The Enhancement and Standardization of Climate-Related Disclosures for Investors"[8] released for public comment on 11 April 2022, appears to face similar difficulties. Conversely, the internal

---

[8]   For the full proposal, please refer to SEC at https://www.sec.gov/rules/proposed/2022/33-11042.pdf.

firm politics that take place at annual meetings through the proposal process appear to have had the intended effect: climate proposals increase climate mitigating technologies that are economically efficient (Tindall, Cole, and Javakhadze 2023), whereas external popular politics often have uncertain and unintended effects. The attorneys general of the states of West Virginia, Arizona, Alabama, Alaska, Arkansas, Florida, Georgia, Idaho, Indiana, Kansas, Kentucky, Louisiana, Mississippi, Missouri, Montana, Nebraska, North Dakota, Ohio, Oklahoma, South Carolina, South Dakota, Utah, Virginia, and Wyoming appear ready to sue the SEC on grounds similar those used to successfully sue the US Environmental Protection Agency in a recent decision by the US Supreme Court.[9] The attorneys general collectively wrote: "We urge you [the SEC] to save everyone years of strife by abandoning the Proposed Rule."[10]

The literature on innovation has shown that policy uncertainty thwarts the innovative process (Bhattacharya et al. 2017; Cong and Howell 2021) and that innovation can suffer in response to mandatory disclosure (Gao and Zhang 2019). In a parallel fashion, the Sarbanes-Oxley Act (SOX) enjoyed near unanimous political support but disproportionately burdened small firms, especially the innovative.

In the view of the authors here, as financial economists, SOX is a bit of a head-scratcher. Is not the very basis of the audit function to ferret out fraud and unintentional misstatement? Why then all the extra tests, specifically for fraud from the fallout of Enron, WorldCom, and Arthur Andersen? It is a bit like requiring "the whole truth and nothing but the truth." If a person (or firm) is going to lie, do the extra descriptors do anything more to compel the truth? As SOX gained momentum toward becoming law, the market did not think so. According to an event study that Litvak (2007) conducted, each step toward the enactment by SOX resulted in a broad market decline. The market reacted negatively each time. The only exception was the suggestion of an exemption from SOX for foreign firms, raised by then-SEC Chairman Harvey Pitt.[11] The single positive market reaction was quickly negated by a stronger negative reaction when the foreign exemption was withdrawn

---

[9]   20–1530 West Virginia v. EPA (06/30/2022) see the full opinion at https://www.supremecourt. gov/opinions/21pdf/20-1530_n758.pdf.

[10]   See their comments to the SEC at https://www.sec.gov/comments/s7-10-22/s71022-20134128-303943.pdf.

[11]   Ironically, Pitt would resign for his endorsement of William Webster, who served as the first president of the Public Company Accounting Oversight Board for weeks before involvement on the audit committee of a technology company being investigated by the SEC (Wikipedia. Public Company Accounting Oversight Board. https://en.wikipedia.org/wiki/Public_Company_Accounting_Oversight_Board).

from SOX. Litvak (2008) also demonstrates the long-term negative effects of SOX on firm value. Even when popular politics has near unanimous support, firms can be penalized by good intentions which may not find commensurate benefit. SOX cannot prevent fraud, as Wirecard[12] and Theranos[13] continue to prove. When popular politics is very divided, as it appears to be for mandatory climate disclosure, the ability of policy to craft economically efficient solutions is further eroded. Given historical precedent, an unintended consequence of mandatory climate disclosure could be climate mitigating technologies. The evidence provided by Tindall, Cole, and Javakhadze (2023) demonstrates that the persuasive elements of shareholder proposals are effective in spurring climate mitigating innovation, whereas required disclosure might distract firm attention from innovating and could potentially focus it on "clever accounting and creative PR [public relations]."[14] Certainly, neither side seeks to thwart firm efforts to address climate change in more meaningful ways, like mitigating and adaptive technologies.

6.4 Substantial Implementation

On 13 July 2022, the SEC issued a press release to amend 3 of the 13 bases for excluding shareholder proposals.[15] Tindall, Cole, and Javakhadze (2023) provide guidance to the SEC on the first of the three, *Substantial Implementation* and, in particular, a proposed "essential elements" test. Currently, a shareholder proposal can be excluded from annual meetings if a firm has already substantially implemented what the shareholder is proposing. (This is the tenth[16] of the thirteen provisions for exclusion in 14a-8.) The proposed amendment on *Substantial Implementation* would provide a test to see if "the company has already implemented the essential elements of the proposal." SEC Commissioner Hester Pierce has expressed her reservations against the amendment for lacking clarity on how to assess essential elements.[17] We agree. Some issues, like auditor ratification, are straightforward to determine essential elements for substantial implementation. Other issues, like climate change

---

12 See *Reuters* (2021) for more information.
13 See the Department of Justice's discussion of its case against Elizabeth Holmes, the former CEO of Theranos at https://www.justice.gov/usao-ndca/us-v-elizabeth-holmes-et-al.
14 See Greta Thunberg's speech at the UN Climate Conference, 11 December 2019, courtesy of NBC News, available at https://www.youtube.com/watch?v=UIRKuUm5P_A.
15 See the proposal at https://www.sec.gov/news/press-release/2022-12.
16 17 CFR § 240.14a-8(i)(10). https://www.govinfo.gov/content/pkg/CFR-2011-title17-vol3/pdf/CFR-2011-title17-vol3-sec240-14a-8.pdf.
17 See her objections at https://www.sec.gov/news/statement/peirce-statement-shareholder-proposals-proposal-071322.

concerns, might be impossible for the SEC's Division of Corporate Finance to identify what has been implemented. To date, prior literature on shareholder proposals (Cuñat, Gine, and Guadalupe 2012; Flammer 2015; Flammer and Bansal 2017) has used changes in environmental, social, and governance (ESG) scores to conceptualize implementation. Indeed, both Cuñat, Gine, and Guadalupe (2012) and Flammer (2015) estimate probability of implementation for passing proposals at 52%, i.e., the flip of a coin. Thus, a "passing" shareholder proposal does not necessarily lead to implementation. The view in this chapter is that a coin flip does not provide the SEC much guidance for judging how substantial implementation has been, much less insight on essential elements, therein. Conversely, when the United States Patent and Trademark Office issues a patent (and even when a firm files one), it has been implemented, complete with all the essential elements necessary to grant it exclusive rights of use. Certainly, when one patent cites another patent, the citations demonstrate substantial implementation. Tindall, Cole, and Javakhadze (2023) make a compelling case that climate proposals lead to more climate mitigating patents and citations. Consequently, it is believed here that the research provides guidance to the SEC as it deliberates not only *Substantial Implementation* grounds for exclusion but also Commissioner Pierce's suggestion "to allow sufficient time to see how our 2020 rules operate (Pierce 2022).[18] The patent data we examine are not subjective. ESG ratings, on the other hand, suffer wide disparities among providers.[19] The same firm has been shown to receive wildly divergent scores by different raters not only on the composite measure of ESG, but also, more alarmingly, on each subcomponent (Berg, Kölbel, and Rigobon 2019), where measurement comprises the largest source of divergence among the six largest rating agencies. (Apparently, whether or not a CEO is also the chairperson is difficult to assess.) Such divergence and subjectivity do not exist with patents. Either a firm files one with the United States Patent and Trademark Office or it does not. Patents either cite other patents or they do not. Even the prescriptions for the Patent and Trademark Office cooperative patent classification for climate mitigating technologies (the Y02 series) are very specific and must withstand the technical scrutiny of a patent officer. Whereas with ESG ratings, a firm can receive praise from one provider and scorn from another. For these reasons, Tindall, Cole, and Javakhadze (2023) inform the

---

[18]   The 2020 rules, Pierce refers to, are the increase in thresholds for resubmission—3%, 6%, and 10% raised to 5%, 15%, and 25% of the vote—and the qualifications to ownership—from a flat $2,000 to variegated ownership: $2,000 owned for 3 years, $15,000 for 2 years, and $25,000 for 1 year.

[19]   Even when rating agencies issue similar ratings, as with bond rating agencies, the outcome of reliance on those ratings can have disastrous consequences, like the failures that gave rise to the 2008 global financial crisis. By extension, relying on ESG ratings for substantial implementation should be seriously questioned.

SEC not only that shareholder proposals serve their intended governance role, but also the degree to which proposals have the intended effect. Endless politics, clever accounting, and public relations gimmicks are unlikely to resolve the climate issues firms face. Rather, when the underlying economics display preference for climate mitigating technologies, firm-level carbon issues are more likely to find resolution and possibly assisting the low carbon energy transition. The view here is that climate-related shareholder proposals in the US since 1994 have provided an invaluable forum for maintaining focus on the economics of innovation.

6.5 Support Thresholds

Since the Benedictine Sisters of San Antonio first sponsored their proposal, average support for climate proposals has increased considerably, as shown in panel A of Figure 6.3. On average, shareholders support for climate proposals did not exceed 20% until 2012. Much like we lean on accounting reasoning (FASB's Statement No. 5) for what it means to book a liability, we also turn to it for what a noncontrolling percentage of shares might mean. The Accounting Principles Board Opinion No. 18 presumes that an investor with over 20% of shares outstanding exerts "significant influence," unless facts and circumstances dictate otherwise. Once 20% is breached, the equity method of accounting must be implemented. It is the opinion here that 20% means "something" for proposal support as well. Exactly what 20% means (or even if 20% is the exact figure), it cannot be said with precision. Tindall, Cole, and Javakhadze (2023) discover that climate-related proposals spur climate innovations that are efficient and valuable. The sample in the paper contained fewer than 10 climate proposals that exceeded 50% support. Given this observation, the paper conjectures that shareholder proposals which gather less than majority are still meaningful even if they "fail." It finds anecdotal reassurance in recent statements made by Shell CEO Ben van Beurden, about voting results. Management appears to listen to shareholder "voice" even when proposals do not "win."

   In the discussion of the Results from the 2021 Annual General Meeting, van Beurden stated of a climate proposal that gained 30% support: "We also note the outcome of the vote on Shareholder Resolution number 21. We will seek to fully understand the reason why shareholders voted as they did..." (Royal Dutch Shell n.d.). The following year, van Beurden again paid homage to the same climate resolution, which declined in support but still garnered 20% of shareholders. "We are also encouraged by the reduced support for Shareholder

Figure 6.3: Average and Range of Climate Proposal Support by Year

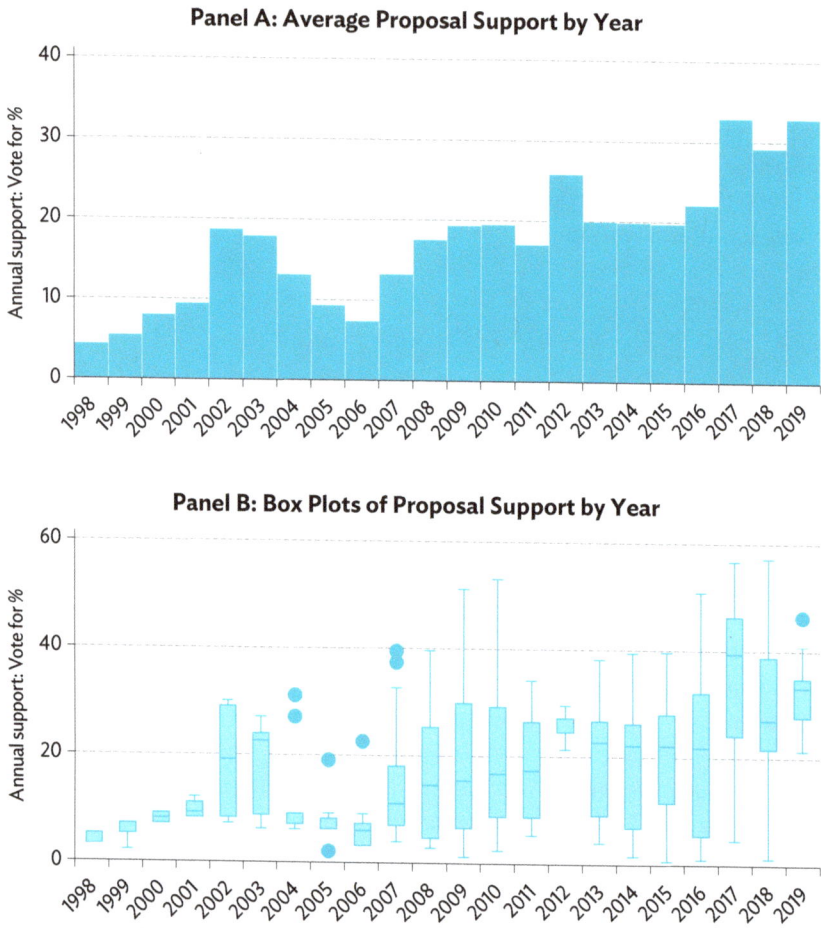

Panel A: Average Proposal Support by Year

Panel B: Box Plots of Proposal Support by Year

Source: Institutional Shareholder Services.

Resolution number 21 but recognise there is still work to do. We will consult shareholders to understand these votes..." Clearly, 20% of the vote is enough to get management's attention, possibly enough to exert significant influence. Even in the United Kingdom, where majority support legally obligates firms to implement a resolution, shareholders can have their "voice" heard. In the US, where majority support remains precatory, shareholder "voice" can resonate enough with management to encourage change in firm policies, as we demonstrate with climate proposals and climate innovations.

With respect to the SEC's 2020 threshold changes now requiring 5%, 15%, and 25% for resubmission and with respect to the unfolding of climate change proposals since 1994, the information in panel A of Figure 6.3 suggests that, on average, shareholder voice would have been silenced long ago. Further, the box plots in panel B of Figure 6.3 display the annual range of shareholder support for climate proposals. The extremes, even as recently as 2017, display the problem of simply taking an average: from almost no support (1.3%) to clear majority (67.3%). Collectively, Figure 6.3 demonstrates that shareholder voice may take more time to find consensus than the 3 years allotted for resolutions to exceed 25% support in order to be resubmitted. If Shell's van Beurden still listens to the 20% of shareholders who voted against him,[20] in the midst of Shell's energy transition, the authors agree with SEC Commissioner Pierce's contention that the SEC might want to refrain from changing 14a-8 any further, at least for the time being.[21] Indeed, the 2020 amendments only became effective at the start of 2022. Her request to allow more time seems prudent given that additional changes to 14a-8 for other grounds to exclude proposals (especially for the *Substantial Implementation* standard and *Essential Elements* test mentioned above) might be obscured by the 2020 change that have been effective for only 1 year. The anecdotal evidence we provide for US climate proposals, the appropriated insight from non-US resolutions, and the borrowed estimation from FASB, all suggest that time may be a key element to compelling owners and agents to ferret out firm interests, as opposed to a hard threshold like 25%.

6.6 Conclusion and Policy Recommendations

When the microcosm of internal firm politics take place through the shareholder proposal mechanism and collectively points in a consistent direction, external policymakers can more comfortably implement their policies, as the decision has been made much easier through mutual consent. Policymakers need not command and control when owners have voiced their opinions and agents have expressed their willingness to listen. More generally, persuasion can be more powerful than coercion. As Tindall, Cole, and Javakhadze (2023) demonstrate, such has been the case for shareholder

---

[20] The authors of this chapter fully recognize the vast differences between the US and the United Kingdom shareholder resolutions (the main one being compulsory implementation if majority support). They speculate that Shell's van Beurden is stating publicly what US CEOs think of proposals that gain significant support. They compound speculation by borrowing 20% from FASB.

[21] For an interesting discussion of the complications with Substantial Implementation and Essential Elements, see Mathew (2023).

proposals related to climate change in encouraging innovations to be not only climate mitigating but also economically efficient. The anecdotal evidence we provide in this chapter suggests that climate-related proposals are not the providence of gadflies. Rather, the Texas Sisters meant serious business and their climate concerns proved to be quite valid, spurring firms to innovate climate mitigating technologies. As can be seen in the debates which attempt to clarify Substantial Implementation and Essential Elements, the SEC has been placed in a difficult position of determining how to apply them at the firm level, fairly and uniformly. Tindall, Cole, and Javakhadze (2023) provide an improvement over prior literature on at least what type of firm outcome might be a better measure: patents over ESG ratings. The most speculative suggestion is for the SEC to reconsider support thresholds. The time trend of climate proposals indicates that a "proper subject on action" might take more than 3 years to exert significant influence. This chapter recognizes that a threshold of support must be drawn at some point in time, but it encourages the SEC to closely monitor its 2020 changes such that its intention to find a good balance between shareholder voice and management's willingness to listen results in the best deployment of firm resources.

References

Berg, F., J. F. Kölbel, and R. Rigobon. 2019. Aggregate Confusion: The Divergence of ESG Ratings. Forthcoming *Review of Finance*. http://dx.doi.org/10.2139/ssrn.3438533.

Bhattacharya, U., P. Hsu, X. Tian, and Y. Xu. 2017. What Affects Innovation More: Policy or Policy Uncertainty? *Journal of Financial and Quantitative Analysis*. 52 (5). pp. 1869–1901.

Brannon, Jr., H. R., A. C. Daughtry, D. Perry, W. W. Whitaker, and M. Williams. 1957. Radiocarbon Evidence on the Dilution of Atmospheric and Oceanic Carbon by Carbon from Fossil Fuels. *Eos, Transactions American Geophysical Union*. 38 (5). pp. 643–650.

Carleton, W. T., J. M. Nelson, and M. S. Weisbach. 1998. The Influence of Institutions on Corporate Governance through Private Negotiations: Evidence from TIAA-CREF. *The Journal of Finance*. 53 (4). pp. 1335–1362.

Cong, L. W. and S. T. Howell. 2021. Policy Uncertainty and Innovation: Evidence from Initial Public Offering Interventions in China. *Management Science*. 67 (11). pp. 7238–7261.

Cuñat, V., M. Gine, and M. Guadalupe. 2012. The Vote Is Cast: The Effect of Corporate Governance on Shareholder Value. *The Journal of Finance*. 67 (5). pp. 1943–1977.

Exxon Mobil. 1998. Definitive Proxy Statement. https://www.sec.gov/Archives/edgar/data/34088/000119312517122538/d182248ddef14a.htm.

_____. 2017. Definitive Proxy Statement. https://www.sec.gov/Archives/edgar/data/34088/000119312517122538/d182248ddef14a.htm#toc182248_23.

Financial Accounting Standards Board (FASB). n.d. Summary of Statement No. 5. https://www.fasb.org/page/PageContent?pageId=/reference-library/superseded-standards/summary-of-statement-no-5.html&bcpath=tff.

Flammer, C. 2015. Does Corporate Social Responsibility Lead to Superior Financial Performance? A Regression Discontinuity Approach. *Management Science*. 61 (11). pp. 2549–2568.

Flammer, C. and P. Bansal. 2017. Does a Long-Term Orientation Create Value? Evidence from a Regression Discontinuity. *Strategic Management Journal*. 38 (9). pp. 1827–1847.

Gao, H. and J. Zhang. 2019. SOX Section 404 and Corporate Innovation. *Journal of Financial and Quantitative Analysis*. 54 (2). pp. 759–787.

Gibson Dunn. 2018. Shareholder Proposal Developments during the 2018 Proxy Season. 12 July. https://www.gibsondunn.com/wp-content/uploads/2018/07/shareholder-proposal-developments-during-the-2018-proxy-season.pdf.

Gillan, S. L. and L. T. Starks. 2007. The Evolution of Shareholder Activism in the United States. *Institutional Investor Activism: Hedge Funds and Private Equity, Economics and Regulation*. Oxford: Oxford University Press. pp. 55–73.

Jacoby, H. D., R. G. Prinn, and R. Schmalensee. 1997. Report #21. Needed: A Realistic Strategy for Global Warming. Massachusetts Institute of Technology. http://web.mit.edu/globalchange/www/rpt21.html.

Kiernan, P. 2021. SEC Asks Dozens of Companies for More Climate Disclosures. *The Wall Street Journal*. 22 September. https://www.wsj.com/articles/regulators-ask-dozens-of-companies-for-more-climate-disclosures-11632341672?mod=article_inline.

Litvak, K. 2007. The Effect of the Sarbanes-Oxley Act on Non-US Companies Cross-Listed in the US. *Journal of Corporate Finance*. 13 (2–3). pp. 195–228.

———. 2008. The Long-Term Effect of the Sarbanes-Oxley Act on Cross-Listing Premia. *European Financial Management*. 14 (5). pp. 875–920.

Mathew, S. J. 2023. How Companies Should Approach Shareholder Proposals this Proxy Season. Harvard Law School Forum on Corporate Governance. https://corpgov.law.harvard.edu/2023/01/03/how-companies-should-approach-shareholder-proposals-this-proxy-season/.

Olson, B. 2017. Exxon Shareholders Pressure Company on Climate Risks. *The Wall Street Journal*. 31 May. https://www.wsj.com/articles/exxon-shareholders-pressure-company-on-climate-risks-1496250039.

Pierce, H. 2022. Exclusion Preclusion: Statement on the Shareholder Proposals Proposal. Statement from the SEC Commissioner. https://www.sec.gov/news/statement/peirce-statement-shareholder-proposals-proposal-071322.

Reuters. 2021. Timeline: The Rise and Fall of Wirecard, a German Tech Champion. 16 March. https://www.reuters.com/article/us-germany-wirecard-inquiry-timeline/timeline-the-rise-and-fall-of-wirecard-a-german-tech-champion-idUSKBN2B811J.

Rich, N. 2018. Losing Earth: The Decade We Almost Stopped Climate Change. *The New York Times.* 1 August.

Royal Dutch Shell. n.d. Result of Annual General Meeting. https://www.shell.com/investors/shareholder-meetings/_jcr_content/root/main/section/simple/list_copy/list_item.multi.stream/1663830795090/e31f2aa8ff0be567ea9577b43011bac4044f0e4e/voting-results-of-the-2021-agm.pdf.

Securities and Exchange Commission (SEC). 2010. SEC Issues Interpretive Guidance on Disclosure Related to Business or Legal Developments Regarding Climate Change. Press release. 27 January. https://www.sec.gov/news/press/2010/2010-15.htm.

_____. 2020. SEC Adopts Amendments to Modernize Shareholder Proposal Rule. Press release. 23 September. https://www.sec.gov/news/press-release/2020–220.

_____. 2022. SEC Proposes Amendments to Shareholder Proposal Rule. Press release. 13 July. https://www.sec.gov/news/press-release/2022-121.

Tindall, G., R. Cole, and D. Javakhadze. 2023. Innovation Responds to Climate Change Proposals. *Working Paper.*

Weiss, P. 2019. ExxonMobil Prevails in Landmark $1.6 Billion Trial Over Climate Change Disclosures. https://www.paulweiss.com/practices/litigation/litigation/news/exxonmobil-prevails-in-landmark-16-billion-trial-over-climate-change-disclosures?id=30337.

Managing Climate Change Risks: Sea Level Rise and Mergers and Acquisitions

John (Jianqiu) Bai, Yongqiang Chu, Chen Shen, and Chi Wan

7.1   Introduction

As climate has changed over the last 4 decades so has awareness of the severe consequences that such changes can bring. Most companies, however, "are underestimating how climate-related risks, such as extreme weather and changing consumer views on environmental issues, could affect their companies' bottom lines, and they need to make climate risk assessments a bigger priority" (Broughton 2019).

This chapter looks at how companies engage in mergers and acquisitions to manage and diversify away from one important long-run climate risk: that associated with sea level rise.[1] It does so for two reasons: First, the accelerating rise of sea level is among the most severe impacts of climate change, with consensus that it is a serious environmental issue that risks disrupting household and business activities in the long run. Hauer, Evans, and Mishra (2016) suggest that a 1.8 meter (roughly 6 feet) rise in sea level would leave areas populated by 6 million Americans uninhabitable. Under these conditions, businesses with commercial properties or operations in low-lying coastal areas might find it increasingly difficult to ensure their assets, making sea level rise a relevant long-term business risk (Balch 2016).

Second, it is a challenge to forecast a rise in sea levels, which makes studying how firms manage such a significant yet uncertain risk particularly urgent and time relevant.

---

[1]   This chapter is an updated version of the paper uploaded in SSRN on 11 May 2021 (https://papers.ssrn.com/sol3/papers.cfm?abstract_id=3739599).

The chapter posits that firms exposed to significant sea level rise diversify away from such risks by acquiring firms unlikely to be affected and that this action is rewarded by the market. It conjectures that, after such a merger, the information environment in the acquiring firms improves as they diversify away an important source of forecast uncertainty, that is, the risk of rising sea levels. The chapter also suggests that the combined firms' environmental, social, and governance scores should improve post-merger.

In a multistep approach, the first set of analyses investigates how exposure to sea level rise risk affects merger likelihood. Because sea level rise is an uncertain yet significant long-term operational risk, the analysis hypothesizes that firms exposed are more (less) likely to become acquirers (targets) in a merger deal. The evidence is consistent with this hypothesis: relative to a group of potential acquirers (targets) in the same industry and similar in size (as well as a book-to-market ratio), firms more exposed to sea level rise are significantly more (less) likely to be an acquirer (target) in a merger deal.

When a firm exposed to the risk of sea level rise announces that it is acquiring a firm, its stock returns are significantly higher (and abnormal) in the announcement period. This is consistent with the notion that the market rewards firms for diversifying away such risk. Indeed, the results hold after controlling for a large number of firms and merger deal characteristics. Importantly, the positive announcement effect concentrates on deals in which target firms are *not* exposed to sea level rise risk, suggesting it is driven by the diversification of sea level rise risk. The positive return is also more pronounced for firms with more analyst coverage.

These findings expand understanding of how environmental and climate change risks influence various market participants and underlying assets. Prior studies have found that institutional investors consider climate risk an important source of risk for their portfolios, such as Krueger, Sautner, and Starks (2018). For instance, mutual fund investors gravitate toward funds with favorable (low) carbon designation by tilting their portfolios toward low fossil fuel and low carbon risk holdings (Bolton and Kacperczyk 2020). Besides, investors pay a premium for green bonds, which use the proceeds for environmental purposes (Baker et al. 2018).

Indeed, the bond markets started to price in sea level rise risk as early as 2011 (Goldsmith-Pinkham et al. 2020). In the real estate market, however, the evidence is somewhat mixed: while some studies find that real estate prices are heavily influenced by sea level rise (Bernstein, Gustafson, and Lewis 2019), others find minimal price impact (Murfin and Spiegel 2020). Acemoglu et al. (2016) take a unique model approach to the competing choices that firms face between clean and dirty technologies and provides empirical evidence that such choices are largely influenced by taxes and subsidies. Bansal, Ochoa, and Kiku (2016) find that equity portfolios with high exposure to climate risk carry a positive risk premium. Adopting a more quantitative approach, Giglio et al. (2018) estimate long-run discount rates for valuing investments in climate change abatement, while Barnett, Brock, and Hansen (2020) highlight the challenges of modeling climate-change risk due to uncertainty. On the corporate side, Jiang, Li, and Qian (2020) find firms' cost of long-term loans increases with sea level rise risk. The analysis in this chapter, meanwhile, provides direct evidence of how firms respond to sea level rise risk in the market for corporate control.

Second, our study contributes to the significant literature on mergers and acquisitions. Empirical studies on mergers and acquisitions largely focus on either the determinants of mergers or the sources of synergistic gains. While many factors such as stock overvaluation (e.g., Shleifer and Vishny 2003; Rhodes-Kropf and Viswanathan 2004), economic, regulatory, and technological shocks (e.g., Harford 2005; Mitchell and Mulherin 1996) lead to merger waves, mergers' synergistic gains range from better resource allocation and product differentiation (e.g., Lichtenberg et al. 1987; Healy, Palepu, and Ruback 1992; McGuckin and Nguyen 1995; Maksimovic and Phillips 2001; Schoar 2002; Hoberg and Phillips 2010; Maksimovic, Phillips, and Prabhala 2011), interest tax shields (Devos, Kadapakkam, and Krishnamurthy 2009; Fee, Hadlock, and Pierce 2012), improvements in product quality (Sheen 2014), to improvements in structured management practices (Bai, Jin, and Serfling 2022). This chapter's analysis contributes to the literature by providing systematic evidence that sea level rise risks are a significant factor that affects merger likelihood and that markets value mergers that diversify away from such long-run risks.

7.2 Literature and Hypothesis

7.2.1 Merger Likelihood

Why would the likelihood of mergers be correlated with environmental risks? On one hand, previous research finds that mergers are clustered by industry and by time and are often motivated by economic, regulatory, and technological shocks (Harford 2005). Because climate change is gradual and slow, it is reasonable to expect merger decisions to be unrelated to environmental risks.

On the other hand, environmental risks pose a unique challenge for today's companies. "Investors, analysts, research firms, and companies are putting more emphasis on how climate issues ranging from rising sea levels to record heatwaves will affect profits and revenues in the United States and what companies are doing to address those risks" (Randall 2019). In the context of managing risks associated with rising sea level, one immediately effective method is to acquire businesses in geographic locations unaffected by such environmental risks. At the same time, it is expected that businesses located in areas severely impacted by rising sea levels are difficult to sell in the market for corporate assets, as these environmental risks are difficult to diversify away and quite salient for any potential acquirers. As a result of these considerations, one can expect a merger likely to be correlated with the risks of sea level rise.

The analysis in this chapter summarizes the above arguments in their null and alternative forms in the following hypotheses:

H1: The likelihood of a firm becoming an acquirer (target) in a merger deal is not correlated with the firm's exposure to the risk of sea level rise.

H1a: The likelihood of a firm becoming an acquirer (target) in a merger deal is positively (negatively) correlated with the firm's exposure to the risk of sea level rise.

H1b: Firms subject to sea level rise risk are more likely to acquire firms subject to no sea level rise risk.

7.2.2 Cumulative Abnormal Returns around Merger Announcements

Following a similar logic, if environmental risks are slow moving and do not affect firms' business strategies or day-to-day operations, investors may not reward acquisitions that diversify away the exposure to these risks. On the other hand, if climate change associated with sea level rise does pose serious operational and business risks, one should expect the market to view acquisitions that diversify away such risks as value improving. The analysis tests these competing predictions by investigating abnormal cumulative returns around merger announcements. The following summarizes these predictions in the second set of hypotheses:

H2: The cumulative abnormal return of the acquiring firms around merger announcements is not correlated with the exposure to risks associated with the sea level rise.

H2a: The cumulative abnormal return of the acquiring firms around merger announcements is positively correlated with the exposure to risks associated with the sea level rise.

7.3 Empirical Methodology

The empirical exercise proceeds in three steps. First, it tests whether exposure to sea level rise risk affects the probability of a firm becoming an acquirer (a target). To this end, it runs conditional logistic, logistic, and ordinary least squares (OLS) regressions. Specifically, it estimates the following specification:

$$Event\ Firm_{i,m,t} = \alpha + \beta_1\ SLR\ Risk_{i,m,t-1} + \beta_2\ X_{i,t-1} + \rho_{t\times s} + \psi_k\ (or\ v_m) + e_{im,t} \quad (1)$$

where i, m, k, t, and s index firm, deal, industry, year, and state, respectively. $Event\ Firm_{i,m,t}$ equals one if firm i is the acquirer (target) in deal m, and zero otherwise. The key independent variable $SLR\ Risk_{i,m,t-1}$ is a dummy variable equal to one if firm i's headquarters would be inundated if the sea level rises by 6 feet, and zero otherwise. The analysis includes the following firm-level characteristics ($X_{i,t-1}$) measured in year $t-1$ to account for firms' observable characteristics on profitability, financial position, and other attributes.

The second set of analyses studies whether acquirers' cumulative abnormal return (CAR) around acquisition announcements is correlated with the sea level rise exposure of the acquiring firms. Specifically, it estimates the following cross-sectional regression:

$$Acquirer\ CAR_{i,m,t} = \alpha + \beta_1\ SLR\ Risk_{i,m,t-1} + \beta_2\ X_{i,t-1} +$$
$$\beta_2\ Deal\ Character_{m,t-1} + \rho_{t \times s} + \psi_k + e_{im,t} \tag{2}$$

where the dependent variable is the acquirer CAR around different windows surrounding the merger announcements. All the other variables are defined analogously to Equation (1).

7.4 Summary of Findings

Testing the first set of hypotheses (i.e., H1 and H1a) by investigating whether sea level rise is an important determinant of a firm engaging in a merger. If sea level rise risks are significant business risks that firms attempt to diversify away through acquisitions, it is expected the sea level rise risk to be positively correlated with a firm's likelihood of becoming an acquirer, and negatively correlated with a firm's likelihood of being a target firm. To operationalize these tests, the analysis estimates Equation (1) on the two matched samples: the industry and size-matched and the industry, size, and M/B ratio matched samples.

Table 7.1 presents the results of these exercises. Panels A and B present the results based on the industry and size-matched sample and industry, size, and M/B ratio-matched samples, respectively. Columns 1–3 of panel A present the coefficient estimates from the conditional logit and logit models, while columns 4–7 display the results using the OLS regression model. Overall, throughout various empirical specifications, it is found that the coefficient estimates on sea level rise risk (Inundated6ft) are positive and statistically significant, suggesting that firms with higher sea level rise risk are more likely to become an acquirer, even after controlling for a variety of firm characteristics. In economic significance, column 1 predicts that if the firm is subject to the inundation risk, then the firm is 4.1% more likely to become an acquirer than the firm not subject to the inundation risk. Although the magnitudes become smaller in columns 4–7 when the linear probability model (i.e., OLS) is employed, the positive relation between sea level rise risk and the probability of becoming an acquirer stays positive and economically meaningful.

Table 7.1, panel B reports the results on the industry, size, and M/B ratio matched sample. The findings are broadly consistent with those in panel A. The coefficient estimates, as well as the economic significance, become larger, which is most likely due to the better-matched sample that ensures that the control firms and treated firms are comparable across more dimensions. For instance, column 1 predicts that if the firm is subject to the inundation risk, the firm is 13.1% more likely to become an acquirer than the firm not subject to the inundation risk. The results are robust to further control for the county fixed effects that absorb the impact of within-county, time-invariant variables.

To examine whether sea level rise is correlated with firms' propensity to become a target in a merger deal, the analysis estimates a similar set of models to examine the likelihood of any given firm becoming a target and presents these results in Table 7.2. Similar to Table 7.1, the table presents the results estimated on the two matched samples in panels A and B separately. Overall, the results show a significant negative relationship between firms' sea level rise risk as proxied by *Inundated6ft* and their probability of becoming a target. For instance, column 1 of panel A shows a negative and statistically significant coefficient of -0.205 on *Inundated6ft*. By economic significance, if the firm is subject to the inundation risk, then the firm is 4.7% less likely to become a target than the firm subject to no inundation risk. Panel B of Table 7.2 repeats these exercises on the industry, size, and M/B matched sample and shows an overall similar pattern as in panel A. In economic significance, if the firm is subject to the inundation risk, then the firm is 5.3% less likely to become a target than the firm subject to no inundation risk.

The analysis next refines the analysis and examines whether high sea level rise risk acquirers are more likely to buy low sea level rise risk firms. It employs the same matching methodology as in earlier sections and for each acquirer (target), up to five control acquirers and targets are found. Next, the analysis follows Bena and Li (2014) to conduct the following test:

$$Merger\ pair_{i,jm,t} = \alpha + \beta_1\ SLR\ Risk_{i,jm,t-1} + \beta_2\ X_{i,j,t-1} + \rho_{t\times s} + \psi_k\ (or\ vm) + e_{i,jm,t} \quad (3)$$

where *Merger pair*$_{i,jm,t}$ equals one if the matching pair is the real merger deal, and zero otherwise. *SLR Risk*$_{i,jm,t-1}$ equals one if the acquirer/target is subject to sea level rise risk/no sea level rise risk. The analysis includes the firm characteristics of both the acquirers and the targets. It also controls for a variety of fixed effects. The results are reported in Table 7.3.

Table 7.1: Sea Level Rise and Likelihood of Becoming an Acquirer

Panel A	Acquirer						
	Conditional Logit	Logit		OLS			
Industry and Size Matched	(1)	(2)	(3)	(4)	(5)	(6)	(7)
Inundated6ft	0.206***	0.184***	0.186*	0.047***	0.046**	0.032***	0.032*
	(0.038)	(0.036)	(0.106)	(0.008)	(0.021)	(0.006)	(0.019)
	0.041	0.029	0.029				
Cluster	Deal	Deal	Zip code	Deal	Zip code	Deal	Zip code
Fixed effects	Deal, State	State, Year, Industry	State, Year, Industry	Deal, State×Year	Deal, State×Year	Industry, State×Year	Industry, State×Year
Control variables	Yes	Yes	Yes	Yes	Yes	Yes	Yes
No. of observations	91,823	100,273	100,273	99,559	99,559	100,364	100,364
R-squared				0.138	0.140	0.061	0.062
Pseudo R-squared	0.087	0.032	0.032				

Panel B	Acquirer						
	Conditional Logit	Logit		OLS			
Industry, Size, and M/B Matched	(1)	(2)	(3)	(4)	(5)	(6)	(7)
Inundated6ft	0.586***	0.542***	0.557**	0.081***	0.082*	0.077***	0.080**
	(0.056)	(0.055)	(0.247)	(0.009)	(0.042)	(0.008)	(0.037)
	0.131	0.056	0.058				
Cluster	Deal	Deal	Zip code	Deal	Zip code	Deal	Zip code
Fixed effects	Deal, State	State, Year, Industry	State, Year, Industry	Deal, State×Year	Deal, State×Year	Industry, State×Year	Industry, State×Year
Control variables	Yes	Yes	Yes	Yes	Yes	Yes	Yes
No. of observations	80,132	83,178	83,178	83,057	83,057	83,293	83,293
R-squared				0.117	0.118	0.086	0.087
Pseudo R-squared	0.068	0.051	0.051				

M/B = market-to-book, OLS = ordinary least squares.
Notes: This table reports coefficient estimates from conditional logit, logit, and OLS models in equation (1). The dependent variable is equal to one for the acquirer, and zero for the matched acquirers that form the control group. The key independent variable is $Inundated6ft$, a dummy variable equal to one if the firm's headquarters would be inundated if the sea level rise by 6 feet, and zero otherwise. Panel A presents the baseline specification for the industry and size-matched sample. Panel B presents the baseline specification for the industry, size, and M/B ratio matched sample. All specifications include fixed effects that are listed at the bottom of the table. Robust standard errors (clustered at the deal or zip code level) are reported in parentheses; *, **, and *** denote significance at the 10%, 5%, and 1% levels, respectively. The analysis reports the marginal effects below the robust standard error in columns 1, 2, and 3.
Source: Authors.

Table 7.2: Sea Level Rise and Likelihood of Becoming a Target

Panel A	Target						
	Conditional Logit	Logit		OLS			
Industry and Size Matched	(1)	(2)	(3)	(4)	(5)	(6)	(7)
Inundated6ft	−0.205*	−0.252**	−0.250	−0.044*	−0.054*	−0.037**	−0.046*
	(0.122)	(0.122)	(0.160)	(0.023)	(0.029)	(0.019)	(0.025)
	−0.047	−0.039	−0.039				
Target control variables	Yes	Yes	Yes	Yes	Yes	Yes	Yes
Cluster	Deal	Deal	Zip code	Deal	Zip code	Deal	Zip code
Fixed effects	Deal, State	State, Year, Industry	State, Year, Industry	Deal, State×Year	Deal, State×Year	Industry, State×Year	Industry, State×Year
No. of observations	8,092	9,180	9,180	9,049	9,049	9,183	9,183
R-squared				0.218	0.217	0.145	0.147
Pseudo R-squared	0.044	0.039	0.039				
Panel B	Target						
	Conditional Logit	Logit		OLS			
Industry, Size, and M/B Matched	(1)	(2)	(3)	(4)	(5)	(6)	(7)
Inundated6ft	−0.609***	−0.513**	−0.511*	−0.061***	−0.060**	−0.054**	−0.054*
	(0.194)	(0.200)	(0.264)	(0.021)	(0.027)	(0.021)	(0.030)
	−0.053	−0.049	−0.048				
Target control variables	Yes	Yes	Yes	Yes	Yes	Yes	Yes
Cluster	Deal	Deal	Zip code	Deal	Zip code	Deal	Zip code
Fixed effects	Deal, State	State, Year, Industry	State, Year, Industry	Deal, State×Year	Deal, State×Year	Industry, State×Year	Industry, State×Year
No. of observations	7,889	8,950	8,950	9,087	9,087	9,099	9,099
R-squared				0.135	0.136	0.168	0.168
Pseudo R-squared	0.104	0.087	0.086				

M/B = market-to-book, OLS = ordinary least squares.
Notes: This table reports coefficient estimates from conditional logit, logit, and OLS models in equation (1). The dependent variable is equal to one for the target, and zero for the matched targets that form the control group. The key independent variable is *Inundated6ft*, a dummy variable equal to one if the firm's headquarters would be inundated if the sea level rise by six feet, and zero otherwise. Panel A presents the baseline specification for the industry and size-matched sample. Panel B presents the baseline specification for the industry, size, and M/B ratio matched sample. All specifications include fixed effects that are listed at the bottom of the table. Robust standard errors (clustered at the deal or zip code level) are reported in parentheses; *, **, and *** denote significance at the 10%, 5%, and 1% levels, respectively. The analysis reports the marginal effects below the robust standard error in columns 1, 2, and 3.
Source: Authors.

Table 7.3: Sea Level Rise and Merger Pair

				Pair			
	Conditional Logit	Logit		OLS			
Panel A							
Size and Industry Matched	(1)	(2)	(3)	(4)	(5)	(6)	(7)
Sea level rise	0.206*	0.118**	0.119*	0.030*	0.031	0.024**	0.025*
	(0.117)	(0.059)	(0.067)	(0.018)	(0.021)	(0.012)	(0.013)
	0.040	0.022	0.022				
Acquirer control	Yes	Yes	Yes	Yes	Yes	Yes	Yes
Target control	Yes	Yes	Yes	Yes	Yes	Yes	Yes
Cluster	Deal	Deal	Zip	Deal	Zip	Deal	Zip
Fixed effects	Deal, State	State, Year, Industry	State, Year, Industry	Deal, State×Year	Deal, State×Year	Industry, State×Year	Industry, State×Year
No. of observations	12,308	13,432	13,357	13,109	13,031	13,166	13,091
R-squared				0.162	0.163	0.086	0.088
Pseudo R-squared	0.052	0.018	0.019				

				Pair			
	Conditional Logit	Logit		OLS			
Panel B							
Size, Industry, and M/B Matched	(1)	(2)	(3)	(4)	(5)	(6)	(7)
Sea level rise	0.454**	0.274**	0.286*	0.047*	0.047	0.033**	0.034**
	(0.202)	(0.127)	(0.162)	(0.024)	(0.031)	(0.014)	(0.016)
	0.102	0.028	0.029				
Acquirer control	Yes	Yes	Yes	Yes	Yes	Yes	Yes
Target control	Yes	Yes	Yes	Yes	Yes	Yes	Yes
Cluster	Deal	Deal	Zip	Deal	Zip	Deal	Zip
Fixed effects	Deal, State	State, Year, Industry	State, Year, Industry	Deal, State×Year	Deal, State×Year	Industry, State×Year	Industry, State×Year
No. of observations	8,562	9,333	9,273	9,261	9,196	9,270	9,206
R-squared				0.162	0.163	0.099	0.100
Pseudo R-squared	0.074	0.042	0.042				

M/B = market-to-book, OLS = ordinary least squares.
Notes: This table reports coefficient estimates from conditional logit, logit, and OLS models in equation (3). The dependent variable is equal to one for the real merger deal, and zero for the matched deal. The key independent variable is $SLR\ Risk_{i,jm,t-1}$ equals one if the acquirer/target is subject to sea level rise risk/no sea level rise risk. Panel A presents the baseline specification for the industry and size-matched sample. Panel B presents the baseline specification for the industry, size, and M/B ratio matched sample. All specifications include fixed effects that are listed at the bottom of the table. Robust standard errors (clustered at the deal or zip code level) are reported in parentheses; *, **, and *** denote significance at the 10%, 5%, and 1% levels, respectively. The analysis reports the marginal effects below the robust standard error in columns 1, 2, and 3.
Source: Authors.

Using various empirical specifications, the analysis finds that the coefficient estimates on *SLR Risk*$_{i,jm,t-1}$ are positive and statistically significant, suggesting that firms with sea level rise risk are indeed more likely to acquire firms subject to no sea level rise risk, even after controlling for a variety of firm characteristics of both the acquirers and the targets. The estimate in column 1 of panel A suggests that if the firm is subject to the inundation risk, the firm is 4.0% more likely to acquire a firm subject to no inundation risk. Although the magnitudes become smaller in columns 4–7 when the linear probability model (i.e., OLS) is employed, the positive relationship between the *SLR Risk*$_{i,jm,t-1}$ and the probability of a merger stays positive and economically meaningful. Panel B reports the results of the same test by using the industry, size, and M/B matched sample.

This section investigates how the market responds to merger announcements by acquirers with high exposure to sea level rise before the merger. Cumulative abnormal returns (CAR) around the merger announcement periods provide a clean estimation of the market's reception of the news announcement and the underlying wealth effects (Li and Prabhala 2007). If sea level rise indeed poses a significant business risk, the market is expected to react positively to acquisition announcements that reduce such risks.

To test this conjecture, the analysis estimates equation (2), in which the dependent variable is the acquirer announcement-period cumulative abnormal return around various windows, and the main independent variable is the acquirer's sea level rise risk. It focuses on several event windows starting from 3 days before the acquisition announcement to 3 days after. The longest window of examination is (-3, +3) while the shortest window is (-1, +1). To estimate the cumulative announcement return, the analysis first uses the Fama and French (1993) three factors model and daily stock returns in the estimation window of (−255, −46) to estimate the factor loadings, which are then applied to returns during the event window to estimate the announcement CARs. Because the stock return analyses use the sample of actual acquisition announcements, we have a different sample size than the one used in the analysis of the probability of a merger.

The results are presented in Table 7.4. It is found that the coefficient estimates of *Inundated6ft* are positive and statistically significant in columns 1–9. The coefficient estimate on *Inundated6ft* in column 1 suggests that acquirers whose headquarters would be inundated if the sea level rises by 6 feet has 0.531% higher CARs than other acquirers over a 2-day window around the announcement. Also, the coefficient estimates on *Inundated6ft* increase with the days of the event window of the CARs. Overall, this evidence is consistent with H2a, suggesting that the market rewards acquirers that diversify away from their sea level rise risk through acquisitions.

Table 7.4: Market Reaction—Acquirers' Announcement Period Returns

CARs	[-1,+1] (1)	[-1,+2] (2)	[-1,+3] (3)	[-2,+1] (4)	[-2,+3] (5)	[-3,+1] (6)	[-3,+1] (7)	[-3,+2] (8)	[-3,+3] (9)
Inundated6ft	0.494*	0.654**	0.730**	0.672**	0.828***	0.925***	0.647**	0.806**	0.900***
	(0.292)	(0.317)	(0.330)	(0.297)	(0.308)	(0.320)	(0.323)	(0.327)	(0.340)
Ln(deal value)	0.493***	0.494***	0.490***	0.534***	0.533***	0.529***	0.583***	0.578***	0.570***
	(0.058)	(0.063)	(0.066)	(0.061)	(0.066)	(0.068)	(0.063)	(0.067)	(0.070)
All cash deal	0.416***	0.400***	0.374***	0.270**	0.262*	0.230	0.207	0.192	0.161
	(0.121)	(0.134)	(0.144)	(0.129)	(0.141)	(0.149)	(0.140)	(0.151)	(0.159)
Diversify deal	0.132	0.011	0.008	0.162	0.049	0.039	0.152	0.035	0.023
	(0.134)	(0.150)	(0.162)	(0.147)	(0.163)	(0.174)	(0.161)	(0.175)	(0.187)
Cluster	Zip	Zip	Zip	Zip	Zip	Zip	Zip	Zip	Zip
Fixed effects	Industry, State× Year	Industry, State× Year	Industry, State× Year	Industry, State× Year	Industry, State× Year	Industry, State× Year	Industry, State× Year	Industry, State× Year	Industry, State× Year
No. of observations	18,645	18,645	18,645	18,645	18,645	18,645	18,645	18,645	18,645
R-squared	0.099	0.094	0.090	0.096	0.092	0.088	0.095	0.093	0.088

CARs = cumulative abnormal returns, OLS = ordinary least squares, R&D = research and development, ROA = return on assets.
Notes: This table reports coefficient estimates for OLS regressions in equation (2) for acquirers. We use the Fama and French (1993) three factors model and daily stock returns in the window (−255, −46) to estimate the deal announcement CARs. We use the Center for Research in Security Prices value-weighted index as the benchmark portfolio. The key independent variable is *Inundated6ft*, a dummy variable equal to one if the firm's headquarters would be inundated if the sea level rise by 6 feet, and zero otherwise. The deal Characteristics include Ln(Deal value), All cash deal, and Diversify deal. Event firm characteristics are *Firm size, Market-to-book* (M/B)*, Leverage, Dividend payer, Ln (Total Sales), ROA, R&D, Capex, Quick ratio, Non-debt tax shield,* and *Cash flow volatility.* All specifications include fixed effects that are listed at the bottom of the table. Robust standard errors (clustered at the zip level) are reported in parentheses; *, **, and *** denote significance at the 10%, 5%, and 1% levels, respectively.
Source: Authors.

7.5 Conclusion

Effective management of environmental risks has become central to the long-term sustainability and success of modern businesses. While there are many types of environmental risks, the inundation risks associated with sea level rise that are both uncertain and significant pose a unique challenge for firms.

The chapter develops and tests the hypothesis that firms manage the sea level rise risk through acquisitions. Using a comprehensive sample of publicly traded firms between 1986 and 2017, the analysis finds that, in the cross-section, firms exposed to high sea level rise risk have a higher probability of becoming acquirers but a significantly lower probability of becoming targets. Also, it finds that the market rewards acquisitions by firms with high sea level rise risk exposure, as a significant and positive relationship is observed between the acquirers' cumulative announcement return and pre-merger sea level rise risk. It is also found that this positive relation is more pronounced for firms with higher analyst coverage. Finally, the analysis finds that sea-level-rise-induced mergers tend to complete faster, and that post-merger, the combined firm experiences a greater increase in analyst coverage; forecast precision; and environmental, social, and governance score when the acquiring firm has a high sea level rise exposure before the merger.

While the results provide the first systematic evidence of how environmental risks associated with sea level rises shape and influence firm behavior in the market for corporate control, many other aspects of such interaction remain unexplored. A deeper understanding of how different types of environmental risks differentially affect firms' investment, financing, and operational policies remains a fruitful area for future research.

References

Acemoglu, D., U. Akcigit, D. Hanley, and W. Kerr. 2016. Transition to Clean Technology. *Journal of Political Economy*. 124 (1). pp. 52–104.

Bai, J., W. Jin, and M. Serfling. 2022. Management Practices and Mergers and Acquisitions. *Management Science*. 68 (3). pp. 2141–2165.

Baker, M., D. Bergstresser, G. Serafeim, and J. Wurgler. 2018. Financing the Response to Climate Change: The Pricing and Ownership of US Green Bonds. *NBER Working Paper*. No. w25194. National Bureau of Economic Research.

Balch, O. 2016. Sea-Level Rises: Why Flooding Is the Next Big Business Risk. *The Guardian*. 18 March.

Bansal, R., M. Ochoa, and D. Kiku. 2016. Climate Change and Growth Risks. *NBER Working Paper*. No. w23009. National Bureau of Economic Research.

Barnett, M., W. Brock, and L. P. Hansen. 2020. Pricing Uncertainty Induced by Climate Change. *The Review of Financial Studies*. 33 (3). pp. 1024–1066.

Bena, J. and K. Li. 2014. Corporate Innovations and Mergers and Acquisitions. *The Journal of Finance*. 69 (5). pp. 1923–1960.

Bernstein, A., M. T. Gustafson, and R. Lewis. 2019. Disaster on the Horizon: The Price Effect of Sea-Level Rise. *Journal of Financial Economics*. 134 (2). pp. 253–272.

Bolton, P. and M. Kacperczyk. 2020. Do Investors Care About Carbon Risk? *NBER Working Paper*. No. w26968. National Bureau of Economic Research.

Broughton, K. 2019. CFOs Are Underestimating the Financial Risks of Climate Change, Executives Say. *Wall Street Journal*. 11 June. https://www.wsj.com/articles/cfos-are-underestimating-the-financial-risks-of-climate-change-executives-say-11560276836.

Devos, E., P. R. Kadapakkam, and S. Krishnamurthy. 2009. How Do Mergers Create Value? A Comparison of Taxes, Market Power, and Efficiency Improvements As Explanations for Synergies. *The Review of Financial Studies*. 22 (3). pp. 1179–1211.

Fama, E. F. and K. R. French. 1993. Common Risk Factors in the Returns on Stocks and Bonds. *Journal of Financial Economics*. 33 (1). pp. 3–56.

Fee, C. E., C. J. Hadlock, and J. R. Pierce. 2012. What Happens in Acquisitions? Evidence from Brand Ownership Changes and Advertising Investment. *Journal of Corporate Finance*. 18 (3). pp. 584–597.

Giglio, S., M. Maggiori, J. Stroebel, and A. Weber. 2018. Cost-Benefit Evaluation of Investments in Climate Change Abatement. Working paper.

Goldsmith-Pinkham, P. S., M. Gustafson, R. Lewis, and M. Schwert. 2019. Sea Level Rise and Municipal Bond Yields. Working paper.

Harford, J. 2005. What Drives Merger Waves? *Journal of Financial Economics*. 77 (3). pp. 529–560.

Hauer, M. E., J. M. Evans, and D. R. Mishra. 2016. Millions Are Projected to Be at Risk from Sea-Level Rise in the Continental United States. *Nature Climate Change*. 6 (7). pp. 691–695.

Haw, I. M., K. Jung, and W. Ruland. 1994. The Accuracy of Financial Analysts' Forecasts after Mergers. *Journal of Accounting, Auditing and Finance*. 9 (3). pp. 465–483.

Healy, P. M., K. G. Palepu, and R. S. Ruback. 1992. Does Corporate Performance Improve after Mergers? *Journal of Financial Economics*. 31 (2). pp. 135–175.

Hoberg, G. and G. Phillips. 2010. Product Market Synergies and Competition in Mergers and Acquisitions: A Text-Based Analysis. *The Review of Financial Studies*. 23 (10). pp. 3773–3811.

Jiang, F., C. W. Li, and Y. Qian. 2019. Can Firms Run Away from Climate-Change Risk? Evidence from the Pricing of Bank Loans. Working paper.

Krueger, P., Z. Sautner, and L. T. Starks. 2020. The Importance of Climate Risks for Institutional Investors. *The Review of Financial Studies*. 33 (3). pp. 1067–1111.

Li, K. and N. R. Prabhala. 2007. Self-Selection Models in Corporate Finance. In B. E. Eckbo, ed. *Handbook of Corporate Finance: Empirical Corporate Finance Vol. 1.* North Holland Handbooks in Finance. Elsevier Science B.V. Chapter 2. pp. 37–86.

Li, Y., M. Lu, and Y. L. Lo. 2019. The Impact of Analyst Coverage on Partial Acquisitions: Evidence from M&A Premium and Firm Performance in China. *International Review of Economics and Finance.* 63. pp. 37–60.

Lichtenberg, F. R., D. Siegel, D. Jorgenson, and E. Mansfield. 1987. Productivity and Changes in Ownership of Manufacturing Plants. *Brookings Papers on Economic Activity.* 18 (3). pp. 643–683.

Maksimovic, V. and G. Phillips. 2001. The Market for Corporate Assets: Who Engages in Mergers and Asset Sales and Are There Efficiency Gains? *The Journal of Finance.* 56 (6). pp. 2019–2065.

Maksimovic, V., G. Phillips, and N. R. Prabhala. 2011. Post-Merger Restructuring and the Boundaries of the Firm. *Journal of Financial Economics.* 102 (2). pp. 317–343.

McGuckin, R. H. and S. V. Nguyen. 1995. On Productivity and Plant Ownership Change: New Evidence from the Longitudinal Research Database. *The RAND Journal of Economics.* pp. 257–276.

Mitchell, M. L. and J. H. Mulherin. 1996. The Impact of Industry Shocks on Takeover and Restructuring Activity. *Journal of Financial Economics.* 41 (2). pp. 193–229.

Murfin, J. and M. Spiegel. 2020. Is the Risk of Sea-Level Rise Capitalized in Residential Real Estate? *The Review of Financial Studies.* 33 (3). pp. 1217–1255.

Randall, D. 2019. Wall Street Taking Closer Look at Climate Change Risks. *Insurance Journal.* 15 November. https://www.insurancejournal.com/news/national/2019/11/15/548563.htm.

Rhodes-Kropf, M. and S. Viswanathan. 2004. Market Valuation and Merger Waves. *The Journal of Finance.* 59 (6). pp. 2685–2718.

Schoar, A. 2002. Effects of Corporate Diversification on Productivity. *The Journal of Finance*. 57 (6). pp. 2379–2403.

Sheen, A. 2014. The Real Product-Market Impact of Mergers. *The Journal of Finance*. 69 (6). pp. 2651–2688.

Shleifer, A. and R. W. Vishny. 2003. Stock Market-Driven Acquisitions. *Journal of Financial Economics*. 70 (3). pp. 295–311.

Tehranian, H., M. Zhao, and J. L. Zhu. 2014. Can Analysts Analyze Mergers? *Management Science*. 60 (4). pp. 959–979.

Wu, J. S. and A. Y. Zang. 2009. What Determines Financial Analysts' Career Outcomes during Mergers? *Journal of Accounting and Economics*. 47 (1–2). pp. 59–86.

Environmental, Social, and Governance Performance and Downside and Upside Risks

Chapter

8

Vina Javed Khan, Searat Ali, and Millicent Chang

8.1 Introduction

The term "environmental, social, and governance (ESG)" was first mentioned during the United Nations Global Compact Leaders' Summit to determine how ESG activities can be integrated into capital markets. Since then, these activities have become a key priority for firms, investors, and other stakeholders.

Sustainable and responsible investment in the United States (US) has grown exponentially, from $639 billion in 1995 to $17.1 trillion in 2020 (US SIF 2020) (Figure 8.1). Firm commitment is growing and increasingly willing to incorporate these activities into business and investment strategies. In 2019, 222 CEOs of the largest US companies signed and issued the "Statement on the Purpose of Corporation" in a business roundtable and committed to lead their companies in the best interests of all stakeholders: employees, customers, suppliers, and shareholders. The statement disregarded shareholder supremacy and reinvigorated contrasting views about shareholder and stakeholder orientations of firms (Harrison, Phillips, and Freeman 2020). Firms holding the shareholder view try to maximize their profits (as the core firm objective), assuming shareholders to be the key stakeholders (Eccles, Ioannou, and Serafeim 2014). In contrast, other companies presume a stakeholder view to account for the externalities of their activities and how they influence other stakeholders (Deegan 2002, Friedman and Miles 2002). To maintain both approaches, effective stakeholder engagement through ESG activities requires not undermining investor interest while delivering value to other stakeholders (Dumitrescu and Zakriya 2021). This raises a question: Do ESG activities undermine investors' interests in practice? One way to answer is to examine the effect of ESG activities on firm risk.

Figure 8.1: Sustainable Investing in the United States, 1995–2020

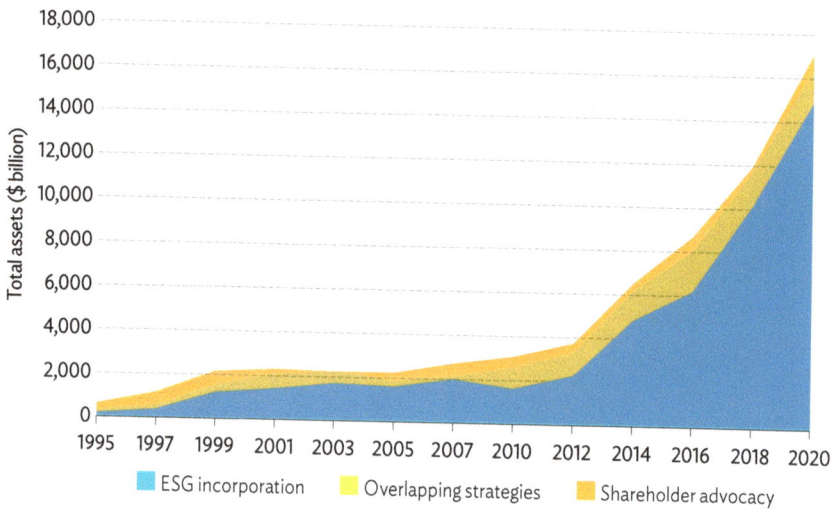

ESG = environmental, social, and governance.
Source: US SIF Foundation.

Traditionalists view risk as unfavorable. The Cambridge dictionary defines risk as "exposing to hazard or danger." An improved description of risk is given by the Chinese symbol for "crisis," which in the first part refers to "danger" and the second to "opportunity," making risk a combination of danger and opportunity (Roggi, Damodaran, and Garvey 2012). So risk management is reducing exposure to downside risk and maximizing exposure to upside potential (Roggi, Damodaran, and Garvey 2012). Economists have long recognized that investors consider downside risk and upside gains differently, showing more sensitivity to downside losses than upside gains and therefore demanding a premium for holding assets that covary with the market when it declines (Ang, Chen, and Xing 2006). Although it has been established that ESG can serve as a risk reduction mechanism, deliberation continues as to whether ESG creates upside potential for investors while protecting against downside risk.

This study thus takes a contemporary risk-taking perspective on ESG to examine whether ESG activities affect downside and upside risk differently. Through risk management and stakeholder theory, the analysis explains the relationship between ESG and firm risk (separated into its downside and upside components).

From the traditional *risk management perspective*, companies pay attention to those activities that are likely to cause damage and take initiatives to minimize financial exposure. For example, firms involve themselves in socially and environmentally responsible practices to legitimize their actions and to avoid fines, penalties, or reputational damage (Godfrey 2005; Kytle and Ruggie 2005). The analysis here argues that as a risk management strategy, ESG performance is expected to reduce overall firm risk. Further, *stakeholder theory* rationalizes that ESG activities reduce financial exposure by developing healthy relations with stakeholders. This strong bond motivates stakeholders to play their role in firm success with the resources they own (Freeman 1984, 2010). Thus, companies with high ESG face less likelihood of boycotts, badmouthing, or scandals, which can decrease downside risk. It also helps firms develop healthy relationships with the financial community and government (McGuire, Sundgren, and Schneeweis 1988), lessen capital constraints (Cheng, Ioannou, and Serafeim 2014), build goodwill (Cornell and Shapiro 1987), improve the company's attractiveness as an employer, and retain a skilled workforce (Greening and Turban 2000). This all increases upside potential.

It may happen that company insiders willingly carry out socially responsible practices, whose costs are greater than benefits to receive recognition or appreciation. This additional cost over benefits translates to lower returns (Barnea and Rubin 2005). Therefore, we argue that ESG activities of firms, having healthy relationships with stakeholders, may not only lower downside risk but also increase or decrease the upside gains for investors (Figure 8.2).

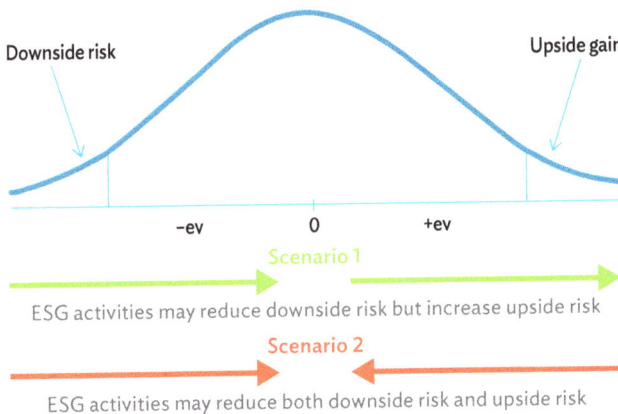

Figure 8.2: Environmental, Social, and Governance Performance and Downside and Upside Risks

ESG = environmental, social, and governance.
Source: Authors.

8.2 Gaps in the Academic Literature

Previous academic research on the ESG and firm risk relationship reports mixed results. For overall ESG and firm risk, the majority of studies show a negative relationship (e.g., Albuquerque, Koskinen, and Zhang 2019; Loof and Stephan 2019; Boubaker et al. 2020); and Becchetti, Ciciretti, and Hasan (2015) find a positive result, while others report no relationship (e.g., Sassen, Hinze, and Hardeck 2016).

Likewise, the literature has drawn unclear conclusions about the relationship between individual ESG pillars (E and S) and firm risk.[1] These inconsistent findings may be due to differences in methodological approaches (Gillan, Koch, and Starks 2021). Most importantly, the earlier classification of firm risk into systematic and idiosyncratic risk is less intuitive for investors because it fails to differentiate between the positive and negative deviation of returns.

Hence, dividing firm risk into its downside and upside fluctuations may accurately capture investors' risk preferences (Harlow 1991). In a recent review, Gillan, Koch, and Starks (2021) note that among all ESG-firm risk related studies, only two studies (Hoepner et al. 2018; Ilhan, Sautner, and Vilkov 2020) have used downside risk: Hoepner et al. (2018) test the impact of ESG shareholder engagement on downside risk while Ilhan, Sautner, and Vilkov (2020) examine the influence of carbon emissions on tail risk.

The analysis here extends this stream of literature by examining for the first time the effect of ESG activities on firm risk, which is divided into downside and upside risks.

8.3 Research Method

8.3.1 Data and Sample

The initial sample includes 5,511 firm-year observations that comprise all S&P 500 companies whose ESG data are available in the Refinitiv database

---

[1] For instance, Bouslah, Kryzanowski, and M'Zali (2013) find a positive relationship between environmental (E) and firm risk for S&P 500 firms but a negative link between the two for non-S&P 500 firms. Contradictory findings are also observed for the social (S) pillar, where Bouslah, Kryzanowski, and M'Zali (2013) highlight a negative as well as no relation with firm risk for different dimensions of social performance, while Lu (2016) finds an inverse linkage between S and firm risk. The governance (G) pillar has also been found to have positive (e.g., Ferreira and Laux 2007), negative (e.g., Bouslah, Kryzanowski, and M'Zali 2013), or no relation (e.g., Sassen, Hinze, and Hardeck 2016) with firm risk.

for 2008–2020. Firm characteristics and stock price data are also sourced from the Refinitiv database. The analysis excludes financial firms because risk-taking may differ for financial (such as banks) and nonfinancial firms. As a final sample, the analysis retains 4,451 firm-year observations for all firms conditioned upon the availability of data for all variables. All the continuous variables are "winsorised"[2] at 1st and 99th percentiles.

8.3.2 Measuring Environmental, Social, and Governance Performance

The analysis uses the ESG score provided by Refinitiv to measure the ESG performance following recent ESG studies (e.g., Ding et al. 2021; and Shi and Veenstra 2021). As shown in Figure 8.3, the score captures firm-level ESG information on more than 630 measures, which are then grouped into 10 different categories, namely emissions, resource use, innovation (environmental categories); human rights, product responsibility, community, workforce (social), management, corporate social responsibility strategy, and shareholders (governance). These categories are further formulated into three individual pillars—environmental, social, and governance—that ultimately formulate an overall ESG score which ranges from 0 (poor performance) to 100 (excellent performance).

Figure 8.3: Refinitiv Environmental, Social, and Governance Score

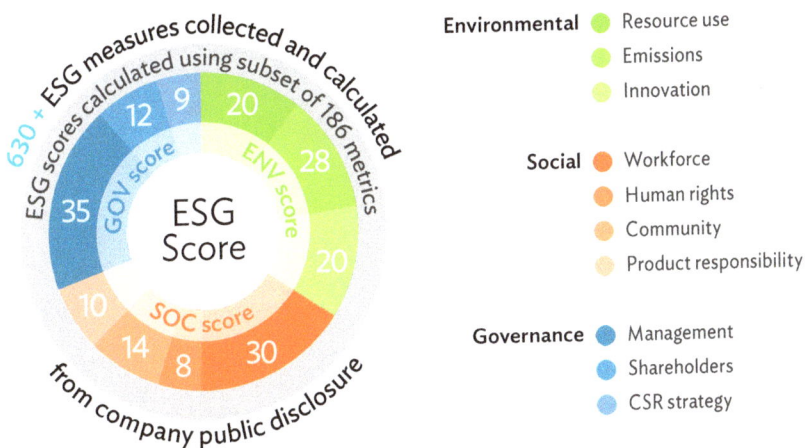

CSR = corporate social responsibility; ESG = environmental, social, and governance.
Source: Refinitiv database, 2022 (accessed 15 January 2023).

---

2   Winsorization is a statistcial procedure used to limit the extreme values in the data to reduce the undue influence of outliers on the regression estimates.

Table 8.1 shows the increasing trend in the average value of overall ESG and its individual pillars from 2008 to 2020. Overall ESG score mean was 45% in 2008, reaching 60.5% in 2020. Among the individual pillars, the E (S) score was at its lowest of 35% (46.7%) in 2008. However, companies started to recognize the importance of being involved in environmentally (socially) friendly practices, which resulted in the highest E (S) score of 56.3% (65.5%), in 2020. Further, the sample firms have average governance performance of above 50% in all years. This was likely due to the introduction of the Sarbanes-Oxley Act in 2002. Cohen, Krishnamoorthy, and Wright (2010) also found a solid post-act corporate governance environment. Overall, the increase in ESG performance may be credited to the introduction of Principles of the Responsible Investment in 2006, which is based on a report "Who Cares Wins," which mentioned that incorporating ESG issues into capital markets generates sustainable markets, results in good business performance, and leads to positive societal outcomes (The Global Compact 2005).

Table 8.1: Environmental, Social, and Governance Scores by Year

Year	N	ESG	E	S	G
2008	243	45.02	35.04	46.66	51.29
2009	336	47.05	38.38	48.61	52.45
2010	349	48.67	40.97	50.17	52.88
2011	356	49.74	42.26	51.58	53.27
2012	359	50.32	43.57	52.04	53.28
2013	354	50.84	43.39	53.04	53.66
2014	374	51.32	44.41	53.28	53.62
2015	398	53.30	45.09	54.83	57.32
2016	404	55.71	46.74	57.76	59.17
2017	413	57.15	49.33	59.52	59.30
2018	414	58.62	52.08	61.16	59.47
2019	402	60.80	54.89	63.64	61.01
2020	54	60.48	56.30	65.53	56.36

E = environment; ESG = environmental, social, and governance; G = governance; N = number of observations; S = social.
Source: Authors.

8.3.3 Measuring Firm Risk

The analysis measures firm risk using three proxies: total risk, downside risk, and upside risk, following Ali, Liu, and Su (2022). In the first measure, total risk depicts the overall variation in stock returns. Following previous studies, such as Albuquerque et al. (2020) and Chollet and Sandwidi (2018), total risk (TR) is measured by the annualized standard deviation of daily stock returns. Daily stock returns for each financial year are calculated using the following formula for continuously compounded returns:

$$R_{it} = \ln \left(\frac{P_t}{P_{t-1}} \right) \tag{1}$$

where P_{t-1} and P_t refer to the closing prices for any two successive periods t and $t-1$, R_{it} denotes daily stock returns, and ln is the natural logarithm.

Firm risk measured through stock return volatility does not distinguish the positive and negative deviation, making this measure less helpful for investors. Separating firm risk into downside and upside fluctuations captures investors' risk preferences (Harlow 1991). Therefore, the second proxy is downside risk, which measures the possible losses over a specific period at a given confidence level (Ali, Liu, and Su 2022). The analysis measures downside risk (DR) using conditional value at risk, the average loss that incurs for the worst possible cases over a given time period, calculated as follows:

$$DR = \left| \sum_{j=1}^{n} R_{ij} / n \right| if\, R_{ij} < -VAR_{it} \tag{2}$$

where R_{ij} is the daily returns for firm i in year t; VAR_{it} is the 5th percentile value of daily returns at the 95% confidence level (left tail); n is the number of daily returns below VAR_{it}. To facilitate interpretation, the value of DR is taken as positive in the empirical analysis.

The third measure is upside risk, which captures the possible gains over a specific time horizon at a given confidence level. It is measured like downside risk, with the main difference being that upside risk is estimated using the right tail (gains) of stock returns, whereas the downside risk shows the left tail (losses). The analysis measures upside risk (UR) using conditional value at risk. It is the average gain that incurs for the best possible cases over a given time period. UP is calculated as follows:

$$UR = \left| \sum_{j=1}^{n} R_{ij} / n \right| if\, R_{ij} > + UP_{it} \tag{3}$$

where R_{ij} is the daily returns for firm i in year t; UP_{it} is the 5th percentile value of daily returns at the 95% confidence level (right tail); n is the number of daily returns above UP_{it}.

8.3.4 Estimation Model

To test the effect of ESG on firm risk, the analysis develops the regression Equation (4) as follows:

$$RISK_{it} = \beta_0 + \beta_1 ESG_{it} + \beta_2 SIZE_{it} + \beta_3 LEV_{it} + \beta_4 R\&D_{it} + \beta_5 PROF_{it} + \beta_6 CASH_{it} + \beta_7 LIQ_{it} + \beta_8 CAPX_{it} + \beta_9 SALESG_{it} + \Psi_j + \omega_t + u_{it} \tag{4}$$

where subscript i denotes individual firms (i = 1,2,3...505) and t refers to the time (t = 2008, 2009,...,2020), β denotes the coefficients to be estimated and u_{it} is the error term. To account for industry-wide and year fluctuations in firm risk, the analysis added year-fixed effects (ω_t), and industry-fixed effects (Ψ_j) in all specifications. $Risk_{it}$ is either total risk (TR), upside risk (UR), or downside risk (DR) and ESG_{it} is either overall score (ESG) or individual pillars (E, S).[3] To conserve space, definitions of control variables are outlined in Table 8.2.

Table 8.2: Variable Definitions

Variable (Notation)	Definitions
Environmental, social, and governance (ESG)	A comprehensive score of company ESG performance, which is based on reported information related to its individual pillars (E, S, G).
Environmental (E)	Environmental pillar (E) reflects the company's performance related to emission reduction, resource use, and green innovation.
Social (S)	Social pillar (S) collects the information whether the firm promoted human rights, worked on community development, considered the welfare of workforce, and fulfilled the product responsibilities for customers.
Total risk (TR)	Annualized standard deviation of daily stock returns
Downside risk (DR)	Conditional value at risk (VAR): An average of the 5% extreme losses if VAR measured at the 95% confidence level
Upside risk (UR)	Conditional upside potential: An average of the 5% best returns if VAR measured at the 95% confidence level
Firm size (SIZE)	Natural logarithm of total assets of firm
Profitability (PROF)	Ratio of net income divided by total assets
Leverage (LEV)	The ratio of firm total debt divided by its total assets
Liquidity (LIQ)	Ratio of current assets to current liabilities
Capital expenditures (CAPX)	Ratio of total capital expenditures divided by total assets
Research and Development intensity (R&D)	Ratio of total R&D expenses divided by total assets
Cash Holding (CASH)	Cash and short-term investment/total assets
Sales Growth (SALESG)	Sales revenue divided by prior year sales revenue minus one, multiplied by 100

Source: Authors.

---

[3] The analysis excludes G factor from the regression model because the relationship of G factor with downside and upside risks has already been examined in Ali, Liu, and Su (2022).

8.4 Empirical Results and Discussion

8.4.1 Descriptive Statistics

Table 8.3 provides the descriptive statistics for all variables consisting of risk-taking measures, ESG variables, and firm characteristics in Panels A, B, and C, respectively. First, panel A of Table 8.3 shows that mean TR is 1.82% and DR and UR have means of 4.17% and 4.06%, respectively. In panel B of Table 8.3, ESG has a mean value of 52.96%, whereas mean E, S, and G are 45.39%, 55.01%, and 55.90%, respectively. Among the three pillars, E has the lowest mean value. The average ESG score reported by Harjoto and Laksmana (2018) for the US sample firms was 27.20%, which is substantially lower than our average ESG score of 52.97%. This difference can be attributed to their ESG data source of MSCI KLD and sample period from 1998 to 2011. According to Wong,

Table 8.3: Descriptive Statistics

	N	Mean	Std. Dev.	p25	Median	p75	min	max
Panel A: Firm Risk Variables								
TR	4,456	1.815	0.85	1.24	1.588	2.121	0.78	6.171
DR	4,450	4.17	2.09	2.79	3.64	4.93	1.63	15.12
UR	4,450	4.06	1.99	2.72	3.51	4.77	1.66	14.30
Panel B: ESG Variables								
ESG	4,456	52.96	19.62	37.93	54.81	68.87	11.00	88.61
E	4,455	45.39	28.73	19.73	50.06	70.41	0.00	92.36
S	4,455	55.01	21.30	37.66	55.70	71.68	11.79	94.67
G	4,456	55.90	21.99	39.66	58.63	73.50	6.22	93.73
Panel C: Control Variables								
LIQ	4,456	1.86	1.24	1.07	1.49	2.24	0.37	7.52
SIZE	4,456	16.41	1.25	15.49	16.42	17.29	12.71	20.52
CASH	4,456	0.14	0.15	0.03	0.09	0.20	0.00	0.67
CAPX	4,456	4.77	4.00	1.91	3.55	6.51	0.00	22.25
SALESG	4,456	8.14	15.92	0.59	6.08	12.86	−35.98	88.96
PROF	4,456	8.31	7.00	4.35	7.67	11.92	−19.32	31.05
LEV	4,456	28.59	17.67	16.25	27.52	38.52	0.00	90.34
R&D	4,456	0.03	0.05	0.00	0.00	0.04	0.00	0.28

Cash = cash holding; CAPX = capital expenditures; DR = downside risk; E = environment; ESG = environmental, social, and governance; G = governance; LEV = leverage; LIQ = liquidity; PROF = profitability; R&D = research and development intensity; S = social; SALESG = sales growth; SIZE = firm size; TR = total risk; UR = upside risk.
Notes: This table displays the statistical description including number of observations (N), mean, standard deviation (std. dev.), first quartile (p25), median, third quartile (p75), minimum (min) and maximum (max) values of 4,456 firm year observations for all the variables. See Table 8.1 for variable details.
Source: Authors.

Brackley, and Petroy (2019), Thomson Reuters, MSCI KLD, Sustainalytics, and Bloomberg are among the top-four ESG rating providers. However, their measurement frameworks significantly differ, which leads to discrepancies in their ESG ratings/scores (Widyawati 2020). Panel C of Table 8.3 presents the control variables where mean liquidity (LIQ) is 1.86%, indicating that the firm's ability to cover current liabilities from current assets while mean cash holding (CASH) is 0.14% showing that sample firms keep less cash and short-term investment. Mean firm size (SIZE) is 16.41 and illustrates that sample firms have average total assets of $16.41 million. The capital expenditure ratio (CAPX) is 4.77 on average and profitability (PROF) ranges from losses of 19.32% to gains of 31.05%. Further, the mean value of 28.59% for leverage (LEV) highlights the financial health of companies. It was interesting to note that more than half of the firms did not engage in R&D activities, as the median value of R&D intensity (R&D) is zero. This figure is consistent with prior studies and implies that R&D distribution is highly right-skewed (Kothari, Laguerre, and Leone 2002). The analysis replaced missing R&D expenditure values to calculate R&D intensity following the suggestion of Koh and Reeb (2015).

8.4.2 Multivariate Regression

Table 8.4 presents the results of the pooled OLS regression estimated using Equation (4), where ESG is a proxy for ESG performance, and TR, DR, and UR are measures of firm risk. The results for TR, DR, and UR are reported in columns 1 to 3. Year-fixed effects and industry-fixed effects are controlled

Table 8.4: Environmental, Social, and Governance and Firm Risk

	(1) TR	(2) DR	(3) UR
ESG	−0.00338**	−0.00676**	−0.00781***
	(−3.29)	(−2.68)	(−3.46)
Controls	Yes	Yes	Yes
Year	Yes	Yes	Yes
Industry	Yes	Yes	Yes
Constant	4.697***	10.71***	11.16***
	(13.22)	(13.15)	(13.77)
N	4,451	4,445	4,445
Adj. R^2	0.632	0.592	0.632

DR = downside risk; ESG = environmental, social, and governance; TR = total risk; UR = upside risk.
Notes: This table shows the results of pooled ordinary least squares (OLS) between ESG and total firm risk (TR), downside risk (DR), and upside risk (UR). The t-statistics in parentheses are based on robust standard errors. Superscripts ***, **, * indicate statistical significance at 1%, 5%, and 10% levels, respectively. See Table 8.2 for variable details.
Source: Authors.

for, in regressions. The *t*-statistics are calculated based on robust standard errors. Equation (4) is well fitted as F-statistic is statistically significant, and adjusted R-square is 63.2%, 59.2%, and 63.2% for TR, DR, and UR, respectively.

Overall, the results show that ESG has a negative influence on firm risk as the ESG coefficient is negative and statistically significant at the 5% level for TR. This implies that high ESG performance decreases the overall risk in firms. These findings are consistent with Jo and Na (2012) and Harjoto and Laksmana (2018), who use MSCI KLD for ESG. Likewise, the coefficient on ESG performance is negative and significant at least the 5% level for DR and UR. These results show that reducing firm risk through high ESG performance is related to downside risk and upside potential. Hoepner et al. (2018) provide corroborative evidence that ESG shareholders engagement reduces downside risk.

However, the analysis does not find evidence for an increase in upside reward. It may be that companies are doing good but not doing well, where managers carry out socially responsible activities to receive recognition or appreciation for being socially responsible. If these activities are not cost-effective, then the excess cost over benefits is revealed through lower shareholder returns (Statman and Glushkov 2009). It also suggests that ESG investors may be happy to accept lower realized returns for a firm's compliance with social norms (Hong and Kacperczyk 2009) as far as they can reduce risk. Another reason for not finding support for an increase in upside reward can be that this high ESG performance may save the firm from greater exposure to risk while holding the fundamental trade-off between risk and return (Lööf, Sahamkhadam, and Stephan 2022).

The analysis also calculates the marginal effects of E and S to see which of the two pillars is driving the results for the different firm risk measures. As seen in Table 8.5, the S pillar's marginal effect proportion (%ME) is greater than E for all firm risk measures. This indicates that most of the negative impact of ESG on firm risk is attributed to the social dimension of ESG. Dumitrescu and Zakriya (2021) provide a rationale for why this social dimension matters by arguing that social initiatives are mainly aimed at primary stakeholders (such as employees and customers), and the market and investors can easily assess their costs and benefits. Also, firms and their managers have the most power over these primary stakeholders. In comparison, environmental initiatives have long-term orientations and are challenging for investors to understand. Since the window of analysis is over the short to medium term, it may be why ESG and its pillars reduce downside risk but not increase upside return, and the impacts are driven by social concerns.

Table 8.5: Marginal Effects of Environment and Social on Firm Risk

		(1) TR	(2) DR	(3) UR
ESG	ME	−0.00338**	−0.00676**	−0.00781***
	p-value	0.001	0.007	0.001
	%ME	−0.285	−0.162	−0.192
E	ME	−0.00147***	−0.00229*	−0.00443***
	p-value	0.000	0.025	0.000
	%ME	−0.124	−0.055	−0.109
S	ME	−0.00191***	−0.00384**	−0.00462***
	p-value	0.000	0.005	0.000
	%ME	−0.161	−0.092	−0.114

DR = downside risk; E = environment; ESG = environmental, social, and governance; S = social; TR = total risk; UR = upside risk.
Notes: The table shows the marginal effects (ME) from pooled ordinary least squares (OLS) shown in Tables 8.3 and 8.4. The ME represents ability of ESG, E, and S to predict firm risk measures (column 1 to column 3). The percentage marginal effect (%ME) is computed as 100 * (ME/mean of dependent variable). Each set of ME, p-value, and %ME represents one regression. See Table 8.1 for variable details.
Source: Authors.

8.5   Conclusion and Policy Implications

This study examines whether overall ESG and its pillars affect downside and upside risk differently. Intuitively, high ESG performance should reduce downside risk and increase upside gains at the same time. Loss aversion behavior and concern for personal benefits may engage conservative strategies that reduce downside risk at the cost of upside gains. It would seem that this analysis is the first to untangle the differential impact of ESG on downside and upside risks. Using a sample of 4,456 US firm-year observations for 2008–2020, the pooled OLS estimation shows that ESG (overall/pillars), measured by Thomson Reuters ESG (overall/pillars) scores in percentage, lower risk taking in firms in terms of total risk, downside, and upside risk.

This finding has implications for regulators who design regulations and disclosure relating to ESG activities. The study suggests that ESG activities can be a device to minimize unanticipated losses but may not be as effective to improve the likelihood of unanticipated gains. From a broader regulatory perspective, these findings imply that ESG-related regulations should be designed so that firms adopting ESG activities cannot only protect investors from downside risk, but also provide an opportunity with significant upside potential. Therefore, the study calls for ESG regulations that aim to minimize the cost and maximize the benefits of adopting ESG activities for firms. In practice, this can be achieved through an appropriate balance between penalizing socially irresponsible firms (lawsuits) and rewarding socially responsible firms (subsidies).

Specifically, for environmental activities, policies should be introduced to encourage firms to invest in environmental activities, including better monitoring by climate agencies on outputs from these activities such as reducing carbon emissions and investment in renewable energy. Since there is no standardized framework for climate change related disclosure which addresses environmental risks and opportunities, a recommendation is to encourage disclosure under the Task Force on Climate-Related Financial Disclosures framework, or make disclosures mandatory, as economies such as Switzerland; the United Kingdom; Hong Kong, China; Japan; Singapore; and New Zealand; and members of the European Union have done.

The Task Force on Climate-Related Financial Disclosures' levels on governance, risk management, strategy and metrics and targets can highlight risks and opportunities in climate change, allowing managers to better understand the impact on the firm and provide better information for investors and other stakeholders. Better monitoring of carbon emissions, including policies to help firms in recordkeeping and management of carbon emission reduction targets can be encouraged and supported through government funding and grant schemes.

For social policies in particular, policies can be introduced to require better disclosure of social activities and the identification of modern slavery risks in operations and supply chains. In modern slavery disclosure of risks and actions, legislation can be introduced for firms, especially large firms, to prepare modern slavery disclosure statements as has been done in Australia and the United Kingdom, to identify and address these risks. Such legislation is especially beneficial to high-risk countries engaging in conflict minerals and textiles. Other social activities, such as employee training schemes, can be introduced via grants and other funding schemes, and awards can be established for firms that prioritize employee welfare. While less attention is paid to social performance in many countries, with the focus worldwide on environmental performance, the study here shows that firms should also pay particular attention to their social performance, and policies and regulations can be launched to support these activities.

Such environmental and social policies should not be designed to increase compliance costs, create a tick box mentality, or promote greenwashing behavior, which provide investors with protection from downside risk at the cost of upside gains. Instead, these policies should be designed to minimize compliance costs and nourish a culture where firms "walk the talk." They should encourage genuine engagement in environmental and social activities to protect the planet and people, which is ultimately favored by the market. This would reward investors with reduced downside risk and increased upside potential.

References

Albuquerque, R., Y. Koskinen, S. Yang, and C. Zhang. 2020. Resiliency of Environmental and Social Stocks: An Analysis of the Exogenous COVID-19 Market Crash. *The Review of Corporate Finance Studies*. 9 (3). pp. 593–621.

Albuquerque, R., Y. Koskinen, and C. Zhang. 2019. Corporate Social Responsibility and Firm Risk: Theory and Empirical Evidence. *Management Science*. 65 (10). pp. 4451–4469.

Ali, S., B. Liu, and J. J. Su. 2022. Does Corporate Governance Have a Differential Effect on Downside and Upside Risk? *Journal of Business Finance and Accounting*. 49 (9–10). pp. 1642–1695.

Ang, A., J. Chen, and Y. Xing. 2006. Downside Risk. *Review of Financial Studies*. 19 (4). pp. 1191–1239.

Barnea, A. and A. Rubin. 2005. Corporate Social Responsibility as a Conflict Between Owners, Social Performance Metrics Conference. *Haas Center for Responsible Business*.

Becchetti, L., R. Ciciretti, and I. Hasan. 2015. Corporate Social Responsibility, Stakeholder Risk, and Idiosyncratic Volatility. *Journal of Corporate Finance*. 35. pp. 297–309.

Boubaker, S., A. Cellier, R. Manita, and A. Saeed. 2020. Does Corporate Social Responsibility Reduce Financial Distress Risk? *Economic Modelling*. 91 (8). pp. 835–851.

Bouslah, K., L. Kryzanowski, and B. M'Zali. 2013. The Impact of the Dimensions of Social Performance on Firm Risk. *Journal of Banking and Finance*. 37 (4). pp. 1258–1273.

Cheng, B., I. Ioannou, and G. Serafeim. 2014. Corporate Social Responsibility and Access to Finance. *Strategic Management Journal*. 35 (1). pp. 1–23.

Chollet, P. and B. W. Sandwidi. 2018. CSR Engagement and Financial Risk: A Virtuous Circle? International Evidence. *Global Finance Journal*. 38. pp. 65–81.

Cohen, J., G. Krishnamoorthy, and A. Wright. 2010. Corporate Governance in the Post-Sarbanes-Oxley Era: Auditors' Experiences. *Contemporary Accounting Research*. 27 (3). pp. 751–786.

Cornell, B. and A. C. Shapiro. 1987. Corporate Stakeholders and Corporate Finance. *Financial Management*. 16 (1). pp. 5–14.

Deegan, C. 2002. Introduction: The Legitimising Effect of Social and Environmental Disclosures. *Accounting, Auditing and Accountability Journal*. 15 (3). pp. 282–311.

Ding, W., R. Levine, C. Lin, and W. Xie. 2021. Corporate Immunity to the COVID-19 Pandemic. *Journal of Financial Economics*. 141 (2). pp. 802–830.

Dumitrescu, A. and M. Zakriya. 2021. Stakeholders and the Stock Price Crash Risk: What Matters in Corporate Social Performance? *Journal of Corporate Finance*. 67. 101871.

Eccles, R. G., I. Ioannou, and G. Serafeim. 2014. The Impact of Corporate Sustainability on Organizational Processes and Performance. *Management Science*. 60 (11). pp. 2835–2857.

Ferreira, M. A. and P. A. Laux. 2007. Corporate Governance, Idiosyncratic Risk, and Information Flow. *The Journal of Finance*. 62 (2). pp. 951–989.

Freeman, R. E. 1984. *Strategic Management: A Stakeholder Approach*. R. Edward Freeman: Pitman.

———. 2010. *Strategic Management: A Stakeholder Approach*. Cambridge: Cambridge University Press.

Friedman, A. L. and S. Miles. 2002. Developing Stakeholder Theory. *Journal of Management Studies*. 39 (1). pp. 1–21.

Gillan, S. L., A. Koch, and L. T. Starks. 2021. Firms and Social Responsibility: A Review of ESG and CSR Research in Corporate Finance. *Journal of Corporate Finance*. 66. 101889.

The Global Compact. 2005. *Who Cares Wins: Connecting Financial Markets to a Changing World*. Geneva: United Nations Global Compact.

Godfrey, P. C. 2005. The Relationship between Corporate Philanthropy and Shareholder Wealth: A Risk Management Perspective. *Academy of Management Review.* 30 (4). pp. 777–798.

Greening, D. W. and D. B. Turban. 2000. Corporate Social Performance as a Competitive Advantage in Attracting a Quality Workforce. *Business and Society.* 39 (3). pp. 254–280.

Harjoto, M. and I. Laksmana. 2018. The Impact of Corporate Social Responsibility on Risk Taking and Firm Value. *Journal of Business Ethics.* 151 (2). pp. 353–373.

Harlow, W. V. 1991. Asset Allocation in a Downside-Risk Framework. *Financial Analysts Journal.* 47 (5). pp. 28–40.

Harrison, J. S., R. A. Phillips, and R. E. Freeman. 2020. On the 2019 Business Roundtable "Statement on the Purpose of a Corporation." *Journal of Management.* 46 (7). pp. 1223–1237.

Hoepner, A. G., I. Oikonomou, Z. Sautner, L. T. Starks, and X. Zhou. 2018. *ESG Shareholder Engagement and Downside Risk.* European Governance Corporate Institute. https://papers.ssrn.com/sol3/papers.cfm?abstract_id=2874252.

Hong, H. and M. Kacperczyk. 2009. The Price of Sin: The Effects of Social Norms on Markets. *Journal of Financial Economics.* 93 (1). pp. 15–36.

Ilhan, E., Z. Sautner, and G. Vilkov. 2020. Carbon Tail Risk. *The Review of Financial Studies.* 34 (3). pp. 1540–1571.

Jo, H. and H. Na. 2012. Does CSR Reduce Firm Risk? Evidence from Controversial Industry Sectors. *Journal of Business Ethics.* 110 (4). pp. 441–456.

Koh, P.-S. and D. M. Reeb. 2015. Missing R&D. *Journal of Accounting and Economics.* 60 (1). pp. 73–94.

Kothari, S., T. E. Laguerre, and A. J. Leone. 2002. Capitalization versus Expensing: Evidence on the Uncertainty of Future Earnings from Capital Expenditures versus R&D Outlays. *Review of Accounting Studies.* 7 (4). pp. 355–382.

Kytle, B. and J. G. Ruggie. 2005. *Corporate Social Responsibility as Risk Management: A Model for Multinationals.* Cambridge: Harvard University.

Lööf, H., M. Sahamkhadam, and A. Stephan. 2022. Is Corporate Social Responsibility Investing a Free Lunch? The Relationship between ESG, Tail Risk, and Upside Potential of Stocks before and during the COVID-19 Crisis. *Finance Research Letters.* 46. 102499.

Lööf, H. and A. Stephan. 2019. *The Impact of ESG on Stocks' Downside Risk and Risk Adjusted Return.* Royal Institute of Technology, CESIS-Centre of Excellence for Science and Innovation Studies.

Lu, W. 2016. *Corporate Social Responsibility and Firm Risk: Implications from Employee Satisfaction.* Paper presented at the Asian Finance Association (AsianFA) 2016 Conference.

Markowitz, H. 1952. Portfolio Selection. *The Journal of Finance.* 7 (1). pp. 77–91.

McGuire, J. B., A. Sundgren, and T. Schneeweis. 1988. Corporate Social Responsibility and Firm Financial Performance. *Academy of Management Journal.* 31 (4). pp. 854–872.

Roggi, O., A. Damodaran, and M. Garvey. 2012. Risk Taking: A Corporate Governance Perspective. Social Science Research Network (SSRN) Electronic Journal. http://papers.ssrn.com/sol3/papers.cfm?abstract_id=2556159.

Roy, A. D. 1952. Safety First and the Holding of Assets. *Econometrica: Journal of the Econometric Society.* 20 (3). pp. 431–449.

Sassen, R., A.-K. Hinze, and I. Hardeck. 2016. Impact of ESG Factors on Firm Risk in Europe. *Journal of Business Economics.* 86 (8). pp. 867–904.

Shi, W. and K. Veenstra. 2021. The Moderating Effect of Cultural Values on the Relationship Between Corporate Social Performance and Firm Performance. *Journal of Business Ethics.* 174 (1). pp. 89–107.

Statman, M. and D. Glushkov. 2009. The Wages of Social Responsibility. *Financial Analysts Journal.* 65 (4). pp. 33–46.

US SIF. 2020. *Report on US Sustainable, Responsible and Impact Investing Trends*. Washington, DC. https://www.ussif.org/files/Trends%20 Report%202020%20Executive%20Summary.pdf.

Widyawati, L. 2020. Measurement Concerns and Agreement of Environmental Social Governance Ratings. *Accounting and Finance*. 61 (S1). pp. 1589–1623.

Wong, C., A. Brackley, and E. Petroy. 2019. *Rate the Raters 2019: Expert Views on ESG Ratings*. The Sustainability Institute by ERM. https://www.sustainability.com/globalassets/sustainability.com/ thinking/pdfs/sa-ratetheraters-2019-1.pdf.

What Should Investors Do about Environmental, Social, and Governance?

Mark Humphery-Jenner, Suman Banerjee, and Vikram Nanda

9.1 Introduction

Company directors and institutional investors often face pressure to pursue environmental objectives from the media, policymakers, or commentators. It is not always from shareholders or investors. Some investors have a clear "impact," "environmental," or "social" mandate. However, other standard investors are often presented with a barrage of environmental, social, and governance (ESG) pressure. What then should they do with this and how should they evaluate ESG in the context of their portfolios?

ESG, sustainability, and climate initiatives have been controversial in business. Environmental impacts are sometimes perceived as "long term" and relevant to short-term decision-making (Kirk 2022). The immediate financial impact of pollution can be opaque. There is a competence deficit in industry (Schumacher 2022). This is exacerbated by a cottage industry of courses, which are not necessarily taught by subject matter experts. Hyperbolic language worsens these concerns (Kirk 2022). This can cause a general distrust of so-called "ESG experts." Thus, CEOs have reportedly become reticent to wade into controversial or hot-button political issues (Kowitt 2023; Rosenbaum 2022).

Investors are thus in a difficult position. Absent a clear ESG mandate, how should they consider ESG factors? Are ESG indexes relevant? What can they reasonably ask officers and directors to do? And what factors might influence corporate performance?

This chapter considers environmental, social, and governance factors within the context of investment. The chapter discusses how investors might consider ESG investors. It first discusses ESG indexes, the problems therewith, and what investors must do about ESG factors within a portfolio. The chapter then considers what officers and directors are obligated to do. And thus, what investors can reasonably expect from officers and directors. It closes with ways ESG factors can influence corporate performance and the associated evidence.

9.2 How Do Environmental, Social, and Governance Factors Fit into a Portfolio?

Institutional investors often face pressure to consider ESG-relate information. Some of this pressure might be from investors. However, outside parties might also pressure investors. This begs the question of what precisely should fund managers do: should they consider ESG factors, especially environmental?

9.2.1 The General Principle: What Should Fund Managers Do?

Fund managers—and institutional investors—often face significant external pressure. However, the issue is then whether this should influence their investment decisions. The answer depends on the fund manager's investment mandate.

The investment mandate tells fund managers what factors should guide their investment decisions. If the mandate contains an ESG impact or environmental focus, then the fund manager must focus on those factors. If the investment mandate is silent on these factors, the fund manager should only consider financial considerations, such as risk and return. Such a fund cannot choose to direct investors' funds to environmental and social initiatives. Rather, the fund must invest capital following their investors' wishes. However, ESG factors can be relevant to those financial considerations.

ESG considerations can be important for financially focused funds, with some nuance. This includes how to frame environmental, social, and governance factors: should they be grouped together or considered separately? Should the manager use an index or should the manager model cash flows? If using an ESG index, what are the dangers and issues with using such an index? Each of these factors is considered below.

9.2.2   Be Careful Combining Environmental, Social, and Governance Factors

Fund managers are often labeled as "ESG" funds. ESG index providers often provide a single ESG score, in addition to overall ratings for E, S, and G individually. However, the constituent parts: E, S, and G are different. This is important because factors that maximize one component need not benefit any other.

Governance is a paradigm example. Traditionally, "governance" has referred to corporate governance. However, some might try to redefine it to suit their own goals. Good corporate governance involves complying with relevant legal obligations, which often include maximizing shareholder value. This is often a legal requirement rather than an option.[1] Disdaining shareholder wealth maximization does not change directors' legal obligations. Thus, if environmental goals undermine shareholder wealth, managers ought not pursue them as this would violate their legal obligations to shareholders.

9.2.3   Environmental, Social, and Governance Indexes Can Be Arbitrary and Bury Nuance

ESG indexes have issues even if they are appropriate to use for a fund. As indicated, ESG indexes arbitrarily group E, S, and G into one index. These factors can have different implications for company performance. However, ESG indexes have additional problems.

ESG indexes can differ significantly in what they measure and how they measure it (Berg, Kölbel, and Rigobon 2022). To see this, one must consider how ESG indexes are created. ESG indexes create subindexes for each of E, S, and G. Each of these subindexes is based on indicators. For example, "G" might be based on the number of anti-takeover provisions, CEO age, tenure, and compensation structure (for example). However, these indicators might differ between rating agencies. Further, they might measure the same concept (i.e., compensation structure) differently (i.e., it could be total compensation, the percentage of bonus, the compensation equity intensity, or its delta). Next, when constructing subindexes (and overall ESG scores), index providers must weight these indicators. But, these weightings might differ. Therefore, indexes might differ due to index providers using different data to measure different concepts, which they weight differently.

---

[1]   For example, see *Corporations Act 2001* (Cth) Section 181. http://classic.austlii.edu.au/au/legis/cth/consol_act/ca2001172/s181.html.

These construction differences can lead to significant deviations between ESG indexes. Berg, Kölbel, and Rigobon (2022) analyze six major ESG indexes: Sustainalytics, S&P Global, Moody's, KLD, Refinitiv, and MSCI. They analyze whether the indexes differ in scope (i.e., the types of things measured), measurement (i.e., the indicators used), and weight (i.e., how the indexes weight the factors). They find a low correlation between indexes and note that 56% of the divergence is due to measurement differences and 38% due to scope differences. That is, the indexes measure different things and do so using different indicators. Despite this, the indexes present themselves as measuring the same underlying idea.

There need not be a problem with ESG indexes differing. However, there are problems if ESG indexes purport to cover the same concept, but they do so differently and produce different results. For example, if the index providers provide a "governance strength" score, but that score is based on different factors, analysts must then determine which score (if any) is correct. This implies that there would be a construct validity issue in one or more ESG indexes.

How then would an analyst—or a company—resolve the problems with ESG indexes? The clear solution is to focus on underlying factors that have a clear demonstrated relationship with corporate performance (or the investor's specific goal). Analysts must then incorporate these considerations into investment decisions, and/or financial modeling, rather than delegating decision-making to an ESG index provider (e.g., Edmans 2023).

9.2.4 Environmental, Social, and Governance Factors Need Not Improve Performance

Investors must also consider whether a high ESG index—or subindex—score improves returns. If ESG (or environmental) indexes are not associated with higher returns, then constructing a portfolio based on them could lower risk-adjusted performance. In turn, this would imply that investors must model the specific cash flow—and risk—implications of firms' environmental policies.

The evidence suggests that higher ESG index scores could be negatively related to returns. Avramov et al. (2022) analyze six major ESG indexes. They explore whether a higher ESG score is associated with higher returns, and whether this is especially the case if the ESG scores are more consistent. This connects with the notion that ESG scores might differ significantly between providers (Berg, Kölbel, and Rigobon 2022). Thus, the firm's ESG (or environmental) strength could be in doubt. Further, the market might be less certain about whether the firm has strong ESG credentials. Avramov et al.(2022) find that higher ESG scores are *negatively* related to stock returns. This is especially the case if there is more certainty about those ESG scores. Similarly, Hartzmark and Sussman (2019, Table 8) show that "higher sustainability" mutual funds *underperform* "lower sustainability" funds.

The negative relationship between ESG indexes (and subindexes) and returns has implications for investors. First, if investors invest in high ESG companies they cannot always expect the company to generate higher returns. Second, the lower returns may suggest—but need not—a lower cost of capital. That is, the market does not demand as high a return from the high-ESG company, due to it having lower risk; and thus, is willing to pay more. In turn, this reduces the realized returns. Third, lower stock returns might imply that the market has erroneously overpriced the company (driving down returns). This is consistent with evidence that investors are susceptible to greenwashing, poorly value the costs of impact, and overpay for perceived impact (Heeb et al. 2023). Such overpayment would manifest in poor future returns.

9.2.5 Consider How Environmental, Social, and Governance Fits into Portfolio Construction

Portfolio managers sometimes impose ESG requirements—or "constraints"—on their portfolios. They might do this by requiring their portfolio to have an ESG index (or subindex) above a certain level. Alternatively, they might screen out companies that they deem to be uninvestable.

The "portfolio constraint" approach can be appropriate if the investment mandate requires that the fund avoid specific companies or maintain an ESG— or environment—score above a certain level. For example, suppose an investor aims to maximize the return per unit of risk subject to the requirement that the portfolio's "environment" score be a certain level (E). Here, if one has n potential stocks, one would have n × 1 vectors of weights (w), expected returns (r), and environment scores (e). One would also have a covariance matrix (Σ). The portfolio optimization approach would then be:

$$\max_{w} \quad w^T r$$

$$s.t.$$
$$w^T \Sigma w = \sigma$$
$$w^T e = E$$

The portfolio constraint approach can have costs. In general, it is mathematically impossible for a constrained portfolio to generate a higher return per unit of risk than an unconstrained portfolio. This is because an unconstrained portfolio can consider the full investment universe. It will mathematically eliminate undesirable companies as they would have poor risk-adjusted returns. For example, if coal companies were to underperform, an unconstrained portfolio would eliminate them. However, not all "undesirable" companies will underperform in the portfolio. And, a constrained portfolio would remove them from consideration.

There are some situations in which portfolio constraints can be non-negative. Some constraints might never be binding. As indicated, if coal mining were to end and coal miners are bad investments in all cases, they would never have been in an unconstrained portfolio. Further, constraints might enable investors to amass—or use—specific expertise. Ideally, this should align with areas where clients want exposure and/or would appreciate pure play companies. For example, a region-specific fund might focus resources on developing expertise in that specific location. This reduces the information asymmetry the fund might otherwise face. In turn, this can make the fund's return and risk predictions more accurate and improve the fund's performance.

What then about environmental constraints? Does eliminating "undesirable" companies or "polluting" companies enable funds to amass more expertise? Or, put differently, does only investing in "clean" companies enable the firm to develop additional expertise? The answer would depend on how that is defined: if the investor only invested in firms with an environmental index score above a certain level, that would not connote expertise. That would connote delegation to an index provider. If the investor only invests in renewables, that can create expertise and/or give investors pure play exposure that they might value.

An example helps to illustrate this. Consider a portfolio that is constrained to only include companies whose names start with "M." If "M" companies always outperformed, this portfolio should perform similarly to an unconstrained portfolio and the constraint should not be binding. However, if companies starting with "Z" sometimes outperform "M" in a portfolio, then the constrained portfolio will underperform.

This analogy applies in the environmental context. If clean companies always outperform, then the constrained portfolio should perform similarly to a rationally constructed unconstrained one. Indeed, it could outperform due to the possibility that unconstrained portfolio managers might erroneously believe clean companies will underperform or "sin" companies will outperform. However, if some sin companies would outperform the clean ones in a portfolio, then the constrained portfolio will underperform.

The constrained portfolio approach thus has issues. It can convey advantages in *specific* situations. These include where investors want a *specific* (cf. vague) exposure, the portfolio can convey genuine expertise, and/or can mitigate value-relevant information asymmetry. However, if the environmental constraint is arbitrary or merely culls companies based on environmental scores or industries, the constrained portfolio will often underperform.

9.2.6   What to Do about Environmental, Social, and Governance?

This discussion has clear implications for portfolio managers: they should not delegate decision-making to ESG index providers or advocates. This flows from the negative relationship between returns and ESG indexes (and, potentially, subindexes). It also is due to construct validity issues in ESG indexes.

Fund managers should start with their investment memorandum. The investment mandate is the fund manager's contract with its clients. If the investment mandate has an ESG objective, then the fund manager should analyze whether specific investments support that objective. Given that ESG indexes (and subindexes) often disagree with each other, fund managers cannot blindly rely on such indexes to make ESG-related decisions.

ESG can be relevant to portfolio returns. If the investment mandate requires the fund manager to maximize performance metrics, ESG and environmental concerns can still be relevant. However, here, fund managers must not generalize or assume that ESG improves returns. Rather, fund managers must model the specific impact of these factors on risk and returns. In so doing, ESG and environmental factors become merely an input into modeling what is relevant to the portfolio.

What then is the nature of this input? The fund manager can explicitly model the impact of the factor on the firm's cash flows and risks. This includes incorporating those factors in financial modeling and/or scenario analysis. Some factors are amenable to this. For example, an analyst could model the impact of carbon taxes or other regulatory interventions based on how polluting the company is. Some factors are not readily amenable to this. For example, what is the specific cash flow impact of a corporate governance attribute. For these factors, investors should consider the precise mechanism of action through which the factor might influence performance. And, they must then analyze the costs of improving that factor (or eliminating it) as is relevant. This chapter discusses factors that the literature shows influence corporate performance.

9.3   What Must Officers and Directors Consider?

Investors and managers must also consider whether there is a business case for considering ESG factors. The starting point for this is to consider whether officers and directors should even consider environmental and social factors. After all, officers and directors must comply with their legal obligations regardless of their personal objectives.

Officers and directors must comply with their legal obligations. What this means varies across jurisdiction. This may—but need not—involve considering environmental (or ESG) factors. In all cases, such decisions must be evidence based and quantified. This section focuses on the Anglo-American approach to corporate governance. And, here, ESG and environmental factors are important to consider but only to the extent they maximize shareholder wealth.

Directors typically owe two overarching duties in the United States (US): a duty of care and a duty of loyalty (Skadden 2020). These are duties to the shareholders. Their precise nature varies across states. Australia has similar directors' duties. In Australia, directors are subject to a duty of care, a duty to act for a proper purpose and in the best interests of the corporation, and a duty not to misuse information, or their position, to obtain an improper benefit or to harm the corporation.

Some countries require directors to consider outside stakeholders. This is not the case in the US or Australia. Indeed, Australia considered widening directors' duties and rejected amending the former corporations law to expand such duties (Senate Standing Committee on Legal and Constitutional Affairs 1989). And, despite being previously considered, Australia's Corporations Act 2001 did not include expanded directors' duties. The question then becomes how environmental and ESG considerations can influence directors' decision-making. This in turn influences what investors can reasonably expect officers and directors to do.

9.3.1   The Duty of Loyalty

Officers and directors owe a duty of loyalty to a company; and thus, the shareholders. If directors violate this duty they potentially risk a securities class action or a derivative litigation. These derivative litigations involve shareholders suing the directors for wrongs done to the company. Thus, if directors act above their authority and misuse company funds for personal reasons, shareholders could sue the director to recover damages.

The duty of loyalty impacts whether—and to what extent—officers and directors should consider social and environmental issues. The duty requires directors to act in "good faith," in the "best interests of the corporation," and "for a proper purpose." This language is codified in Australia,[2] and similar language exists in the US case law and/or statute. In general, the best interests of the corporation involve maximizing corporate value and/or shareholder wealth.

The next issue is whether officers and directors should act for short-term or long-term shareholders. These groups can have disparate interests (Fried 2015). This can be especially the case since investors might underappreciate long dated, hard-to-value, or risky investments (Martin 2012). However, the "short-term" vs "long-term" divide is often a distinction without a difference.

Activists often raise concerns about myopia in relation to dividend payments or repurchases, which involve a present-day cash distribution. Such distributions tautologically reduce the cash available for investment. However, this is beneficial. There are well-documented agency conflicts of "excess" free cash flow (Jensen 1986), or cash holdings (Harford 1999). Here, managers with access to large amounts of capital make increasingly self-interested investments, consume excess perquisites, or simply shirk. They might also pursue suboptimal investments, either motivated by self-interest or a "money chasing deals" problem (see analogously Diller and Kaserer 2009). Thus, distributing cash to shareholders—only some of whom might hold short-term—benefits the corporation and long-term shareholders (Edmans 2017; PwC 2019).

---

[2]   *Corporations Act 2001* (Cth) Section 181 states that officers and directors must act "in good faith in the best interests of the corporation" and "for a proper purpose."

Acting in good faith for short-term shareholders will ordinarily benefit long-term shareholders, and vice versa. Usually, the firm's stock price should reflect the present value of all future expected cash flows. Thus, if capital is freely available, corporations should pursue all value-creating projects, regardless of whether they are short or long term. Capital rationing can force a short-term focus. However, even here, we must note that a firm will only get to focus on the long term if it can survive the short term. And thus, a manager acting in "good faith" to "properly" benefit short-term shareholders should also benefit long-term shareholders, and vice versa.

Environmental and social factors can fit into the duty of loyalty. Firms must generally comply with environmental and social regulations in order to continue as a going concern. For example, stronger workplace laws is associated with fewer accidents (Banerjee et al. 2022a). They can face negative publicity from safety or environmental incidents. Satisfied workers can be more productive, thereby improving corporate performance (Boustanifar and Kang forthcoming). Thus, environmental and social considerations may, but need not automatically, square with satisfying the duty of loyalty.

9.3.2   The Duty of Care

Directors and officers owe a duty of care to the company. This requires directors and officers to exercise the level of care and skill that would be expected of a director in the company's circumstances. The duty of care would generally require officers and directors to turn their minds to environmental and social factors.

The duty of care implies that directors should consider factors that might impact the firm's access to capital and the cost thereof. It would be imprudent to ignore capital requirements. Sustainability may influence the firm's cost of equity (Ng and Rezaee 2015), and cost of debt (Eichholtz et al. 2019; Jung, Herbohn, and Clarkson 2018), depending on the company's specific circumstances. Worker well-being can boost productivity, which could improve corporate performance (Boustanifar and Kang forthcoming). Therefore, officers and directors must consider environmental and social factors; however, they must do so in the context of maximizing corporate value.

In some locations, the duty of care might be relatively moot due to the "business judgment rule." Depending on the jurisdiction, making a genuine business judgment is sufficient to satisfy this duty. Thus, in states such as

Delaware, it would be relatively straightforward for directors to argue that they satisfied the duty of care. However, in other locations,[3] directors might also need to show they rationally believed the decision was in the companies' best interests, the judgment is made in good faith and for a proper purpose, and the directors had no material personal interest in the decision.

The duty of care also implies that officers and directors must consider the financial costs of environmental and social considerations. In this context, acting with "care" or "skill" involves focusing that "care" and "skill" on the corporation's interests. For example, it is mostly irrelevant whether the officers and directors exercise "care" when deciding the color scheme for their personal offices. Rather, the duty focuses on directing that care and skill toward improving corporate value, which is inherent in how the duty of care sits alongside the duty of loyalty. Therefore, if the director enables ESG considerations to undermine returns, then they are not acting "with care" or "with skill" in the relevant sense. Similarly, if the officers and directors fail to consider ESG's financial implications, they will also not act with care or skill. This implies that financial considerations are to be the overarching guide when deciding whether to pursue environmental and social initiatives.

9.3.3   How Are These Duties Relevant to Environmental, Social, and Governance Investing?

Officers' and directors' duties directly influence how investors might engage with managers on ESG-related topics. These duties circumscribe directors' behaviors. An investor—ESG mandate or not—cannot expect an officer or director to act contrary to the duties.

Investors cannot expect officers and directors to pursue environmental or social initiatives that undermine shareholder returns. This has several corollaries. First, officers and directors act for all shareholders, not merely the largest or the loudest shareholder. This has created some shareholder conflicts in which environmentally-focused investors attempt to exert influence over officers and directors (Humphery-Jenner 2022a). Second, when engaging with managers over ESG-issues, investors must do so through a financial lens and must understand managers' objective function and duties. The following section discusses some of the factors that have been documented to be associated with performance.

---

[3]   For example, see *Corporations Act 2001* (Cth) Section 180(2).

9.4 How Might Environmental Factors Impact Business?

The issue is then how environmental factors might impact corporate performance. Whether and how these factors are relevant depends on the nature of the portfolio. If the portfolio has an explicit environmental or sustainability mandate, this will circumscribe the nature of the investments. If the portfolio's objective is to maximize performance metrics, the fund manager must consider the impact of environmental factors on risk and return. That is, they should consider environmental and social factors much like they would any other corporate characteristic.

The literature contains some interesting findings on how environmental and social factors may enhance, or potentially worsen, corporate performance. And the findings point toward how investors might analyze environmental and social factors when constructing a portfolio, or how officers and directors might target expenditure to increase shareholder wealth. Some of these factors could be specifically incorporated into cash flow models. For other factors, investors should identify the clear mechanism-of-action through which the factor influences returns and establish the likely costs (if any) and benefits associated with pursuing such a factor.

9.4.1 How Environmental Factors Can Influence Performance

Environmental considerations can influence corporate performance. However, investors must consider the specific mechanism of action through which they are alleged to do so. And investors must consider environmental initiatives on a case-by-case basis rather than overgeneralizing.

Take a coal power plant, for example. Coal-fired power plants are decreasingly popular and will have a finite life. At the end of that life, there are also cash flows. The power plant might have some salvage value. But, conversely, the owner might need to engage in environmental rectification work. During its life, the coal power plant will generate revenues. These revenues might decrease over time. Environmental taxes *may* but *need not* reduce that revenue. Whether this is the case will depend on myriad political and economic considerations. Thus, how does an investor evaluate the coal-fired power plant?

The investor must consider two overarching factors for the coal power plant. First, investors must forecast the returns. This includes forecasting the power plant's useful life and likely revenues. Second, investors must analyze the "cost of capital." This is the rate of return that an investor would demand in order to invest in such a project. Investors would also benefit from undertaking a scenario analysis to determine the asset's performance in possible future states of the world and the probability thereof. For a non-ESG investor, the investment decision turns on these factors.

Environmental performance can influence firms' cost of capital: this includes both the cost of debt and the cost of equity. Environmental factors can influence these in different ways. Lenders have reportedly become concerned about social pressure when lending to "polluters." They have also become concerned about business risks to polluting companies. For example, a lender would worry about risks to that coal power plant's future cash flows. Therefore, Eichholtz et al. (2019) find that US-based real estate investment trusts' (REITs) borrowing costs are lower for more environmentally friendly buildings. And REITs with a greater proportion of environmentally friendly buildings have a lower corporate cost of debt.

Environmental factors can also influence firms' cost of equity. The implied cost of equity is the rate of return that shareholders require to be willing to invest in a firm. Better environmental performance is associated with a lower *implied* cost of equity (Gupta 2018; Yang and Yulianto 2022). This appears to concentrate in firms in an environmentally sensitive industry and for firms with a greater associated risk exposure. Further, firms with higher ESG indexes—which often heavily feature environmental matters—have lower realized stock returns (Avramov et al. 2022), which is consistent with such firms having a lower cost of equity (but which could also suggest such firms simply underperformed).

The lower cost of equity could be due to several factors. First, if environmental risks make cash flows more volatile or increase regulatory risks, then firms that mitigate such risks could be "safer." This would cause a lower cost of equity. Second, the rise of ESG-focused funds could create more demand for green-looking companies. In turn, this could create either more demand for such firms' stock issuances and/or more demand and support for those firms' stocks in the secondary market. Third, investors seemingly underestimate the costs and/or overestimate the benefits of environmental initiatives (Heeb et al. 2023). In turn, this could support prices and lower the implied cost of equity while also risking long-run underperformance.

Environmental considerations can be relevant to firms' cash flows. However, investors must assess whether such a benefit is quantifiable, realistic, and offsets the cost. For example, a polluter might face greater regulatory risk. This could impact cash flows. Some customers might be concerned about the environmental credentials of their supply chains. Corporations (and thus investors) should consider whether it is necessary to preemptively improve environmental performance to reduce the risk of climate-related taxes and penalties.

Companies might also look to environmental initiatives for cash flow benefits. For example, Occidental Petroleum—most known for its oil operations—generates revenues from carbon capture technology (Valle 2022). Mawson Infrastructure—most known for cryptocurrency mining—generates revenues from carbon credits and heavily emphasizes environmental initiatives in its investor documentation (Mawson Infrastructure Group 2022). Therefore, investors must also consider whether environmental initiatives can generate revenue rather than merely incur costs.

Environmental factors can also have an indirect effect. Workers dislike working in polluted environments. Thus, corporations might need to pay more to convince employees to work in locations with poor air quality (Banerjee et al. 2022b). Further, given that employee satisfaction can improve performance (Boustanifar and Kang forthcoming), corporations might consider how to support their local environment. In turn, this could increase employee productivity and lower labor costs.

The foregoing environmental factors can influence the investment case: environmental considerations can influence firms' cost of capital, cash flows, and the risk thereof. However, corporations and investors must scrutinize these initiatives on a case-by-case basis and all such benefits should be clearly quantified. Investors should be cautious to avoid greenwashing, or token initiatives, which might cost money, trick inattentive investors, and might ultimately yield limited financial upside.

9.4.2　How Specific Social Factors Can Influence Corporate Performance

Social-related factors *can* influence corporate performance. This can arise in several ways. However, investors and shareholders must always scrutinize whether claimed benefits are evidence-backed and quantifiable.

A frequent claim is that social initiatives might convey public relations benefits (Liang and Vansteenkiste 2020). This may, but need not, be the case. For example, in the context of disaster relief, corporate philanthropy can often have limited commercial benefit. However, it yields greater gains for firms in need of image enhancement, or around high profile attention-grabbing disasters with greater media coverage. Corporate philanthropy might also improve staff morale (Rice 2022). However, corporations should be cautious of polarizing or contentious issues, which might increase staff division or aggravate staff members. Corporations must also ensure that any such actions are seen as "authentic," rather than performative, condescending, fake (Garg 2022). Thus, shareholders and investors must analyze whether there is such a benefit, whether it outweighs the expenditure, and whether the social initiative risks alienating a corporate market segment.

The market might underappreciate the wealth-effects of employee happiness. Boustanifar and Kang (forthcoming) argue that satisfied employees are more productive and associated with lower employee turnover. They highlight that the market might overemphasize the costs of employee-satisfaction initiatives and underemphasize the benefits. Therefore, as long as employee welfare remains underappreciated, investors might earn abnormal returns by investing in (at least moderately) employee-friendly companies.

Workplace accidents are often associated with worse corporate performance. This can stem from several factors. Accidents are often associated with significant fines, lost labor hours, and reduced morale. Workplace accidents can also trigger greater regulatory scrutiny or union activity. Accident rates can also be associated with worse training and reduced productivity. Therefore, investors might consider firms' workplace safety practices and the governance structures in place that might influence workplace accidents (Banerjee et al. 2022a). Such accident-reduction steps could ultimately improve corporate value. However, investors should scrutinize such activities on a case-by-case basis.

Social factors need not always improve performance and investors should scrutinize them. Executives might gain "utility" from doing "good" acts. This might encourage them to engage in philanthropic causes, especially those with which they have a personal connection. However, executives might experience all the "benefits" of helping these causes while shareholders bear the costs. This can drive self-interested philanthropic activities, which benefit executives but that do not benefit shareholders (Masulis and Reza 2015). Therefore, shareholders and investors must critically analyze any philanthropic or social initiatives that companies propose.

9.4.3   Do Not Forget Corporate Governance!

Strong corporate governance tautologically is a positive. The "G" in "ESG" pertains to corporate governance. It is separate and distinct from social and environmental considerations. Strengthening corporate governance involves aligning managers' objectives and actions with those of shareholders. Thus, any attempt to enhance such an alignment is an attempt to benefit shareholders. Corporate governance is often neglected when investors refer to ESG. Corporate governance is a broad topic. However, there are some general factors to consider.

Investors must consider whether the board of directors is appropriate. For example, a more independent board of directors can help restrain CEOs that are either overconfident (Banerjee et al. 2015), or otherwise powerful (Humphery-Jenner et al. 2022). Independent directors are also more likely to discipline underperforming CEOs for their poor performance (Guo and Masulis 2015). However, independent directors might lack firm-specific knowledge or might be poorly incentivized. Thus, independent directors might become distracted and focus their time on companies that they deem to be "more important" (Liu et al. 2020). Thus, it is important to have an appropriate number of sufficiently skilled and motivated independent directors while also drawing insights from executive directors.

Executive compensation practices are important considerations. When analyzing executive compensation, investors should not delegate decision-making to ESG indexes, which can bury nuance. In general, incentive-based compensation is desirable: this helps to better align executives' incentives with shareholders' objectives. However, the appropriate nature of that compensation can depend on the CEO's behavioral attributes (Humphery-Jenner et al. 2016) and the broader regulatory environment (Humphery-Jenner et al. 2021). Further, compensation levels and structures can be the result of a complex trade-off with other factors. For example, firms might adjust compensation in order to convince a CEO to work in a more polluted environment (Banerjee et al. 2022b).

The nature of the firm's shares can also be important. This can include whether the firm has a dual class share structure. Dual-class structures provide an uneven distribution of voting power in favor of a specific group of shareholders. This arrangement allows the dominant shareholders and their connected insiders to reap the private benefits of control. Within this framework, they can pursue investments and expenses driven by self-interest, enjoying outsized benefits while avoiding the full costs of such outlays.

Dual class share structures are typically associated with worse corporate performance, but higher CEO compensation (Masulis, Wang, and Xie 2009). They have created issues at tech companies such as Snap (Humphery-Jenner 2017), and Meta (Humphery-Jenner 2022b).

Potential investors should also consider the company's broader governance attributes. This includes the presence of anti-takeover provisions. Such provisions are generally associated with worse corporate performance as they "entrench" managers and enable them to resist disciplinary acquisitions (Harford, Humphery-Jenner, and Powell 2012; Masulis, Wang, and Xie 2007). Anti-takeover provisions include structures such as poison pills, which enable targets to dilute putative acquirers, stymieing a takeover attempt. These can sometimes benefit younger or more innovative companies by enabling managers to focus on long-term value creation without worrying about "opportunistic" takeover bids (Humphery-Jenner 2014; Johnson et al. 2022). However, the benefits diminish for larger incumbent firms (Humphery-Jenner and Powell 2011). Thus, investors should consider whether the firm has such provisions in place, and the extent to which managers might unilaterally adopt such provisions in a manner that harms shareholders.

The nature of the other investors can also significantly influence corporate governance. Institutional and activist investors can often engage with firms' managers (McCahery, Sautner, and Starks 2016). This can involve direct interactions with the manager, which can help encourage managers to act consistent with shareholders' best interests. Further, being able to credibly threaten to sell shares can discipline managers ex ante (Edmans and Manso 2011; Gallagher, Gardner, and Swan 2013). Therefore, investors might consider the nature of the other investors in the company. This includes analyzing whether the other investors have similar ESG objectives.

The foregoing factors are some of the governance attributes investors might consider. Governance is an important part of ESG investing and is vital to ensuring that managers act in shareholders' best interests. Indeed—both FTX and Adani have touted their ESG credentials—but both FTX and Adani have been the subject of major governance scandals.

9.5 What Should Investors Do about Environmental, Social, and Governance?

The question is then how investors might consider environmental, social, and governance factors in their portfolio construction. If investors have a specific impact, social, or environmental objective, they should act according to that objective. If the investors' investment mandate is to maximize shareholder wealth, then ESG factors can be relevant to the extent that they are consistent with that mandate.

When considering ESG factors, investors should be cautious. They should note that E, S, and G are different. They have different implications and influence cash flows and risks differently. ESG indexes that combine these factors risk becoming a "black box." This is clear from the relatively low correlation between the ESG indexes. High ESG indexes also need not be associated with better performance. And a naïve approach of simply requiring the portfolio's ESG index to be above a specific level, or screening out firms with ESG indexes below a level, could harm returns.

Investors must also consider the appropriate role of the firm's officers and directors. The officers and directors act for all shareholders and must comply with their legal obligations. Therefore, they cannot merely act for the most aggressive shareholder or even the largest shareholder. They must also comply with their duties, which are generally to maximize shareholder wealth. Therefore, any impact-related pressure must be within the context of what officers and directors are legally allowed to do. Attempting to push directors to act contrary to their duties is liable to result in performative corporate actions.

When considering environmental and social factors, investors should consider specific ways in which they can influence firms' cash flows and returns. For example, better corporate governance is associated with better corporate performance because better governance is focused on aligning shareholders' and executives' actions. Environmental performance can reduce firms' cost of capital and might reduce cash flow risk. Better social performance may—but need not—enhance employee welfare, which can improve returns.

The overall approach should be quantitative. When assessing specific ESG indexes, or ESG factors, investors should be sure to quantify their impact rather than relying on generalizations or heuristics. The literature indicates that investors are susceptible to unscrupulous greenwashing and might overpay for impact. Thus, investors should, overall, specifically model how factors might influence cash flows and risks, and/or establish a clear mechanism of action through which the factor might improve performance.

References

Avramov, D., S. Cheng, A. Lioui, and A. Tarelli. 2022. Sustainable Investing with ESG Rating Uncertainty. *Journal of Financial Economics*. 145 (2). pp. 642–664. https://doi.org/10.1016/j.jfineco.2021.09.009.

Banerjee, S., M. Humphery-Jenner, P. Jain, and V. K. Nanda. 2022a. Safety First! Overconfident CEOS and Reduced Workplace Accidents. UNSW Business School Research Paper.

Banerjee, S., M. Humphery-Jenner, and V. Nanda. 2015. Restraining Overconfident CEOs through Improved Governance: Evidence from the Sarbanes-Oxley Act. *Review of Financial Studies*. 28 (10). pp. 2812–2858.

Banerjee, S., M. Humphery-Jenner, V. Nanda, and X. Zhang. 2022b. Location Matters: The Impact of Local Air Quality on CEO Compensation. University of New South Wales (UNSW) Business School Research Paper.

Berg, F., J. Kölbel, and R. Rigobon. 2022. Aggregate Confusion: The Divergence of ESG Ratings. *Review of Finance*. 26 (6). pp. 1315–1344. https://doi.org/10.1093/rof/rfac033.

Boustanifar, H. and Y. D. Kang. 2022. Employee Satisfaction and Long-Run Stock Returns, 1984–2020. *Financial Analysts Journal*. 78 (3). pp. 129–151. https://doi.org/10.1080/0015198X.2022.2074241.

Diller, C. and C. Kaserer. 2009. What Drives Private Equity Returns? Fund Inflows, Skilled GPs, and/or Risk? *European Financial Management*. 15 (3). pp. 643–675.

Edmans, A. 2017. The Case for Stock Buybacks. *Harvard Business Review*. 15 September. https://hbr.org/2017/09/the-case-for-stock-buybacks.

———. 2023. The End of ESG. *Financial Management*. 52 (1). pp. 3–17. https://doi.org/10.1111/fima.12413.

Edmans, A. and G. Manso. 2011. Governance Through Trading and Intervention: A Theory of Multiple Blockholders. *Review of Financial Studies*. 24 (7). pp. 2395–2428.

Eichholtz, P., R. Holtermans, N. Kok, and E. Yonder. 2019. Environmental Performance and the Cost of Debt: Evidence from Commercial Mortgages and REIT Bonds. *Journal of Banking and Finance*. 102. pp. 19–32.

Fried, J. M. 2015. The Uneasy Case for Favoring Long-Term Shareholders. *Yale Law Journal*. 124 (5). pp. 1346–1835.

Gallagher, D. R., P. Gardner, and P. L. Swan. 2013. Governance through Trading: Institutional Swing Trades and Subsequent Firm Performance. *Journal of Financial and Quantitative Analysis*. 48 (2). pp. 427–458.

Garg, N. 2022. Why Companies Need to Be Authentic About Brand Activism. UNSW Business School. *BusinessThink*. 12 April.

Guo, L. and R. Masulis. 2015. Board Structure and Monitoring: New Evidence from CEO Turnovers. *The Review of Financial Studies*. 28 (10). pp. 2770–2811.

Gupta, K. 2018. Environmental Sustainability and Implied Cost of Equity: International Evidence. *Journal of Business Ethics*. 147 (2). pp. 343–365.

Harford, J. 1999. Corporate Cash Reserves and Acquisitions. *The Journal of Finance*. 54 (6). pp. 1969–1997.

Harford, J., M. Humphery-Jenner, and R. G. Powell. 2012. The Sources of Value Destruction in Acquisitions by Entrenched Managers. *Journal of Financial Economics*. 106 (2). pp. 247–261.

Hartzmark, S. M. and A. B. Sussman. 2019. Do Investors Value Sustainability? A Natural Experiment Examining Ranking and Fund Flows. *The Journal of Finance*. 74 (6). pp. 2789–2837. https://doi.org/10.1111/jofi.12841.

Heeb, F., J. F. Kölbel, F. Paetzold, and S. Zeisberger. 2023. Do Investors Care about Impact? *The Review of Financial Studies*. 36 (5). pp. 1737–1787. https://doi.org/10.1093/rfs/hhac066.

Humphery-Jenner, M. L. 2014. Takeover Defenses, Innovation, and Value-Creation: Evidence from Acquisition Decisions. *Strategic Management Journal* 35 (5). pp. 668–690.

———. 2017. Disappearing Votes: Why Investors Should Steer Clear of Snapchat's Dual-Class Shares. *The Conversation*. 24 January. https://theconversation.com/disappearing-votes-why-investors-should-steer-clear-of-snapchats-dual-class-shares-71710.

———. 2022a. Should Billionaires Drive Company Policy? Even If They're Doing Good? UNSW Business School. *BusinessThink*. 11 October.

———. 2022b. Mark Zuckerberg Can Sack 11,000 Workers But Shareholders Can't Dump Him: It's Called 'Management Entrenchment.' *The Conversation*. 10 November.

Humphery-Jenner, M., E. Islam, V. Nanda, and L. Rahman. 2021. Litigation Risk and Managerial Contracting: Evidence from Universal Demand Laws. Working paper.

Humphery-Jenner, M., E. Islam, L. Rahman, and J.-A. Suchard. 2022. Powerful CEOs and Corporate Governance. *Journal of Empirical Legal Studies*. 19 (1). pp. 135–188. https://doi.org/10.1111/jels.12305.

Humphery-Jenner, M. L. Lisic, V. Nanda, and S. Silveri. 2016. Executive Overconfidence and Compensation Structure. *Journal of Financial Economics*. 119 (3). pp. 533–558.

Humphery-Jenner, M., and R. G. Powell. 2011. Firm Size, Takeover Profitability and the Effectiveness of the Market for Corporate Control: Does the Absence of Anti-Takeover Provisions Make a Difference? *Journal of Corporate Finance*. 17 (3). pp. 418–437. https://doi.org/10.1016/j.jcorpfin.2011.01.002.

Jensen, M. C. 1986. Agency Costs of Free Cash Flow, Corporate Finance, and Takeovers. *The American Economic Review*. 76 (2). Papers and Proceedings of the Ninety-Eighth Annual Meeting of the American Economic Association. pp. 323–329.

Johnson, W. C., J. M. Karpoff, and S. Yi. 2022. The Life Cycle Effects of Corporate Takeover Defenses. *Review of Financial Studies*. 35 (6). pp. 2879–2927.

Jung, J., K. Herbohn, and P. Clarkson. 2018. Carbon Risk, Carbon Risk Awareness and the Cost of Debt Financing. *Journal of Business Ethics*. 150 (4). pp. 1151–1171.

Kirk, S. 2022. Why Investors Need Not Worry about Climate Risk. Presentation at the FT Live Moral Money Summit Europe Conference. 20 May. https://www.youtube.com/watch?v=bfNamRmje-s.

Kowitt, B. 2023. The Shortlived Era of the Woke CEO Is Already Over. *Australian Financial Review*. 10 January.

Liang, H. and C. Vansteenkiste. 2020. Disaster Relief, Inc. *European Corporate Governance Institute - Finance Working Paper*. No. 709–2020.

Liu, C., A. Low, R. Masulis, and L. Zhang. 2020. Monitoring the Monitor: Distracted Institutional Investors and Board Governance. *The Review of Financial Studies*. 33 (10). pp. 4489–4531. https://doi.org/10.1093/rfs/hhaa014.

Martin, I. 2012. On the Valuation of Long-Dated Assets. *Journal of Political Economy*. 120 (2). pp. 346–358.

Masulis, R. W. and S. W. Reza. 2015. Agency Problems of Corporate Philanthropy. *Review of Financial Studies*. 28 (2). pp. 592–636.

Masulis, R. W., C. Wang, and F. Xie. 2007. Corporate Governance and Acquirer Returns. *Journal of Finance*. 62 (4). pp. 1851–1889.

_____. 2009. Agency Problems at Dual-Class Companies. *Journal of Finance*. 64 (4). pp. 1697–1727.

Mawson Infrastructure Group. 2022. Q3 FY2022 Investor Presentation.

McCahery, J., Z. Sautner, and L. Starks. 2016. Behind the Scenes: The Corporate Governance Preferences of Institutional Investors. *Journal of Finance*. 71 (6). pp. 2905–2932.

Ng, A. C. and Z. Rezaee. 2015. Business Sustainability Performance and Cost of Equity Capital. *Journal of Corporate Finance*. 34. pp. 128–149. https://doi.org/10.1016/j.jcorpfin.2015.08.003.

PwC. 2019. Share Repurchases, Executive Pay, and Investment. *BEIS Research Paper*. No. 2019/011. Department for Business, Energy & Industrial Strategy.

Rice, A. 2022. When Corporate Philanthropy Keeps Staff Happy. *Chinese University of Hong Kong Business School*. 17 November. https://cbk.bschool.cuhk.edu.hk/when-corporate-philanthropy-keeps-staff-happy/.

Rosenbaum, E. 2022. There's an ESG Backlash Inside the Executive Ranks at Top Corporations. *CNBC*. 29 September. https://www.cnbc.com/2022/09/29/the-esg-backlash-inside-the-executive-ranks-at-top-corporations.html.

Schumacher, K. 2022. Environmental, Social, and Governance (ESG) Factors and Green Productivity: The Impacts of Greenwashing and Competence Greenwashing on Sustainable Finance and ESG Investing. APO Productivity Insights. 2-11. Asian Productivity Organization.

Senate Standing Committee on Legal and Constitutional Affairs. 1989. Company Directors' Duties: Report on the Social and Fiduciary Duties and Obligations of Company Directors. No. 395 of 1989. Parliament of the Commonwealth of Australia.

Skadden. 2020. Directors' Fiduciary Duties: Back to Delaware Law Basics. https://www.skadden.com/insights/publications/2020/02/directors-fiduciary-duties.

Valle, S. 2022. Occidental Plans Up to $1 Bln for Facility to Capture Carbon from Air. *Reuters*. 24 March.

Yang, A. S. and F. A. Yulianto. 2022. Cost of Equity and Corporate Social Responsibility for Environmental Sensitive Industries: Evidence from International Pharmaceutical and Chemical Firms. *Finance Research Letters*. 47 (A). 102532. https://doi.org/10.1016/j.frl.2021.102532.

Sustainable Private Capital Markets

Chapter 10

Jongsub Lee, Sehoon Kim, Nitish Kumar, and Junho Oh

10.1 Introduction: The Rise of Environmental, Social, and Governance and Private Markets

Environmental, social, and governance (ESG) issues in corporate policies have moved vigorously to the center of discussion in recent years. Indeed, estimates suggest that "sustainable" investing has surged in the United States (US), commanding about $15 trillion under management as of 2022, up nearly tenfold in 10 years.[1]

Understandably, this remarkable trend has spurred inquiry into the forces driving the demand, with one fitting financial or economic explanation being that it reflects widespread concern among investors that a poor ESG profile may pose an important risk. In other words, the pursuit of sustainability from the standpoint of investors is still within the risk-return objective framework.

For example, large institutional investors have expressed concern about climate change related risks, particularly regulatory risk associated with policy responses to climate change (Krueger, Sautner, and Starks 2020). An organization's commitment to ESG is increasingly viewed as protection against such risks (Albuquerque et al. 2020; Hoepner et al. 2022; Lins, Servaes, and Tamayo 2017).

An alternative view is that investors derive nonfinancial utility from reflecting their environmental and social preferences in their investments.

[1]   For information, see the US SIF Foundation 2022 report at https://www.ussif.org/.

Hart and Zingales (2017) argue that if investors have such preferences, companies should implement policies that maximize shareholder "welfare" that incorporate these preferences, rather than pursuing only financial values. This "prosocial" preference is empirically documented (Riedl and Smeets 2017; Humphrey et al. 2021), and is now increasingly incorporated into theoretical models of sustainable investing (Pastor, Stambaugh, and Taylor 2021; Pedersen, Fitzgibbons, and Pomorski 2021; Goldstein et al. 2023).

In recent years, these possibilities and hypotheses have been studied and tested extensively in *public capital markets,* which consist of companies that issue publicly listed securities such as stocks or bonds and investors who invest in them either directly or indirectly.

One rich body of research examines how public equity investors respond to information about corporate ESG risk (Hartzmark and Sussman 2019), whether investor portfolio choice reflects their preferences for sustainability (Gibson Brandon et al. 2022), how investors affect the sustainability of portfolio firms (Heath et al. 2023), how investor demand for sustainability is affected by macroeconomic conditions (Döttling and Kim 2022), and how the financial conditions of publicly listed firms affect the sustainability of their corporate policies (Bartram, Hou, and Kim 2022; Kim and Xu 2022), among others. Another extensively studies how public debt investors value and price sustainability in green bonds (Flammer 2021; Tang and Zhang 2020; Zerbib 2019; Baker et al. 2022).

However, public capital markets are only a small part of how companies can raise capital. *Private capital markets,* which encompass markets such as unlisted private equity or corporate syndicated loans, represent a much larger segment of corporate external financing. According to J.P. Morgan, private capital markets were more than twice as large as public capital markets in the amount of investments made in 2020. Surprisingly, however, we have only begun to scratch the surface in understanding demand for sustainable investing and its implications in private capital markets. This is a gaping hole not only in the academic literature, but also in policy dialogues, given how economically important private markets are for the economy and how much we can learn from them.

This chapter examines what we can learn about sustainable investing from recent developments in private capital markets, what challenges may lie ahead, and how policymakers can help to overcome these challenges.

10.2 Sustainable Investing: The Case of Private Equity

A substantial part of the private market landscape, the private equity industry constitutes a significant part of the economy. In 2021, the industry controlled over $4.5 trillion in assets under management. Private equity firms typically raise funds from institutional investors such as pension funds, endowments, and wealthy individuals, and then use that capital to acquire controlling stakes in companies or to fund management buyouts of publicly traded companies. The goal of private equity is usually to improve the performance of the companies they invest in and then sell their stakes at a profit.

However, there is widespread perception among the general public that private equity investments, or ownership by private equity firms, are heavily focused on short-term profits principally at the expense of stakeholder value. For example, US Senator Elizabeth Warren famously accused the private equity industry of "buying companies, loading them up with debt, and then extracting value from them... at the expense of workers and their families, as well as communities and small businesses" and that private equity firms are "simply not good for America."[2] As private equity funds whose future fund flows have historically been principally dependent on their financial performance (Kaplan and Schoar 2005), this is a critique potentially not without merit.

On the other hand, it is possible that the ESG preferences of investors in private equity, namely large institutions, can influence private equity firms to be more committed to sustainability. The largest class of investors (i.e., limited partners) in private equity, among them pension funds and sovereign wealth funds, are increasingly concerned about ESG-related issues including system-level effects of climate change and inequality (Eccles et al. 2022). For example, several Dutch pension funds now grade and rank general partners (or the private equity firms) based on key performance indicators related to ESG issues.

Given the economic importance of the private equity industry, public concerns about the industry, and increasing investor pressure for higher ESG standards, it is important to analyze and understand the implications of private equity investments for sustainability. Recently, academic researchers started to systematically examine whether private equity ownership really hurts stakeholder values. The evidence to date provides unique insights.

---

2   See Senator Warren's website at https://www.warren.senate.gov/.

On the environmental front, Bellon (2022) studies the effects of private equity ownership on corporate pollution. The study finds that private equity-backed firms reduce pollution, only when such firms face higher environmental regulatory risk or political risk. On the other hand, firms that do not face such risks conversely increase their pollution after being owned by private equity firms. These findings shed important light on whether private equity firms promote sustainability genuinely for the sake of stakeholder values. This does not seem to be the case. Rather, the results are consistent with private equity investors primarily seeking financial returns, and only ensuring sustainability when failing to do so may cost significant shareholder value due to regulatory enforcement.

Along social dimensions, Lambert et al. (2021) study changes in employee satisfaction around leveraged buyout transactions. While the type of deals varies substantially, the authors document an overall decline in employee satisfaction after a leveraged buyout deal. The results seem to indicate that private equity firms are not primarily interested in improving the welfare of employees when they target portfolio firms.

Fang, Goldman, and Roulet (2022) examine pay gaps within private equity portfolio firms and show that leveraged buyout target firms experience a reduction in within-firm wage inequality between men and women, managers and non-managers, and older and younger employees. While on the surface this seems to suggest that private equity firms promote equality, additional analysis in the study conveys a more nuanced message. Much of the reduction in inequality is in fact driven by a change in employee composition, where "expensive" employees in the high pay categories (such as older men in managerial positions) are replaced with cheaper and younger ones. Moreover, the authors show that these separated expensive employees had been paid more before the buyout than similar employees at other firms and have worse career outcomes after the deal. Therefore, the key findings of the study are consistent with private equity firms "cutting fat" in mismanaged companies and improving their operational efficiency.

The common thread across these studies is that private equity investments, by focusing on improving shareholder value, also benefit some stakeholders under certain circumstances that align their incentives. However, there is no evidence yet that private equity firms would promote sustainability as a priority in and of itself. An important policy implication of these recent findings is that if stakeholder value protection is an important societal objective, incentive structures need to be designed to align the financial incentives of private market investors with such stakeholder-oriented goals. In particular, Bellon (2022) highlights the role that regulations can play in setting up incentives such that a profit maximizing investor like a private equity firm can also ensure that certain externalities, such as those of pollution, are internalized.

10.3 Transparency and Disclosure of Sustainability in Private Markets

An increasingly important issue related to corporate incentives and the role of regulation in sustainability is how much information companies should be required to disclose regarding their sustainable practices. There has been a general push for more transparent corporate disclosure about their ESG footprints (Ilhan et al. 2023; Ioannou and Serafeim 2019). For example, in March 2022, the US Securities and Exchange Commission proposed rule changes that would require companies to include climate-related disclosures in their financial statements, including disclosure of firms' greenhouse gas emissions, among other material information.[3]

This demand for transparency of corporate sustainability is not limited to public markets. Notably, skepticism has been growing around the validity of sustainability-related clauses and commitments that are purportedly reflected in an increasing number of privately negotiated contracts—such as sustainability-linked loans (Kim et al. 2022)—for which detailed information is typically not available to the outside stakeholders or the general public. This concern has opened the door to a potential debate over whether to implement policies that require a certain level of public transparency on sustainability in private contracts.

However, it is not immediately obvious that disclosure-related policies should be taken that far, given that contractual details in most private contracts are by their nature not required to be disclosed to parties outside of the contract. The question of what disclosure should be required in private contracts ultimately boils down to whether there is a potential conflict of interest or infringement on other stakeholders' interests that arises from the contract. When it comes to sustainability-linked contracts, a few important reasons for such conflicts might be of concern, which are ultimately related to firm incentives.

---

3   See climate risk disclosure guidelines proposed by the Securities and Exchange Commission at https://www.sec.gov/news/press-release/2022–46.

Chief among these reasons is that such contracts can be and are often used as signaling mechanisms whereby the contracting parties (e.g., corporations) might have incentives to impress outside stakeholders that they are ESG-conscious or socially responsible along some dimensions. It is then not unreasonable to view outside stakeholders also as parties of interest, as the ESG commitments signaled by the private contract may affect their decisions about the company as customers, investors, or potential employees. With limited public disclosure, the asymmetry of information in the genuineness of the ESG commitment may lead to adverse selection problems because firms could make empty promises of sustainability, in other words, engage in forms of greenwashing.

The fact that private contracts are often relationship-driven could exacerbate this problem. For example, relationship banking may foster mutually beneficial greenwashing arrangements in sustainability-linked lending between borrowers and lenders at the expense of other stakeholders. While lending relationships might facilitate more effective tailoring and monitoring of ESG commitments specific to the borrower, they can make it substantially easier for banks to falsely label the revolving credit lines of their existing relationship borrowers' as sustainability-linked loans when they renew or roll over these loans in the spirit of greenwashing.

10.4 Transparency and Disclosure: The Case of Sustainability-Linked Loans

As seen above, a case in point for the issue of transparency and disclosure is the market for *sustainability-linked loans*, which has grown exponentially from $3 billion in 2017 to roughly $600 billion in 2021 (Figure 10.1). Sustainability-linked loans are general purpose corporate syndicated loans that tie loan pricing terms to the ESG performance of the borrowing firm. These loans are also called *ESG-linked loans*. The loan spreads are pegged explicitly to key performance indicators incorporating sustainability goals. These indicators may be ESG scores assigned to borrowers by external rating agencies (e.g., MSCI or Sustainalytics) or specific measures such as greenhouse gas emissions or gender equality. The proceeds from sustainability-linked loans can be used to fund general operations without being tied to green projects. In contrast, the conventionally available instruments for green financing (e.g., green bonds) require that the capital raised be used only for specific sustainable projects (e.g., renewable power plants, energy-efficient buildings).

Figure 10.1: Sustainability-Linked Loan Issuance

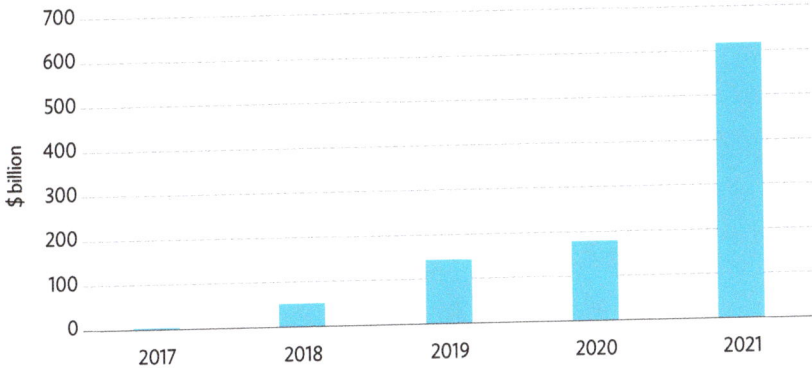

Source: Refinitiv DealScan.

In response to the growth of these loans into perhaps the most important sustainable private financing market, other studies have emerged to investigate its nature (Kim et al. 2022; Caskey and Chang 2022; Du, Harford, and Shin 2022; Dursun-de Neef, Ongena, and Tsonkova 2022; Loumioti and Serafeim 2022). The first of these studies, Kim et al. (2022) pay particular attention to the availability of public information on the sustainability-linked contract features of these loans and relates the level of transparency to potential greenwashing incentives on the part of borrowers and lenders. The following discusses this study's implications for sustainability disclosure in private markets.

Amid the rapid development of this sustainability-linked private financing market, practitioners and the general public are significantly concerned that it is difficult to verify ESG loan labels or assess the real impact of sustainability-linked loans in disciplining borrowers on sustainability issues.[4] To gauge the credibility of ESG commitments signified by the issuance of sustainability-linked loans, investors must rely on publicly disclosed information about the contractual details, such as what the specific key performance indicators are and how they are tied to the loan terms. The sustainability-linked loan principles, developed by a working party consisting of representatives from leading financial institutions, provide guidelines to borrowers about disclosures and reports that need to be made available to *lenders*. However, in the absence of regulations or public disclosure requirements in the emerging ESG lending market, this information is voluntarily and selectively disclosed by borrowers and lenders to the larger public. Practitioners commonly criticize the limited availability of this information, making it difficult for investors

---

4   See Bloomberg 2020, 2021a, and 2021b.

and other stakeholders of the firm to verify the validity of ESG loan labels and navigate the opaque market. The lack of detail or quality of such disclosures is in turn skeptically viewed as an indication of greenwashing. It is therefore important to examine the quality of key performance indicator information disclosures in sustainability-linked loans.

Kim et al. (2022) classify sustainability-linked loans for which there is no public information about the indicators or how they are tied to loan terms as "low public information" (LPI) loans. "High public information" (HPI) loans are those with loan terms linked to some metric of ESG performance (e.g., CO_2 emissions per tonne of transported cargo per nautical mile, percent of women in workforce, Sustainalytics score). The study finds that the disclosure quality of sustainability-linked loans is generally poor. Roughly half of the sustainability-linked loans in the sample are classified as LPI loans (i.e., 510 LPI loans vs. 617 HPI loans). The large fraction of LPI loans is rather surprising given how generous the study is in classifying loans as HPI loans (i.e., it loosely classifies them as such, as long as they have some information on the ESG-related key performance indicators). Even among HPI sustainability-linked loans that disclose such indicators, firms asymmetrically disclose the rewards (i.e., more likely to disclose, or 22% of HPI loans) and penalties (i.e., less likely to disclose, or 13% of HPI loans) to be applied to loan spreads conditional on ESG performance.

Kim et al. (2022) argue that borrowers are more likely to refrain from publicly disclosing information on sustainability features of their ESG-linked loan contracts when the sustainability features have no "bite," i.e., when key performance indicator targets are not ambitious enough or when the penalty for not meeting the targets is not financially material. In such cases, borrowers aim to benefit from the ESG label while never intending to devote resources toward improving their ESG profile. Put differently, they engage in greenwashing. To empirically assess whether the lack of disclosure in sustainability-linked loans is a potential manifestation of greenwashing and therefore should be improved through policy, this study examines how borrower ESG performance is related to the issuance of ESG loans with high or low public information availability. Kim et al. (2022) investigate this issue using firm-level ESG scores from the Refinitiv Asset4 database.[5]

---

[5]   Acknowledging recent concerns about the subjective nature and inconsistency of some third-party ESG scores (Berg, Fabisik, and Sautner 2021; Berg, Koelbel, and Rigobon 2022), the study here further analyzes components of Asset4 scores that are plausibly more objective (e.g., emissions, resource usage, etc.), and finds similar results.

The study finds that both borrowers and lenders of ESG loans have significantly higher ex ante ESG scores than those of matched non-ESG loans, consistent with firms that face greater scrutiny from stakeholders issuing sustainability-linked loans.[6] If sustainability-linked loans credibly signal commitment to ESG-friendly practices, one would expect the superior ex ante ESG profiles to improve or at least persist after sustainability-linked loan issuance. On the other hand, a deterioration of ESG performance ex post could indicate greenwashing around sustainability-linked loan issuance.

Consistent with the latter, the study here finds that borrowers' ESG profiles deteriorate after sustainability-linked loan issuance. To further delineate whether the ex post within-firm deterioration in ESG performance is consistent with greenwashing, the study exploits the cross-sectional heterogeneity across sustainability-linked loans in the availability of public information about how the loan terms are tied to specific key performance indicators. Figure 10.2, which plots coefficients from dynamic difference-in-differences regressions, paints an interesting picture. HPI sustainability-linked loans are not associated with post-issuance decline in borrower ESG scores. Such borrowers, who have high ESG scores to begin with, continue to maintain their superior ESG scores. On the other hand, consistent with a greenwashing hypothesis, this study finds

Figure 10.2: Borrower Environmental, Social, and Governance Performance around Sustainability-Linked Loan Issuance

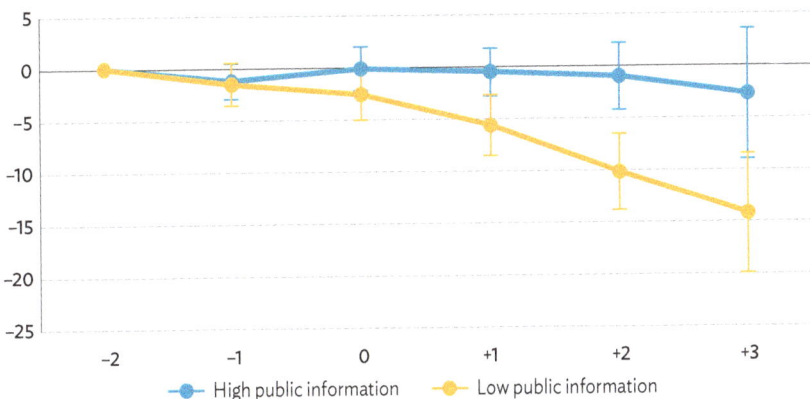

Source: Kim et al. (2022).

---

[6] The results are also consistent with recent findings that borrowers and lenders with similarly high ESG ratings tend to form lending relationships (Kacperczyk and Peydró 2022; Houston and Shan 2022).

a sharp deterioration in ESG performance following the issuance of LPI sustainability-linked loans. This indicates a form of greenwashing in which companies enter sustainability-linked loans that have lax loan terms when it comes to punishment for missing sustainability targets or loans that lay out unambitious targets to begin with and choose not to publicize this information.

Taken together, the study here finds that ESG loan issuance itself has no positive impact on ex post borrower ESG performance, but in fact is followed by within-borrower deterioration in ESG performance. This ex post deterioration is driven by LPI sustainability-linked loans with little information available about their key performance indicators, raising concerns about greenwashing in a large segment of the market. There is no deterioration in ESG scores following the issuance of HPI loans, suggesting greater commitments to high ESG standards among such borrowers. The analysis also shows that shareholders—outside stakeholders from the perspective of the loan contracts—express their concerns about greenwashing, whereby public stock market reactions are positive for HPI sustainability-linked loans (i.e., only when there is enough informational detail about the sustainability-linked aspect of the loan contract) but negligible or negative for LPI loans. It seems that more transparent disclosure would be a welcome development for the evolution of the sustainability-linked loan market as a pillar of sustainable private contracts.

10.5 Conclusion and Policy Guidelines

Stakeholders increasingly demand transparency in corporate ESG policies. While much academic research has looked at public capital markets, much less work is available on private capital markets. Early research thus far suggests that private equity firms can have a positive impact on the sustainability of their portfolio firms' businesses, but only if their profit-maximization incentives are aligned with stakeholder values. Rules and regulations may play an important role in helping companies and investors internalize externalities.

One potential and hotly debated regulation is requiring sustainability-related disclosures. Even in private capital markets, such rules could make sense when companies have incentives to engage in greenwashing. Mounting stakeholder pressure does indeed give firms this incentive. In the corporate syndicated loan market, where sustainability-linked loans have proliferated in recent years, such incentives are pervasive. This is apparent in the poor quality with which companies disclose the sustainability-linked contractual features of these loans to the general public. Not only is this information often unavailable publicly, but it is presented selectively even when it is available. More importantly, borrowing companies who do not make the contractual information public tend to perform worse on ESG-related performance metrics after they take out sustainability-linked loans. This indicates that sustainability-linked contractual features are in place as a signaling device to affect stakeholder decisions without following through on concrete and ambitious commitments.

Overall, the early evidence thus far builds a reasonable case for advancing policy discussions to design and implement regulations to align shareholder-oriented corporate incentives with stakeholder values. Rules requiring the transparency of purported sustainability commitments seem a reasonable starting point.

References

Albuquerque, R., Y. Koskinen, S. Yang, and C. Zhang. 2020. Resiliency of Environmental and Social Stocks: An Analysis of the Exogenous COVID-19 Market Crash. *The Review of Corporate Finance Studies.* 9 (3).pp. 593–621.

Baker, M., D. Bergstresser, G. Serafeim, and J. Wurgler. 2022. The Pricing and Ownership of US Green Bonds. *Annual Review of Financial Economics.* 14. pp. 415–437.

Bartram, S., K. Hou, and S. Kim. 2022. Real Effects of Climate Policy: Financial Constraints and Spillovers. *Journal of Financial Economics.* 143 (2). pp. 668–696.

Bellon, A. 2022. Does Private Equity Ownership Make Firms Cleaner? The Role of Environmental Liability Risks. Working paper.

Berg, F., K. Fabisik, and Z. Sautner. 2021. Is History Repeating Itself? The (Un) Predictable Past of ESG Ratings. Working paper.

Berg, F., J. Koelbel, and R. Rigobon. 2022. Aggregate Confusion: The Divergence of ESG Ratings. *Review of Finance.* 26 (6). pp. 1315–1344.

Bloomberg. 2020. Leveraged Loan Market's ESG Push Offers Window into Opaque Deals. 3 February.

———. 2021a. Wall Street's ESG Loans Charge Corporate America Little for Missed Goals. 8 September.

———. 2021b. Ethical Label Is Hard to Verify in Secretive World of ESG Loans. 22 June.

Caskey, J. and W-H. Chang. 2022. Do ESG-Linked Loans Enhance the Credibility of ESG Disclosures? Working paper.

Döttling, R. and S. Kim. 2022. Sustainability Preferences Under Stress: Evidence from COVID-19. *Journal of Financial and Quantitative Analysis.* pp. 1–39. https://doi.org/10.1017/S0022109022001296.

Du, K., J. Harford, and D. Shin. 2022. Who Benefits from Sustainability-Linked Loans? Working paper.

Dursun-de Neef, O., S. Ongena, and G. Tsonkova. 2022. Green versus Sustainable Loans: the Impact on Firms' ESG Performance. Working paper.

Eccles, R. G., V. Shandal, D. Young, and B. Montgomery. 2022. Private Equity Should Take the Lead in Sustainability. *Harvard Business Review*. July–August 2022.

Fang, L. H., J. Goldman, and A. Roulet. 2023. Private Equity and Pay Gaps Inside the Firm. Working paper.

Flammer, C. 2021. Corporate Green Bonds. *Journal of Financial Economics*. 142 (2). pp. 499–516.

Gibson Brandon, R., S. Glossner, P. Krueger, P. Matos, and T. Steffen. 2022. Do Responsible Investors Invest Responsibly? *Review of Finance*. 26 (6). pp. 1389–1432.

Goldstein, I., A. Kopytov, L. Shen, and H. Xiang. 2023. On ESG Investing: Heterogeneous Preferences, Information, and Asset Prices. Working paper.

Hart, O. and L. Zingales. 2017. Serving Shareholders Doesn't Mean Putting Profit Above All Else. *Harvard Business Review*. 12 October.

Hartzmark, S. M. and A. B. Sussman. 2019. Do Investors Value Sustainability? A Natural Experiment Examining Ranking and Fund Flows. *The Journal of Finance*. 74 (6). pp. 2789–2837.

Heath, D., D. Macciocchi, R. Michaely, and M. C. Ringgenberg. 2023. Does Socially Responsible Investing Change Firm Behavior? *ECGI Working Paper Series in Finance*. No. 762/2021. Brussels: European Corporate Governance Institute.

Hoepner, A. G. F., I. Oikonomou, Z. Sautner, L. T. Starks, and X. Zhou. 2022. ESG Shareholder Engagement and Downside Risk. *ECGI Working Paper Series in Finance*. No. 671/2020. Brussels: European Corporate Governance Institute.

Houston, J. F. and H. Shan. 2022. Corporate ESG Profiles and Banking Relationships. *The Review of Financial Studies*. 35 (7). pp. 3373–3417.

Humphrey, J., S. Kogan, J. S. Sagi, and L. T. Starks. 2021. The Asymmetry in Responsible Investing Preferences. Working paper.

Ilhan, E., P. Krueger, Z. Sautner, and L. T. Starks. 2023. Climate Risk Disclosure and Institutional Investors. *The Review of Financial Studies*. 36 (7). pp. 2617-2650.

Ioannou, I. and G. Serafeim. 2019. The Consequences of Mandatory Corporate Sustainability Reporting. *The Oxford Handbook of Corporate Social Responsibility: Psychological and Organizational Perspectives*. Chapter 20. pp. 452–489.

Jung, H., R. F. Engle, and R. Berner. 2023. CRISK: Measuring the Climate Risk Exposure of the Financial System. Working paper.

Kacperczyk, M. T. and J.-L. Peydró. 2022. Carbon Emissions and the Bank-Lending Channel. Working paper.

Kaplan, S. N. and A. Schoar. 2005. Private Equity Performance: Returns, Persistence, and Capital Flows. *The Journal of Finance*. 60 (4). pp. 1791–1823.

Kim, S., N. Kumar, J. Lee, and J. Oh. 2022. ESG Lending. Working paper.

Kim, T. and Q. Xu. 2022. Financial Constraints and Corporate Environmental Policies. *The Review of Financial Studies*. 35 (2). pp. 576–635.

Krueger, P., Z. Sautner, and L. T. Starks. 2020. The Importance of Climate Risks for Institutional Investors. *The Review of Financial Studies*. 33 (3). pp. 1067–1111.

Lambert, M., N. Moreno, L. Phalippou, and A. Scivoletto. 2021. Employee Views of Leveraged Buy-Out Transactions. Working paper.

Lins, K. V., H. Servaes, and A. Tamayo. 2017. Social Capital, Trust, and Firm Performance: The Value of Corporate Social Responsibility during the Financial Crisis. *The Journal of Finance*. 72 (4). pp. 1785–1824.

Loumioti, M. and G. Serafeim. 2022. The Issuance and Design of Sustainability-Linked Loans. Working paper.

Pastor, L., R. F. Stambaugh, and L. A. Taylor. 2021. Sustainable Investing in Equilibrium. *Journal of Financial Economics*. 142 (2). pp. 550–571.

Pedersen, L. H., S. Fitzgibbons, and L. Pomorski. 2021. Responsible Investing: The ESG-Efficient Frontier. *Journal of Financial Economics*. 142 (2). pp. 572–597.

Riedl, A. and P. Smeets. 2017. Why Do Investors Hold Socially Responsible Mutual Funds? *The Journal of Finance*. 72 (6). pp. 2505–2550.

Tang, D. Y. and Y. Zhang. 2020. Do Shareholders Benefit from Green Bonds? *Journal of Corporate Finance*. 61. 101427. https://doi.org/10.1016/j.jcorpfin.2018.12.001.

Zerbib, O. D. 2019. The Effect of Pro-Environmental Preferences on Bond Prices: Evidence from Green Bonds. *Journal of Banking and Finance*. 98. pp. 39–60.

Climate-Related Risks to Financial Stability and Greening Policies by Central Banks

Ramkishen S. Rajan and Cyn-Young Park[1]

11.1 Introduction

The economic impacts of climate change and environmental degradation are far-reaching, with significant implications for financial stability and the profitability of commercial enterprises. As such, central banks are increasingly stepping up efforts to account for climate risks in their operations and analysis. This chapter discusses the role of central banks in combating climate change and its associated effects on macrofinancial stability.

Climate change is a negative externality which poses a "systemic risk" (Aglietta and Espagne 2016) or "green swan risk,"[2] defined as "potentially extremely financially disruptive events that could be behind the next systemic financial crisis" (Bolton et al. 2020, iii). Studies have illustrated a significant negative correlation between greater vulnerability of a country to climate risks and higher risk premiums on its sovereign bonds, lower credit ratings, and a higher probability of sovereign default (Cevik and Jalles 2020a, 2020b, 2020c).

Kling et al. (2021) further demonstrate that a higher sensitivity to climate impacts and lower capacity for response increased the sovereign cost of debt for a country by almost 1.2 percentage points over the past 10 years or so. The causal mechanisms underpinning these findings stem from the adverse

---

[1] Valuable research and editorial assistance by Bhavya Gupta is gratefully acknowledged. The views expressed are those of the authors and do not necessarily reflect the views and policies of the Asian Development Bank (ADB) or its Board of Governors or the governments they represent.

[2] The term "green swan" draws inspiration from the concept of "black swan," which refers to events that are unexpected and difficult to account for in risk-based accounting; have wide-ranging and extreme impacts; and are rationalized ex-post (Taleb 2010) but have two additional characteristics, i.e., unanimity on their eventual occurrence (though the timing is unknown) with irreversible consequences (Svartzman et al. 2021).

impact of extreme-weather events on a country's fiscal and macroeconomic indicators, apart from contributing to financial and political instability, and a balance of payments impact through changes in international trade and finance flows (Volz et al. 2020).[3]

Against this backdrop, climate change has emerged as a policy area for central banks. In 2015, the then-Bank of England Governor Mark Carney gave a landmark speech outlining the exposure of the United Kingdom's insurance sector to the increasing frequency of climate risks. He argued that policymakers are unable to take decisive and significant action on climate change as they face a "tragedy of the horizon," i.e., an inability to envisage the adverse consequences of climate change during their lifetime or term of office (Carney 2015). He articulated the risks posed by climate change to financial and macroeconomic stability, thereby necessitating a more prominent role for central banks in mitigating these risks given their requisite expertise and nuanced skills.

In more recent years, central banks in Europe, Asia, and elsewhere have increasingly become cognizant of the systemic risks that climate change poses to financial stability. In addition, central banks have been proactive in forming a coalition to coordinate and conduct research on "green finance,"[4] called the Network for Greening the Financial System. Steps toward promoting "green finance" have also been taken by emerging and developing countries, including Bangladesh, Brazil, the People's Republic of China, India, Indonesia, and Singapore.

The chapter reviews the risks posed by climate change to financial stability. It then looks at central bank responses to mitigate these climate-related financial risks and the implementation or "greening" of prudential policies, including the uneven diffusion of these policies across countries and the various policy tools being used or considered. The chapter empirically examines the characteristics of the economies where green prudential policies are adopted and concludes with policy implications for Asia.

---

[3] For instance, a 2020 report by ADB attributes a higher risk premium of around 155 basis points on sovereign bond yields due to the greater vulnerability of Association of Southeast Asian Nations (ASEAN) economies to climate change (Volz et al. 2020).

[4] Green finance, or the greening of finance, broadly encompasses an impetus to financing geared toward nonfossil fuel or climate-friendly sectors, enabling a smooth transition to a low-carbon economy.

11.2 Impact of Climate Change on Financial Stability

Climate change impacts financial stability primarily through physical risk and transition risk,[5] which in turn exacerbates various financial risks to firms. First, a "physical risk" arises from the adverse impacts of extreme-weather events and the more gradual rise in global temperatures and sea levels on the balance sheets of firms and households (Dafermos, Nikolaidi, and Galanis 2018; Molico 2019). On the financial side, risks in this regard are likely to arise, for instance, within insurance companies where the unprecedented scale of catastrophic losses unleashed by climate events would send insurance claims soaring. Since insurance companies are highly integrated within the overall financial system, a decline in their profitability and/or increased operational risk is likely to present a source of systemic risk for overall financial stability (Tooze 2019).

Second, a "transition risk" is posed by the current economic architecture, which still relies predominantly on fossil fuels for energy supply and production. An unexpected shift, or an expected but unplanned-for shift in the current carbon emission standards, precipitating a "hard landing" from a high-carbon to low-carbon emitting economy (Schoenmaker and Van Tilburg 2016), can prompt an abrupt move away from fossil fuels and carbon-intensive production methods, which in turn will result in supply side shocks and a subsequent need for central bank intervention (Batten, Sowerbutts, and Tanaka 2016). Such an unexpected shift is likely for private investment in carbon-intensive sectors, because research has demonstrated that commercial and private investment is currently not very sensitive to the reality of global carbon emission reduction agreements (Ameli et al. 2020; Morgan 2020). Other sources of transition risk are policy changes that penalize brown investments, technological breakthroughs that further the case of green energy production methods, and large-scale shifts in consumer preferences toward more environment-friendly technologies and products (Gabor et al. 2019). Campiglio (2016) argues that central banks can facilitate this shift away from carbon intensive to low-carbon standards, especially in emerging economies, by incentivizing commercial banks to fund the latter projects through directed lending, differential reserve requirements, and macroprudential policies.

---

[5]   Reference is also sometimes made to "liability risks," which arise specifically for financial entities such as insurance agencies and businesses, due to the "uncertainty surrounding potential financial losses and compensation claims stemming from various damages caused by climate change-related natural hazards" (Dikau and Volz 2018).

Physical and transition risks are somewhat negatively correlated. A gradual transition from a high-carbon to low-carbon economy can minimize transition risks but can exacerbate physical risks, owing to the longer period of transition, which will be correlated with an increase in extreme climate events (Table 11.1, bottom-right and bottom-left columns). On the other hand, a sudden shift from a carbon-intensive to an environment-conscious economic architecture can lower physical risks at the cost of imposing hefty transition costs on economic agents, including private firms in fossil fuel-intensive sectors, banks, insurance and reinsurance agencies, and allied players. This could occur by triggering a massive realignment in asset valuations which do not currently fully reflect climate-associated risks (Kyriakopoulou, Chye, and Thio 2020; Pointner and Ritzberger-Grünwald 2019), a so-called "hard landing" from a high-carbon to low-carbon economy (Table 11.1, top-left column). In this context, the job of financial supervisors and central banks is to design policies to prepare for a "soft-landing" from a high-carbon to low-carbon economy in the medium term (Table 11.1, top-right column). Both these climate-related risks could exacerbate financial risks to firms, including credit risk, market risk, liquidity risk, operational, reputational, and systemic risk (Gruenewald 2020; Pointner and Ritzberger-Grünwald 2019). Since these risks are encountered at the individual firm-level, microprudential instruments, such as differential capital conservation buffers and various liquidity coverage ratios (D'Orazio and Popoyan 2019; Goodhart and Perotti 2013) can minimize such risks. However, microprudential policies targeting risks associated with individual financial institutions are inadequate to deal with the system-wide threats posed by climate-related financial risks.

From a system-wide perspective, higher physical and transition risks arising from the inability of financial institutions to adequately account for climatic risks in their risk framework and short-termism in asset allocation to brown versus green sectors can raise the probability of default and write-offs of brown assets. This can aggravate overall financial instability and systemic risk. Similarly, abrupt and messy decarbonization can cause large-scale corrections in asset prices and lead to "stranded assets," which could destabilize the entire financial sector.

Table 11.1: Scenarios of Interconnected Physical and Transition Risks Based on Degree and Timing of Corrective Responses

		Strength of Response	
		STRONG	**WEAK**
Timing of Response	**EARLY**	Hard landing Limit physical risk, but cause high transition risk	Soft landing Limit, but not eliminate, both physical and transition risks
	DELAYED	Too little too late Both high physical and transition risk	Hot house earth Extremely elevated levels of physical risk associated with considerable transition risks

Source: By authors based on Gruenewald (2020).

11.3 Role of Central Banks and Green Prudential Policies

Central banks should be key actors in mitigating the adverse impacts of climate-related financial risks on the financial system. Likewise, they are key actors in facilitating a smooth transition to a decarbonized net-zero carbon economy, in line with the globally agreed Conference of the Parties (COP) 21 Paris Agreement, and more recently, the COP28 meetings in Egypt. Central bank responses to climate change can be categorized based on their policy motives for intervention in financial markets.

Conceptually, Isabel Schnabel, member of the Executive Board of the European Central Bank (ECB), envisages central bank responses as falling into two categories—market-fixing or market-shaping (Kyriakopoulou, Chye, and Thio 2020; Schnabel 2020). In market-fixing policies, central banks work at the peripheries of the market to fix the information asymmetry surrounding the carbon pricing of assets. This could be accomplished by creating green taxonomies and encouraging climate-related disclosures by private firms. Market-shaping policies are more proactive and involve the incorporation of climate objectives into the setting of monetary and prudential policies by central banks to directly influence credit allocation to green vs. brown sectors[6] (Gruenewald 2020).

---

[6]   Other central bank responses include incorporating green principles into the management of their own asset portfolios, operations, and foreign reserves (OMFIF 2019), which do not unambiguously fall into either of the above two categories but have formed a key aspect of central banks' response to climate change.

Baer, Campiglio, and Deyris (2021) propose a somewhat different yet complementary classification of financial policies' motives as prudential or promotional. They argue that while promotional policies are aimed at facilitating the transition to a low-carbon economy, they are premised on a market-shaping approach. On the other hand, policies with a prudential motive are aimed at identifying, monitoring, and mitigating the risks to financial stability arising from climate change.

An alternative classification of central bank responses to climate change can focus on whether the policies undertaken are preventive or mitigative. In this context, policies to preempt and minimize the adverse effects of climate change on financial stability—including the creation of green taxonomies, disclosures, calibration of risk weights, etc.—can be termed preventive. In contrast, ex-post central bank policies, implemented after the realization of climate-related financial risks—such as tackling of stranded assets and nonperforming loans—can be classified as mitigative.

Disagreements are rife in the central banking policy domain and academia about the "correct" role for central banks in tackling climate change, with concerns articulated particularly about the "greening" of monetary and macroprudential policies (Brunnermeier and Landau 2020; Cochrane 2020; Honohan 2019). Dikau and Volz (2021) analyze central bank mandates using the International Monetary Fund's (IMF) Central Bank Legislative Database to assess the de jure support for central banks incorporating climate-related risks into their policy frameworks and responses. They find that 52% of central banks in their 135-country database explicitly or implicitly include sustainable growth as a policy objective.[7] Thus, a little less than half (48%) of central banks in their sample do not have de jure support per se for promoting green finance, but some of them still have taken policy measures to address climate risk. The authors argue that it is imperative for central banks to take account of climate-related financial risks regardless of their legal mandate insofar as it impedes or affects the attainment of other central bank policy objectives of price stability, growth, and financial stability. Similarly, a survey of 18 central banks in Asia and the Pacific reveals considerable de facto support among the central banking community to introduce policies for promoting green finance and mitigating climatic risks to the financial system (Durrani, Rosmin, and Volz 2020).

[7]   Of this 52%, 12% of central banks explicitly have sustainable growth as a policy objective, while the other 40% have a broader and vaguer mandate of supporting their governments' respective policy priorities. The large proportion of these central banks belong to emerging markets and developing countries (Dikau and Volz 2021).

Advocates of green central banking argue that the current economic architecture is implicitly biased against green funding options, particularly due to the Basel III macroprudential regulations which were formulated after the 2008 global financial crisis. Basel III norms assign higher risk weights to green sector financing since their gestation period is longer, green technology is still not mainstreamed, and project completion is subject to higher uncertainty compared to traditional fossil fuel "brown" sectors (Gruenewald 2020; Schnabel 2020). Thus, reversing this implicit bias by promoting green finance and incorporating climatic risks into asset prices to facilitate full price discovery is just leveling the playing field. However, the impact of wading into the climate change debate on the independence of otherwise technocratic and neutrally perceived central banks, as well as questions on the severity of climatic risk perceptions themselves, are posed as counterarguments to this claim (Cochrane 2020; Honohan 2019).

The response to these charges is also divided sharply along geopolitical and ideological lines. ECB strongly supports an activist role for central banks to include climate-sensitive policies into central bank mandates, because climate change poses a direct risk to price stability through large price and output shocks affected by climate-related physical risks. However, the United States Federal Reserve endorses the view that such policies are the territory of elected policymakers (Brunnermeier and Landau 2020; Randow 2020; Schnabel 2020).

Asian economies have largely been "nonvocal" in these policy discussions. They have, however, implemented voluntary or mandatory policies incorporating green criteria into their credit allocation, risk disclosure, and macroprudential policies, to mitigate the impact of climate-related financial risks. This could be partly because their central bank mandates are not premised on price stability alone, but also include supporting the design and implementation of the government's economic policies. This is a broad mandate which is able to incorporate climate-related risks to financial stability (Dikau and Ryan-Collins 2017) without much controversy or ambiguity about the scope and appropriateness of central bank policymaking in these areas.

Against this backdrop, the Network for Greening the Financial System lays out six recommendations for policymakers, central banks, and financial institutions to mitigate the impact of climate-related financial risks on financial stability. These are "(i) integrating climate-related risks into financial stability monitoring and microsupervision, (ii) integrating sustainability factors into own-portfolio management, (iii) bridging the data gaps, (iv) building awareness and intellectual capacity and encouraging technical assistance and knowledge sharing, (v) achieving robust and internationally consistent climate and environment-related disclosures, and (vi) supporting the development of a taxonomy of economic activities" (NGFS 2019, 4).

Microprudential regulation has increasingly become a major component of central banks' toolkits in responding to climate-related financial risks. Green microprudential policies focus on the incorporation of environmental and social safeguards by individual financial entities to ensure their resilience to climatic risks. At the minimum, this involves supervision and climate disclosures by individual firms.

In contrast, green macroprudential policy is simultaneously concerned with the preservation of financial stability while trying to minimize climatic risks to the financial system and enabling a smooth transition to a low-carbon economy by promoting green finance. These policies are more suited to combat systemic risks arising from the interconnected and synergistic nature of financial firms (IMF-FSB-BIS 2016). To mitigate climate-related financial risks, some commonly used and/or discussed green macroprudential tools include countercyclical capital buffers, differential equity margin requirements, differential risk weights for assets based on their carbon content, and climate-related stress testing (Dikau and Ryan-Collins 2017; Schoenmaker and Van Tilburg 2016).

However, an argument against the use of green prudential policies is that financial and climate-related risks are not perfectly correlated. Moreover, the relationship between climate change and financial stability is not unidirectional. A few financial policies calibrated toward a climate objective can also have unintended consequences and can end up exacerbating financial instability (Restoy 2021; Schydlowsky 2020). For instance, proposals to artificially reduce risk weights on capital devoted to green sectors by introducing a green supporting factor (GSF) could end up backfiring. Although such a policy could incentivize/nudge financial institutions to increase their capital exposures to green sectors, a green supporting factor does not necessarily provide a complete account of the financial viability and/or creditworthiness of green projects. If these green projects subsequently turn out to be unprofitable and/or unviable (evidenced by contemporary concerns of a green bubble and greenwashing by firms), the ensuing volume of nonperforming assets could exacerbate credit/liquidity risk to financial entities and end up worsening financial stability.

The most widely discussed and/or implemented green policies across countries are climate-related disclosure requirements for listed companies and financial institutions (currently under discussion or implemented in 27 jurisdictions), followed by the inclusion of broadly encompassing "green financial principles" in financial regulators' operations.

Developing economies, in particular, have largely resorted to credit allocation policies (lending requirements and differentiated reserve requirements) to achieve sustainability goals. For instance, different "equity margin requirements" for green versus brown assets (which is akin to differential capital conservation buffers) are mandatory in Bangladesh (Dikau and Ryan-Collins 2017), the People's Republic of China (Durrani et al. 2020), and Lebanon (D'Orazio and Popoyan 2019), while these are in the discussion phase in Europe (D'Orazio and Popoyan 2019). Variants of priority sector lending are evident in India and Bangladesh.[8] Climate-related stress testing, on the other hand, is mandatory in many developing and developed economies including Brazil; Hong Kong, China; Japan; Singapore; the United Kingdom; and in some European economies (Kyriakopoulou, Chye, and Thio 2020). Various other economies are actively considering proposals to include climate-related risks in their risk assessment frameworks (D'Orazio and Popoyan 2019).

Enhanced disclosure requirements appear to be witnessing the most activity at the international level and through cross-country collaboration. The Task Force on Climate-Related Financial Disclosures led by the Financial Stability Board and a technical working group formed by the European Commission have adopted a consultative and collaborative approach to lay down common standards for climate risk disclosures by private financial firms. Among emerging economies in Asia and Latin America, Bangladesh, Brazil, the People's Republic of China, Indonesia, and Singapore also have such disclosure requirements in place for financial entities (Dikau and Ryan-Collins 2017; Durrani, Rosmin, and Volz 2020).

---

[8]   Bangladesh requires banks to extend minimum 5% of their loan portfolio toward green activities. India included credit to renewable sectors under its long-standing Priority Sector Lending scheme, which mandates banks to lend up to 40% of their total loan portfolio to specified sectors (Durrani, Rosmin, and Volz 2020).

11.4 Empirics

11.4.1 Methodology

Although the introduction of green prudential measures across countries is a recent phenomenon and its effectiveness in mitigating climate-related financial risks can only be judged over time, here we explore the question of what factors determine the likelihood of adoption of green prudential regulations by central banks.[9] In particular, we examine whether countries that are more vulnerable to climate change tend to be more likely adopters of green prudential policies, hypothesizing a positive correlation between the two variables.

A probit model is employed for analysis since the dependent variable—the imposition of green prudential policies—is a bivariate dummy. The baseline considers a simple bivariate regression estimating the effect of climate vulnerability of countries on their likelihood of implementing green prudential policies. The model specification is as follows:

$$GMI_i = f(X_i) \tag{1}$$

where GMI_i is a binary dummy indicating whether any green prudential policy is implemented in country i in 2018 (data discussed in next section); f(.) is a function and X_i represents a vector of variables that determine the imposition of green prudential regulations.

The analysis includes the Climate Vulnerability Index by Paun, Acton, and Chan (2018) in the baseline model as the main determinant (independent variable). It adopts a specific-to-general approach in assessing the determinants of imposition of green prudential regulations, starting by only including climate risk-related indicators in the baseline using a probit model.

Having established the baseline, the analysis then conjectures that a country which has previously imposed macroprudential policy instruments in general is more likely to adopt green prudential practices.[10] Accordingly, the analysis includes an aggregate macroprudential policy index in a previous

---

9 Parts of this section draw on Cheng, Gupta, and Rajan (2022).
10 It is likely that countries that are already familiar with and have used prudential policy tools in the previous year are more likely to implement "green" prudential policies, since they only require a recalibration to incorporate green criteria.

year to capture how intensively countries have engaged in prudential measures overall. The analysis uses the Macroprudential Index compiled by Cerutti, Claessens, and Laeven (2017) based on the IMF survey on the Global Macroprudential Policy Instruments database.

Following that, the analysis further includes a proxy for institutional capacity using the indicator "potential to respond to climate risks" from Paun, Acton, and Chan (2018) to capture the overall institutional capacity of a country. It hypothesizes that given the same vulnerability to climate risks, the greater the institutional capacity of an economy, the less likely it is (relatively) to impose green prudential measures. Therefore, we generate interaction terms between the three climate risk indexes and the potential to respond to climate risks and include them in the model to test whether a country with higher institutional capacity is less likely to implement green prudential regulation, everything else being equal.

11.4.2 Data

The dependent variable is a bivariate dummy generated based on the Green Macroprudential Index (GMI) developed by D'Orazio and Popoyan (2019), which gives the status of adoption of green prudential policies—under discussion, voluntary, or mandatory—by 56 countries for 2018.[11] This dataset surveys existing green prudential regulations and instruments by documenting official central bank and financial institution reports. The GMI constructed by the authors has three categories and takes values from zero to two. It equals zero when the measures are under discussion, indicating that countries are discussing the possibility of introducing green prudential regulation; it equals one when countries have developed a voluntary green regulation; and it equals two when countries have adopted a green prudential regulation which is mandatory in nature. We make use of this classification but define a country as having adopted green prudential policies no matter if it is voluntary or mandatory. Hence, a binary dummy variable indicating green regulation adoption is generated and it equals one when the GMI is either equal to one or two and zero when the GMI equals zero.

---

[11]   From the initial database of 56 countries by D'Orazio and Popoyan (2019), the sample size for the probit regressions is 41 countries, because 8 countries in the dataset had missing values for status of implementation of green prudential policies, leaving 48 countries with values for the dependent variable, and 7 that were not overlapping with the HSBC Climate Risks Index dataset, the key independent variable.

The key independent variable of interest is the vulnerability of a country to climatic risks. This measure is operationalized through an index created based on the Climate Vulnerability Index developed by The Hongkong and Shanghai Banking Corporation Limited (HSBC). The Fragile Planet Report by HSBC ranks 67 countries on the basis of their vulnerability to climate change by primarily focusing on the period between 2006 and 2016 (and in some cases going back to 1995 such as the level and change in temperatures) (Paun, Acton, and Chan 2018). It assesses countries based on both the physical risks posed to them by climate change, including a greater frequency of extreme weather-related events as well as the risks involved in transitioning to a low-carbon economy, which is a function of adequate public and private investment in renewable energy initiatives. It also includes the availability of innovative technology to harness energy from water, hydrogen, and other replenishable sources, as well as the policy architecture and capacity that exists to facilitate and promote the decarbonization of the economy. A country's overall rank is determined by an equal weightage given to four subindexes of climate risks: "(1) physical impacts; (2) sensitivity to extreme weather events; (3) energy transition risks; and (4) a country's potential to respond to climate change, covering financial resources and national governance indicators" (Paun, Acton, and Chan 2018).[12] A lower country score based on these four measures corresponds to a higher vulnerability of the country to climate risks.[13]

For the statistical analysis, a new climate risk index is developed by aggregating the first two subindexes in the HSBC report measuring physical impacts and sensitivity to extreme weather events, assigning a 50% weight to each of the sensitivity score and physical impacts score. The aggregate score is then reversed by subtracting the value from 10 for interpretation (since a lower initial score implies a higher vulnerability to climate risks and scores across all four HSBC subindexes range from 0 to 10).

The analysis also uses the fourth subindex in Paun, Acton, and Chan (2018) separately as a proxy for institutional capacity. This index describes how well countries are placed to respond to the physical and transition risks from climate change. The indicator captures a country's financial soundness, including its gross domestic product per capita, public debt, sovereign wealth funds and capital costs, as well as the strength of its institutions, including rule of law, corruption, inequality, and tertiary education.

---

[12]   For more details on the composition of the each of subindexes, refer to Annex Table A.1 on p. 197.
[13]   The survey findings report two interesting trends—that countries in South Asia and Southeast Asia are most vulnerable to climate change; and that developed countries in general are less vulnerable to climate shocks than developing countries.

For proxying conventional macroprudential policy, the analysis uses the Macroprudential Index compiled by Cerutti, Claessens, and Laeven (2017) based on the IMF survey on Global Macroprudential Policy Instruments database. In this database, there are two broad types of macroprudential measures. The first type consists of two instruments that target borrowers, which specifically include caps on the loan-to-value (LTV) ratio and limits to the debt-to-income (DTI) ratio. The second type consists of 10 other instruments that focus on financial institutions (lenders). These 12 macroprudential instruments are time series dummy indicators on the usage of each instrument for the sample countries. The aggregated macroprudential policy index (MPI) takes the sum of policy action indicators of all 12 individual instruments. We use the lagged aggregated MPI in 2017 to capture previous experience with conventional macroprudential regulation.

All variables, along with their respective data sources and hypothesized causal impact on the dependent variable, are summarized in Table 11.2.

Table 11.2: Variables, Data Sources, and Direction of Impact

Variable	Source	Direction of Impact on Dependent Variable (Likelihood of Imposition of Green Macroprudential Policies)
Climate Risks Index (2017)	New aggregate index developed based on the HSBC Climate Vulnerability Index	**+** Countries more vulnerable to climate change are more likely to implement green macroprudential policies.
Aggregate macroprudential index (lagged by 1 year—2017)	Macroprudential Index compiled by Cerutti, Claessens, and Laeven (2017) based on the International Monetary Fund survey on Global Macroprudential Policy Instruments database	**+** Countries with prior experience of macroprudential policies are more likely to align them with a "green" objective.
Overall institutional capacity	Paun, Acton, and Chan (2018)—subindex on "potential to respond to climate risks"	**–** Countries with higher institutional capacity are more likely to have the resources and wherewithal to implement fiscal responses to climate change. Prudential policies, considered as a substitute to fiscal policies, are more likely to be implemented in a country with lower institutional capacity.

HSBC = The Hongkong and Shanghai Banking Corporation Limited.
Source: Authors.

11.4.3 Results

The analysis estimates the probit model as discussed. It starts with a bivariate regression model establishing the relationship between GMI and the index capturing physical impacts of climate change. Results are presented in Table 11.3, column (1). MPI is then added to the model and results are reported in column (2). Column (3) presents the results of the impact of sensitivity of a country to extreme weather events on GMI. MPI is then added to the model and results are reported in column (4). Similarly, an aggregate indicator (consisting of an equally weighted average of the first two indexes) is then created and added to the model and results are reported in column (5). MPI is then included in the model and results are reported in column (6). Robust standard errors are used to correct for potential heteroscedasticity.

Table 11.3: Climate Risks and Green Prudential Policies—Probit Model

Variables	(1) GMPI	(2) GMPI	(3) GMPI	(4) GMPI	(5) GMPI	(6) GMPI
Phyrisk_rev	0.417***	0.495***				
	(0.156)	(0.184)				
Sensirisk_rev			0.327***	0.327***		
			(0.0959)	(0.101)		
Aggrisk_rev					0.788***	0.803***
					(0.192)	(0.200)
mpi_2017		0.202		0.00285		0.103
		(0.128)		(0.138)		(0.135)
Constant	−2.076***	−3.425***	−1.838***	−1.849***	−4.080***	−4.652***
	(0.748)	(1.262)	(0.546)	(0.680)	(0.989)	(1.275)
Observations	41	41	41	41	41	41

GMPI = global macroprudential policy index.
Notes:
1. Phyrisk_rev refers to physical risk scores from Paun, Acton, and Chan (2018), which are reversed for ease of interpretation.
2. Sensirisk_rev refers to sensitivity scores from Paun, Acton, and Chan (2018), which are reversed for ease of interpretation.
3. Aggrisk_rev refers to an equally weighted average of physical risk scores and sensitivity scores from Paun, Acton, and Chan (2018), which are reversed for ease of interpretation.
4. Mpi_2017 refers to the aggregate macroprudential index developed by Cerutti, Claessens, and Laeven (2017).
5. Probit coefficients are reported. Robust standard errors are adopted.
6. *** $p < 0.01$, ** $p < 0.05$, * $p < 0.1$.
7. T-statistics are reported in parentheses.
Source: Authors.

Results indicate that all three climate risk indicators are positive and highly significant, even after controlling for past record of implementing macroprudential policies (captured by mpi_2017). This confirms our initial hypothesis—countries that are more vulnerable to climate risks are more likely to implement green prudential policies.

Next, we examine whether the overall institutional capacity of a country is a mechanism that can mediate the impact of higher vulnerability to climate risks on the likelihood of imposition of green prudential policies. We hypothesize that a country with a higher overall capacity—captured by the fourth subindex in Paun, Acton, and Chan (2018), which includes proxies of both a country's financial soundness and the strength of its institutions—will be less likely to implement green prudential policies, since these policies are considered a second-best or second-order response to combat climate change (Villeroy de Galhau 2020; Weidmann 2020). The first-best response would be levy of carbon taxes, emissions trading schemes, and greening of other fiscal policies (Breman 2020; Elderson 2020). To assess this hypothesis, we interact the proxy for institutional capacity with the aggregate climate risk indicator.

Table 11.4 shows that for countries with a given level of climate risks (proxied first by the two subindexes on physical impacts of climate change and sensitivity to extreme-weather events, and then an aggregate of the two), a higher institutional capacity reduces the likelihood of imposition of green prudential policies in all three cases. The results are highly statistically significant at the 1% level and remain robust to the inclusion of past record of using macroprudential policies.[14]

---

[14]   Institutional capacity by itself has only a weak impact on the likelihood of undertaking green prudential policies. Only in the case of aggregate risks as the independent variable, the coefficient on overall capacity is significant at the 5% level but with a positive sign, indicating that a higher institutional capacity leads to a greater chance of implementing green prudential policies, notwithstanding the degree of vulnerability to climate change.

Table 11.4: Interaction Effects of Climate Risks with Overall Capacity

Dependent Variable: GMI Dummy	(1)	(2)	(3)
Sensirisk_rev	0.746**		
	(0.337)		
Sensitivity score*Overall capacity	−0.117**		
	(0.0538)		
Phyrisk_rev		1.318**	
		(0.562)	
Physical impacts*Overall capacity		−0.176**	
		(0.0858)	
Aggrisk_rev			2.587***
			(0.804)
Aggregate*Overall capacity			−0.355***
			(0.110)
Overall capacity	−0.0110	0.219	1.200**
	(0.311)	(0.397)	(0.552)
mpi_2017	0.0816	0.227	0.167
	(0.141)	(0.165)	(0.194)
Constant	−1.531	−4.441	−11.17**
	(1.987)	(3.192)	(4.491)
Observations	41	41	41

GMI = green macroprudential index.
*** $p<0.01$, ** $p<0.05$, * $p<0.1$.
Notes: See Table 11.3.
Source: Authors.

11.5 Conclusion

Increasingly, financial supervisors and central banks are being called upon to undertake the task of mitigating the impact of climate-related financial risks on financial stability. Accordingly, financial supervisors and central banks may need to embrace green prudential policies as part of their policy toolkit and use them to facilitate the transition to a more sustainable economy. Since climate change affects both the balance sheets of individual financial entities and poses system-wide risks affecting the entire financial system, both micro- and macroprudential policy tools are being considered and implemented in different countries to mitigate its impact. The preliminary empirical evidence in this chapter suggests that countries that are more vulnerable to climate change tend to more likely be adopters of green prudential policies.

From a policy perspective, even though debate rages on regarding the degree to which central banks should incorporate green objectives in their mandates and overall regulatory and monetary policies, most agree that central banks can play a vital role in facilitating the development of taxonomies and climate-related disclosures. Even as many central banks are adopting a degree of green policy and regulations at the domestic level, international coordination and collaboration is vital in this regard. Steps are needed to harmonize green standards internationally to ensure cross-border consistency of regulations and to prevent green washing. At the global level, several standard-setting bodies have been established with this mandate, such as the Taskforce on Climate-Related Financial Disclosures and the Taskforce on Climate-Related Financial Risks under the Bank for International Settlements, the International Organization for Securities Commissions Sustainable Finance Task Force, the Network for Greening the Financial System, and so on. However, an international global agreement on taxonomies and disclosures remains elusive.

Several Asian economies have emerged as global frontrunners in implementing policies to encourage green finance and to create a conducive environment for an orderly transition to a decarbonized economy. The uptake of green prudential policies of a mandatory nature is the highest in Asia as compared with other regions of the world, and this is perhaps partly due to the higher vulnerability of Asian economies to extreme weather-related events and global warming. The "greening" of prudential policies (both micro and macro), undertaken particularly by Asian central banks, are aimed both at nudging investors toward low-carbon "green" sectors, as well as mitigating the climate-related risks to financial stability. Asian central banks also promote green finance through preferential allocation of credit to low-carbon sectors and away from high-carbon ones, and a recalibration of central banks' own balance sheets and reserves to reflect climate priorities.

However, since most of these policies are implemented individually by countries at the national level, greater discussions could also be done on issues relating to the greening of prudential regulations, which may need to be coordinated across countries to prevent cross-border regulatory arbitrage given greater regionalization of financial markets. The Association of Southeast Asian Nations (ASEAN) Task Force on the Roles of Central Banks in Managing Climate and Environment-Related Risks set up by nine central banks of ASEAN countries in 2019 is an important initiative in this regard.

Annex

Table A.1: Four Climate Risk Subindexes from the
HSBC Fragile Planet Report 2018

Subindex	Description
Physical impacts of climate change	Composite score is based on "temperature levels (35% of the score), water availability (50%), and extreme weather events (15%)."
Sensitivity to extreme weather events	Extreme weather events are defined as droughts, floods, extreme temperatures, storms, and wildfires, normalized by adjusting for land mass. Sensitivity is measured across three dimensions—"cost of damage (40% weightage), number of deaths (30%), and number of people affected (30%)."
Energy transition risks	Measured by including "the level and change over the past 10 years for fossil rents (economic profit) as a percentage of GDP (33.3%), share of fossil fuels in exports (33.3%), and share of fossil fuels in primary energy use (33.3%)."
Potential to respond to climate change	A 50% weightage each is assigned to financial capacity and strength of institutions, or institutional capacity. Metrics to capture financial capacity include GDP per capita at PPP, public debt, sovereign wealth funds, and cost of capital. Strength of institutions is proxied using measures of rule of law, corruption, inequality, and tertiary education.

GDP = gross domestic product, PPP = purchasing power parity.
Source: Paun, Acton, and Chan (2018).

References

Aglietta, M. and É. Espagne. 2016. Climate and Finance Systemic Risks, More than an Analogy? The Climate Fragility Hypothesis. *CEPII Working Paper*. No. 2016-10. Paris: CEPII.

Ameli, N., P. Drummond, A. Bisaro, M. Grubb, and H. Chenet 2020. Climate Finance and Disclosure for Institutional Investors: Why Transparency Is Not Enough. *Climatic Change*. 160 (4). pp. 565–589. https://doi.org/10.1007/s10584-019-02542-2.

Baer, M., E. Campiglio, and J. Deyris. 2021. It Takes Two to Dance: Institutional Dynamics And Climate-Related Financial Policies. *Centre for Climate Change Economics and Policy Working Paper*. No. 384 / Grantham Research Institute on Climate Change and the Environment Working Paper*. No. 356. https://www.lse.ac.uk/granthaminstitute/wp-content/uploads/2021/04/working-paper-356-Baer-et-al.pdf.

Batten, S., R. Sowerbutts, and M. Tanaka. 2016. Let's Talk about the Weather: the Impact of Climate Change on Central Banks. *Bank of England Staff Working Paper*. No. 603. London: Bank of England.

Bolton, P., M. Despres, L. A. P. da Silva, R. Svartzman, and F. Samama. 2020. *The Green Swan: Central Banking and Financial Stability in the Age of Climate Change*. Basel: Bank for International Settlements.

Breman, A. 2020. *How the Riksbank Can Contribute to Climate Policy*. Speech by the Deputy Governor of Sveriges Riksbank. Royal Swedish Academy of Engineering Sciences, Stockholm. 3 March. https://www.bis.org/review/r200304g.pdf.

Brunnermeier, M. K. and J-P. Landau. 2020. Central Banks and Climate Change. *VoxEU / Centre for Economic Policy Research (CEPR)*. 15 January. https://voxeu.org/article/central-banks-and-climate-change.

Campiglio, E. 2016. Beyond Carbon Pricing: The Role of Banking and Monetary Policy in Financing the Transition to a Low-Carbon Economy. *Ecological Economics*. 121. pp. 220–230. https://doi.org/10.1016/j.ecolecon.2015.03.020.

Carney, M. 2015. *Breaking the Tragedy of the Horizon – Climate Change and Financial Stability*. Speech. 29 September. https://www.bankofengland.co.uk/-/media/boe/files/speech/2015/breaking-the-tragedy-of-the-horizon-climate-change-and-financial-stability.pdf?la=en&hash=7C67E785651862457D99511147C7424FF5EA0C1A.

Cerutti, E., S. Claessens, and L. Laeven. 2017. The Use and Effectiveness of Macroprudential Policies: New Evidence. *Journal of Financial Stability*. 28. pp. 203–224. https://doi.org/10.1016/j.jfs.2015.10.004.

Cevik, S. and J. T. Jalles. 2020a. *An Apocalypse Foretold: Climate Shocks and Sovereign Defaults* (20/231). International Monetary Fund. https://www.elibrary.imf.org/doc/IMF001/29355-9781513560403/29355-9781513560403/Other_formats/Source_PDF/29355-9781513562285.pdf?redirect=true.

Cevik, S. and J. T. Jalles. 2020b. *Feeling the Heat: Climate Shocks and Credit Ratings*. International Monetary Fund. https://www.imf.org/en/Publications/WP/Issues/2020/12/18/Feeling-the-Heat-Climate-Shocks-and-Credit-Ratings-49945.

Cevik, S. and J. T. Jalles. 2020c. *This Changes Everything: Climate Shocks and Sovereign Bonds*. International Monetary Fund. https://www.imf.org/en/Publications/WP/Issues/2020/06/05/This-Changes-Everything-Climate-Shocks-and-Sovereign-Bonds-49476.

Cheng, R., B. Gupta, and R. S. Rajan. 2022. Why Are Some Countries Greening Macroprudential Regulations Faster than Others? Mimeo.

Cochrane, J. 2020. Central Banks and Climate: A Case of Mission Creep. *Hoover Institution*. 13 November. https://www.hoover.org/research/central-banks-and-climate-case-mission-creep.

D'Orazio, P. and L. Popoyan. 2019. Dataset on Green Macroprudential Regulations and Instruments: Objectives, Implementation and Geographical Diffusion. *Data in Brief*. 24. 103870–103870. https://doi.org/10.1016/j.dib.2019.103870.

D'Orazio, P. and L. Popoyan. 2019. Fostering Green Investments and Tackling Climate-Related Financial Risks: Which Role for Macroprudential Policies? *Ecological Economics*. 160. pp. 25–37. https://doi.org/10.1016/j.ecolecon.2019.01.029.

Dafermos, Y., M. Nikolaidi, and G. Galanis. 2018. Climate Change, Financial Stability and Monetary Policy. *Ecological Economics*. 152. pp. 219–234.

Dikau, S. and J. Ryan-Collins. 2017. *Green Central Banking in Emerging Market and Developing Country Economies*. London: New Economics Foundation. https://neweconomics.org/uploads/files/Green-Central-Banking.pdf.

Dikau, S. and U. Volz. 2018. *Central Banking, Climate Change and Green Finance*. Tokyo: Asian Development Bank Institute. https://www.adb.org/publications/central-banking-climate-change-and-green-finance.

Dikau, S. and U. Volz. 2021. Central Bank Mandates, Sustainability Objectives and the Promotion of Green Finance. *Ecological Economics*. 184. 107022. https://doi.org/10.1016/j.ecolecon.2021.107022.

Durrani, A., M. Rosmin, and U. Volz. 2020. The Role of Central Banks in Scaling Up Sustainable Finance—What Do Monetary Authorities in the Asia-Pacific Region Think? *Journal of Sustainable Finance and Investment*. 10 (2). pp. 92–112. https://doi.org/10.1080/20430795.2020.1715095.

Elderson, F. 2020. *We Should Aim for a 1,5 Degree Economy When Designing the Recovery Path*. Basel: Bank for International Settlements. https://www.bis.org/review/r200804g.pdf.

Gabor, D., Y. Dafermos, M. Nikolaidi, P. Rice, F. van Lerven, R. Kerslake, A. Pettifor, and M. Jacobs. 2019. Finance and Climate Change: A Progressive Green Finance Strategy for the UK. Report of the Independent Panel commissioned by Shadow Chancellor of the Exchequer John McDonnell MP. Labour Party. https://labour.org.uk/wp-content/uploads/2019/11/12851_19-Finance-and-Climate-Change-Report.pdf.

Goodhart, C. A. E. and E. Perotti. 2013. Preventive Macroprudential Policy. *Journal of Financial Management, Markets and Institutions*. 1 (1). pp. 115–123.

Gruenewald, S. N. 2020. Climate Change as a Systemic Risk – Are Macroprudential Authorities up to the Task? *European Banking Institute Working Paper Series*. No. 62. https://ssrn.com/abstract=3580222 or http://dx.doi.org/10.2139/ssrn.3580222.

Honohan, P. 2019. *Should Monetary Policy Take Inequality and Climate Change into Account?* Washington, DC: Peterson Institute for International Economics. https://www.piie.com/sites/default/files/documents/wp19-18.pdf.

International Monetary Fund, Financial Stability Board, and Bank for International Settlements (IMF-FSB-BIS). 2016. Elements of Effective Macroeconomic Policies: Lessons from International Experience. https://www.imf.org/external/np/g20/pdf/2016/083116.pdf.

Kling, G., U. Volz, V. Murinde, and S. Ayas. 2021. The Impact of Climate Vulnerability on Firms' Cost of Capital and Access to Finance. *World Development.* 137. 105131. https://doi.org/10.1016/j.worlddev.2020.105131.

Kyriakopoulou, D., B. Chye, and L. Thio. 2020. *Tackling Climate Change: The Role of Banking Regulation and Supervision.* Official Monetary and Financial Institutions Forum. https://www.omfif.org/tacklingclimatechange/.

Molico, M. 2019. *Researching the Economic Impacts of Climate Change.* Ottawa: Bank of Canada. https://www.bankofcanada.ca/2019/11/researching-economic-impacts-climate-change/.

Morgan, J. 2020. *Financing Fossil Fuels Risks a Repeat of the 2008 Crash. Here's Why.* Geneva: World Economic Forum. https://www.weforum.org/agenda/2020/01/financing-fossil-fuels-repeat-2008-crash-heres-why/.

Network for Greening the Financial System (NGFS). 2019. *A Call for Action: Climate Change as a Source of Financial Risk.* Paris. https://www.ngfs.net/sites/default/files/medias/documents/ngfs_first_comprehensive_report_-_17042019_0.pdf.

Official Monetary and Financial Institutions Forum (OMFIF). 2019. *Central Banks and Climate Change.* OMFIF Special Report. https://www.omfif.org/wp-content/uploads/2020/02/ESG.pdf.

Paun, A., L. Acton, and W-S. Chan. 2018. *Fragile Planet: Scoring Climate Risks Around the World.* HSBC Global Research. London: HSBC. https://www.sustainablefinance.hsbc.com/carbon-transition/fragile-planet.

Pointner, W. and D. Ritzberger-Grunwald. 2019. Climate Change as a Risk to Financial Stability. *Financial Stability Report*. 38. pp. 30–45.

Randow, J. 2020. Lagarde Leverages Virus to Press for Greener Monetary Policy. *Bloomberg*. 15 September. https://www.bloomberg.com/news/articles/2020-09-15/christine-lagarde-fights-climate-change-through-monetary-policy-despite-covid.

Restoy, F. 2021. *The Role of Prudential Policy in Addressing Climate Change*. Basel, Switzerland: Bank for International Settlements. https://www.bis.org/speeches/sp211008.htm.

Schnabel, I. 2020. *Never Waste a Crisis: COVID-19, Climate Change and Monetary Policy*. Speech in Frankfurt am Main. 17 July. https://www.ecb.europa.eu/press/key/date/2020/html/ecb.sp200717~1556b0f988.en.html.

Schoenmaker, D. and R. Van Tilburg. 2016. What Role for Financial Supervisors in Addressing Environmental Risks? *Comparative Economic Studies*. 58 (3). pp. 317–334. https://doi.org/10.1057/ces.2016.11.

Schydlowsky, D. M. 2020. Prudential Regulations for Greening the Financial System: Coping with Climate Disasters. *Latin American Journal of Central Banking*. 1 (1–4). 100010. https://doi.org/10.1016/j.latcb.2020.100010.

Svartzman, R., P. Bolton, M. Despres, L. A. P. Da Silva, and F. Samama. 2021. Central Banks, Financial Stability and Policy Coordination in the Age of Climate Uncertainty: A Three-Layered Analytical and Operational Framework. *Climate Policy*. 21 (4). pp. 563–580. https://doi.org/10.1080/14693062.2020.1862743.

Taleb, N. N. 2010. *The Black Swan: The Impact of the Highly Improbable*. New York: Random House.

Tooze, A. 2019. Why Central Banks Need to Step Up on Global Warming. *Foreign Policy*. 20 July. https://foreignpolicy.com/2019/07/20/why-central-banks-need-to-step-up-on-global-warming/.

Villeroy de Galhau, F. 2020. *Speech by François Villeroy de Galhau: Paris 2020 Climate Finance Day*. Governor of the Bank of France. 29 October. https://www.bis.org/review/r201030b.pdf.

Volz, U. J., J. Beirne, N. A. Preudhomme, A. Fenton, E. Mazzacurati, N. Renzhi, and J. Stampe. 2020. *Climate Change and Sovereign Risk*. A. D. B. I. SOAS University of London, World Wide Fund for Nature Singapore, and Four Twenty Seven. https://eprints.soas.ac.uk/33524/1/Climate%20Change%20and%20Sovereign%20Risk_final.pdf.

Weidmann, J. 2020. *Combating Climate Change - What Central Banks Can and Cannot Do*. Bank for International Assessments. Speech at the European Banking Congress. 20 November. https://www.bis.org/review/r201120e.pdf.

Chapter 12

Central Banks and Climate Change

Jonathan Kearns, Anna Park, and Serena Alim[1]

12.1 Introduction

Given the broad and pervasive effects of climate change on economies, financial markets, and investor tolerance for risk, central banks are increasingly turning their attention to climate change.

Human activity is significantly contributing to climate change. Globally, average surface air temperatures have warmed by over 1°C since the mid-1800s and average sea levels have risen about 25 centimeters since 1880 (CSIRO 2002). And the frequency and severity of extreme weather events—heat waves, storms, etc.—has increased. In Australia, for example, average days with mean temperature above the 99th percentile rose from 1 day every 3 years in 1920–1930 to 14 days each year in 2010–2020 (Australian Government 2021).

The broad impact on society includes effects on economic activity and financial markets, both through the impact on the economy and market participants' risk tolerance. Central banks have taken action, as noted by expanding analysis and response to these developments.

[1] This work was completed while the authors were all working at the Reserve Bank of Australia. The authors would like to thank Ashvini Ravimohan for assistance on this work.

Categorizing the effects of climate change

The effects fall under three broad categories:

- *Acute physical risks* are the effects of extreme one-off events—floods, cyclones, bushfires, etc.—that damage infrastructure, harm livestock and crops, and disrupt the economy more broadly by hampering people's ability to work and hindering transportation.
- *Chronic physical risks* are the ongoing effects of climate change from rising temperatures, greater frequency of very hot days, and changes in rainfall patterns that reduce productivity of some economic activity, such as by lowering crop yields or discouraging tourists from visiting particular areas.
- *Transition risks* arise from changes in government policies, technology, and consumer preferences in reaction to climate change that can, for example, reduce the income generated from particular activities or assets, and so erode their value.

Because central banks' primary objectives relate to economic and financial market outcomes, they need to account for climate change in their policy decisions. Some central banks also have broader reasons for responding to climate change.

Overall, four issues in central banks' objectives and operations warrant a response. These include their (i) inflation and employment mandates; (ii) financial stability mandates; (iii) own operations including management of their portfolios of assets; and (iv) for some central banks, financial market development and supporting government policy objectives.

Central banks generally assess the impact of climate change on the first two of these objectives in a similar way. On the third objective—their own operations—some central banks have been more active than others. However, the greatest disparity in central banks climate change positions is on the fourth issue: whether or not to actively promote financial market developments that would help the economy better respond to the threat of climate change and support associated government policies.

Inflation and employment mandates

Almost all central banks have an inflation target (or, for a few, another nominal anchor such as an exchange rate target). In most cases, this target is one part of a dual mandate that also focuses on full employment or economic spare capacity.

The realization of acute risks of climate change can affect the dynamics of inflation and output and, at least in the near term, the level of inflation.

Climate change can result in more frequent and extreme supply shocks. Significant flooding in Australia in recent years, for example, has reduced supply and increased prices of fruit and vegetables. Before that, widespread droughts raised the price and reduced the availability of meat. Supply shocks can have wide-ranging effects on economic output. For example, flooding and storms can reduce mining output and disrupt shipping and other transport, which can in turn reduce exports or manufacturing output and retail sales. Short-term supply shocks tend to have less impact on employment, as employers generally do not permanently reduce employment in response to a transient shock, but short-term layoffs may result.

Central banks with flexible inflation targets can typically look through the effects of any such transient supply shocks, including those from extreme weather. However, if increases in inflation and, importantly, inflation expectations from a supply shock are persistent (including those at least partly attributable to climate change), then central banks may need to tighten policy.

Chronic physical risks and transition risks result in structural change in the economy as some economic activities become unprofitable, and others (eventually) take their place. How disruptive this structural change is will depend on whether it is anticipated and how rapidly it occurs. If structural change is abrupt then the productive capacity, and potential growth rate, of the economy will be lower, at least for a period of time. This would mean that a given level of output, or growth, would be more inflationary than otherwise, and so require a tighter setting of monetary policy.

When setting monetary policy, central banks should account for anything that influences their core mandates of inflation and employment, including the impact of weather events and the climate. Hence, analyzing the effects of climate change and responding to those effects has become a standard approach among most central banks. For example, the Bank of Canada states that "to fulfil its monetary policy mandate of keeping inflation low and stable, the Bank needs to understand the potential impacts of climate change on the macroeconomy and price stability (BOC 2021)." In the words of the Federal Reserve, "it is vital for monetary policymakers to understand the nature of climate disturbances to the economy, as well as their likely persistence and breadth, in order to respond effectively" (Brainard 2021). Table 12.1 provides examples of central banks' climate-related objectives.

Table 12.1: Examples of Central Bank Climate- or Sustainability-Related Objectives

Bank of Canada
- Assess the effects of climate change on the macroeconomy and price stability
- Evaluate the Canadian financial system's exposures to climate-related risks and improve associated risk management capacities
- Measure, mitigate, and report on the central bank's operational risks related to climate change
- Engage and collaborate with Canadian and international partners

Bank of England
- Ensuring the financial system is resilient to climate-related financial risks
- Supporting an orderly economy-wide transition to net zero emissions
- Promoting the adoption of effective TCFD-aligned climate disclosure
- Contributing to a coordinated international approach to climate change
- Demonstrating best practice through own operations

Bank of Japan
- Support the private sector's efforts on climate change
- Support financial institutions in identifying and managing their climate-related financial risks
- Deepen analysis on how climate change would affect the macroeconomy, including economic activity and prices, financial markets, and the financial system
- Strengthen efforts to promote investment in climate-related financial products, such as green bonds to foster development of financial markets

European Central Bank
- Managing and mitigating the financial risks associated with climate change and assessing its economic impact
- Promoting sustainable finance to support an orderly transition to a low-carbon economy
- Sharing expertise to foster wider changes in behavior

Monetary Authority of Singapore
- Strengthen the Singapore financial sector's resilience to environmental risks
- Develop a vibrant sustainable finance ecosystem to support Asia's transition to a low-carbon future
- Integrate climate risks and opportunities into our investment framework
- Reduce own carbon and environmental footprint to support Singapore's broader climate ambitions and commitment

Reserve Bank of New Zealand
- Monitor and manage its impact on climate
- Understand and incorporate the impact of climate change in its core functions
- Provide leadership as an institution

Riksbank (Swedish central bank)
- Work to ensure that its own operations gradually comply with international agreements such as the Paris Agreement
- Help to increase knowledge of the effects of climate change on the economy by contributing its own research and analyses
- Take a sustainability perspective in its asset purchases and in the management of the foreign exchange reserves under the framework of the Riksbank's mandate
- Promote increased transparency and reporting related to its climate footprint
- Promote regulations in the financial markets to reduce the risks climate change may entail for the financial system
- Actively participate in various international networks and partnerships to help reduce the risks of climate change at a global level

TCFD = Task Force on Climate-Related Financial Disclosures.
Source: Authors.

Some central banks see a broader objective to support the transition to a low-carbon economy as flowing from primary mandates. The Bank of Japan notes that supporting the private sector's efforts on climate change will help stabilize the macroeconomy in the long run, which is consistent with its mandate of achieving price stability and ensuring the stability of the financial system (BOJ 2021a). Similarly, some central banks highlight their role, drawing on research and analysis to raise awareness of the impacts of climate change. For example, one of the three core climate objectives for the European Central Bank (ECB) is "sharing our expertise to foster wider changes in behaviour" (ECB 2022a). The Reserve Bank of New Zealand's climate strategy includes "providing leadership as an institution," by helping support policy development and closing information gaps (RBNZ 2022). Many central banks also note the importance of contributing to collective efforts on climate and sustainability issues. The Bank of England, for example, aims to contribute to a coordinated international approach to climate change, including through its involvement with international groups.

Financial stability

Most central banks have a responsibility for the stability of the financial system. Some are also the prudential regulator and so have a direct role in overseeing the risks of individual institutions.

Climate change has the potential to increase both the likelihood of borrowers defaulting and the potential size of the lender's loss if borrowers default. Climate change can reduce the ability of borrowers to meet their repayments if it results in sustained decline in their income or makes it less reliable. Climate change can also lead to lower asset valuations if it reduces the assets' cash flows or makes them more volatile. Where those assets have been used as security for loans, asset price declines increase the potential losses that lenders face if borrowers default.

Individual financial entities can also be exposed to liability risk if they mismanage their climate risks. If the risks from climate change are not well managed by financial institutions, and they result in large losses for individual institutions or erode confidence in parts of the financial system, it could be detrimental to financial stability.

Many central banks highlight their role in understanding and managing the risks that climate change poses to financial institutions and financial stability. For example, the Monetary Authority of Singapore works to "strengthen the Singapore financial sector's resilience to environmental risks" (MAS 2022). The Bank of England has committed to "ensuring that the financial system is resilient to climate-related financial risks" (BOE 2022). Even where central banks are not prudential regulators, as part of a responsibility to support financial stability, they identify a role in improving the ability of firms and investors to understand and manage climate-related risks. For example, the Bank of Canada has committed to "evaluate the Canadian financial system's exposures to climate-related risks" (BOC 2021). The Reserve Bank of Australia, as part of the Australian Council of Financial Regulators, has a role to play in creating the framework that enables participants to manage climate change risks and opportunities (Kearns 2022).

Central bank operations and assets

Many central banks are also seeking to understand and manage the climate-related risks associated with their own operations. Central banks hold portfolios of assets to implement monetary policy, to facilitate foreign exchange transactions for the government and in case of the need for foreign exchange intervention. Since climate change could result in declines in asset prices, it is a risk affecting the value of the central bank's portfolio. How significant this risk is for a central bank depends on the composition of their portfolio. Central banks that hold only sovereign debt are likely to be less exposed than those that also hold debt or equity issued by firms with significant exposure to climate change. Some central banks have also examined the greenhouse gas emissions associated with their holdings of financial assets.

The Bank of Canada, for example, has committed to "measure, mitigate and report on the Bank's operational risks related to climate change," and to "review its financial market operations to consider climate-related financial risks and opportunities" (BOC 2021). As discussed later, central banks' actions associated with meeting their own risk management needs can also support other objectives, including the development of green financial markets or taking a leadership role. The Bank of England, for example, aims to "demonstrate best practice through our own operations" (BOE 2022).

Financial market development and support for government policies

Some central banks also have objectives for developing their financial system—in particular, greening their financial system—or supporting the government's policy objectives. Typically, these additional objectives are described as secondary to the central bank's primary inflation and employment goals.

Some central banks identify as an objective supporting an orderly economy-wide transition to net zero emissions, including by promoting sustainable finance. This includes central banks with explicit secondary objectives to support government policies in general, or climate policies specifically. For example, the Bank of England Act states that in relation to monetary policy, the objectives of the Bank of England shall be (i) to maintain price stability; and (ii) subject to that, to support the economic policy of Her Majesty's Government, including its objectives for growth and employment. And in a 2021 letter to the Bank of England governor, the United Kingdom treasurer has stated that the government's economic strategy includes "transition to an environmentally sustainable and resilient net zero economy" (HM Treasury 2021). Similarly, under the European Union (EU) Treaties, the ECB has a secondary objective to support general economic policies which help achieve EU objectives, acting within its mandate and without prejudicing its primary objective. The ECB notes that this includes protecting the environment (ECB 2021a).

As part of supporting the transition to a low-carbon economy, some central banks identify the development of markets for sustainable finance as an objective, which stems from their role in promoting the development of financial markets more broadly. For example, the Monetary Authority of Singapore's mission includes promoting a sound and progressive financial center, and aims to "work with financial institutions to develop a vibrant sustainable finance ecosystems to support Asia's transition to a low carbon future" (MAS 2022). The ECB lists "promoting sustainable finance to support an orderly transition to a low carbon economy" as one of its three core climate objectives (ECB 2022a). More broadly, many central banks have historically played a role in developing markets and guiding credit allocation.

Other central banks, in contrast, see their roles as more limited. The Federal Reserve, for example, has noted that while it has a responsibility to oversee climate-related financial risks as a bank regulator, broader policies addressing climate change would have distributional effects across firms and regions that are best made by governments. Indeed, the Federal Reserve has noted that "it would be inappropriate for us to use our monetary policy or supervisory tools to promote a greener economy or to achieve other climate-based goals" (Powell 2023).

Indeed, central banks often emphasize that while their actions can support climate mitigation, primary responsibility for climate change policy sits with government. For example, the ECB states that "governments should take the lead because they are primarily responsible for climate policy and have the most effective tools" while also noting that "the ECB also have a strong interest in helping address climate change...because climate risks affect how we do our job of keeping prices stable" (ECB 2021b). Or in the words of the Reserve Bank of New Zealand, "No single institution working alone can achieve meaningful progress on a global challenge such as climate change. Furthermore, it is not for financial policymakers to drive the transition to a low-carbon economy, nor is it our role to advocate one policy response over another. That is the role of government" (RBNZ 2022).

12.2 Central Bank Actions Related to Climate Objectives

Central banks' climate-related actions are similar in some dimensions but vary widely across others, reflecting differences in mandates and stated climate objectives. This section illustrates the range of climate-related actions by drawing on central banks' own statements. It is important to note that some actions may serve more than one of the four climate-related objectives noted earlier.

Given climate risks are becoming much more prominent, undertaking research and analysis has been important for central banks to understand the implications of climate change for their macroeconomic and financial stability mandates. This work is also seen as contributing to a leadership role. This has included developing analytical tools and models, as well as contributing to work to identify and address important gaps in the data. A number of central banks working with financial institutions have undertaken climate scenario exercises to help measure the potential financial risks to banks and understand how banks may adjust their business models in response.

Those with financial stability mandates and prudential responsibilities are also providing guidance and developing frameworks to support the management of climate-related risks by financial entities. While the specific actions vary considerably in line with individual central banks' role on financial stability, this can include providing supervisory guidance, improving disclosures, and developing sustainable finance taxonomies and frameworks (or supporting this work where responsibility sits with other policymakers).

Central banks may also, through their own actions, model good practice in the management of climate-related risks. The Bank of England, for example, in aiming to demonstrate "best practice though our own operations" is publishing the Taskforce for Climate-Related Disclosures-aligned climate-related financial disclosures, setting out how its 2050 net zero pledge will be met across all its physical operations and is greening its corporate bond portfolio (BOE 2022).

Some central banks frame their climate-related measures as "protective," designed to reduce the climate-related risks associated with their financial portfolios or market operations (Network for Greening the Financial System 2021). Sweden's Riksbank, for example, only buys bonds issued by companies deemed to comply with sustainability standards covering human rights, working conditions, environment, and anti-corruption. The Riksbank describes this approach as considering the financial risks associated with the purchase of those bonds, as "it is riskier to purchase bonds issued by companies that are in breach of these principles" (Sveriges Riksbank 2021).

Other central banks are implementing or considering "proactive" measures designed to promote a transition to a lower emissions economy. Often these central banks have explicit mandates to support their government's net zero objectives or to foster financial market development. The Bank of England, for example, has introduced climate-related criteria for corporate bonds to be eligible for purchases in its operations, with purchases "tilted" toward eligible firms with stronger climate credentials (BOE 2021). This aims to achieve a 25% reduction in the carbon intensity of their portfolio, and is aimed at supporting an orderly economy-wide transition to net zero. Some central banks also provide lending facilities for green or sustainable activities to support an orderly transition to a low-carbon economy. The Bank of Japan, for example, provides loans at a lower interest rate to banks that contribute to Japan's actions to address climate change, noting that this is "with a view to supporting private sector efforts on climate change" (BOJ 2021b).

The distinction between protective and proactive actions, however, is not always clear cut. Protective central bank actions associated with meeting their own risk management needs, like requiring climate-related disclosures in collateral frameworks, are also proactive because they support the development of green financial markets by improving the information available to price and manage these risks. In announcing its plan to decarbonize its corporate bond holdings, for example, the ECB said that "this aims to mitigate climate-related financial risks to the Eurosystem balance sheet. It also provides incentives for issuers to improve their disclosures and reduce their carbon emission in future" (ECB 2022b). Table 12.2 provides more examples.

Table 12.2: Examples of Changes to Monetary Policy Operations

Monetary Policy Portfolio	
Riksbank	Only buys bonds issued by companies deemed to comply with sustainability standards covering human rights, working conditions, environment, and anti-corruption.
European Central Bank	Tilting corporate bond holdings toward issuers with better climate performance.
Bank of England	Climate-related eligibility criteria for corporate bond purchase, with purchases "tilted" toward eligible firms that are stronger climate performers, targeting a 25% reduction in the carbon intensity of the portfolio.

Foreign Reserves Portfolio	
Sveriges Riksbank	A "sustainability perspective" is applied in the selection of assets in the foreign exchange reserves portfolio.
People's Bank of China	Will further increase the share of green bonds, limit investment in carbon-intensive assets, and incorporate climate risk factors into our risk management framework.
Reserve Bank of New Zealand	Purchased $100 million of BIS Green Bond Investment Pool. Considering taking a more "holistic" approach when choosing assets for foreign reserves portfolio, by considering expanding universe of sustainability-linked investment opportunities. They will look to support the development of sustainability-linked markets.

Collateral Framework	
European Central Bank	Will limit share of assets issued by entities with a high carbon footprint that can be pledged as collateral. The new regime aims to reduce climate-related financial risks in ECB credit operations.
Bank of England	Collected climate-related information in its due diligence questionnaires since 2019 and recently started asking counterparties prepositioning residential loan collateral to submit additional information on energy efficiency.
People's Bank of China	Expanded collateral for medium-term lending facility to include SMEs and green bonds.

Investment or Other Portfolios	
Norges Bank (Norway)	Manages the government's sovereign wealth fund (Government Pension Fund Global) and engages in "responsible investment" practices. Norges Bank has divested from assets due to concerns around climate-related risks.
Monetary Authority of Singapore	Taking actions to reduce the equities portfolio emissions intensity, set expectations for external managers and exclude investments in thermal coal mining and oil sands activities.
Bank of Canada	Developing practical steps to integrate ESG considerations into investment decisions and reporting.

Lending Facilities	
People's Bank of China	Offering low interest loans to banks that help firms cut carbon emissions.
Bank of Japan	Provide loans at a lower interest rate to banks that use the funds to invest in climate-friendly projects in Japan.
Reserve Bank of India	Added green projects to its quota for "priority lending," which banks must hit when they make loans.

BIS = Bank for International Settlements; ECB = European Central Bank, ESG = environmental, social, and governance; SMEs = small and medium-sized enterprises.
Source: Authors.

Challenges for central banks

Central banks are making significant progress in assessing the impact of climate change and tailoring their response. But the economic and financial impacts of climate change raise challenges for central banks, just as they do for financial institutions, businesses, households, and government entities.

There is a good scientific understanding of the impact of climate change on mean temperatures; however, there is significant uncertainty about the effect on the frequency and severity of extreme weather events. More frequent and severe extreme weather events are likely to result in greater structural change and more persistent supply shocks, which increases the uncertainty for central banks in how to respond to climate change. Central banks are accustomed to dealing with uncertainty about the future state of the economy, but with climate change there is less information to characterize the scale of the uncertainty.

A second challenge is that the time frame over which climate change is playing out is much longer than the horizon central banks typically consider. Central banks generally focus on the next 2–3 years when setting monetary policy and perhaps out to 10 years when considering the longer dynamics relevant for financial stability. In contrast, the horizon over which the impacts of climate change are playing out is much longer; typically climate change projections are made for many decades, often out to the end of the century.

A third challenge for central banks is that climate change is likely to result in more frequent and larger supply shocks. But monetary policy is best able to respond to changes in demand, monetary policy usually does not respond to supply shocks since it cannot address their underlying cause. Larger and more frequent supply shocks could then make it harder for central banks to achieve their objectives, for example, if climate change induced supply shocks were to make inflation expectations less stable.

A fourth challenge for central banks is that the drivers of climate change, and the issues that arise from it, are very different to those that central banks are used to analyzing. As a result, central banks are needing to invest in a new range of skills, new data, and different models (for example, with longer horizons and finer granularity of industries or geographic representations) as they continue to assess how ongoing climate change affects all aspects of their objectives and operations.

References

Australian Government. 2021. 2021 SoE Climate Changes in Number of Days When the Australian Area-Averaged Mean Temperature Is above the 99th Percentile. Canberra. https://data.gov.au/data/dataset/2021-soe-cli-010.

Bank of Canada (BOC). 2021. Bank of Canada Announces Climate Change Commitments for COP26. Press release. 3 November. https://www.bankofcanada.ca/2021/11/bank-canada-announces-climate-change-commitments-for-cop26/.

Bank of England (BOE). 2021. Greening Our Corporate Bond Purchase Scheme. London. https://www.bankofengland.co.uk/markets/greening-the-corporate-bond-purchase-scheme.

_____. 2022. Climate-Related Financial Disclosure. London. https://www.bankofengland.co.uk/prudential-regulation/publication/2022/june/the-bank-of-englands-climate-related-financial-disclosure-2022.

Bank of Japan (BOJ). 2021a. Strategy on Climate Change. The Bank of Japan's Strategy on Climate Change. Speech at the Japan National Press Club. 27 July. https://www.boj.or.jp/en/about/release_2021/rel210716b.pdf.

_____. 2021b. Outline of Climate Response Financing Options. https://www.boj.or.jp/en/mopo/mpmdeci/mpr_2021/rel210922c.pdf.

Brainard, L. 2021. Why Climate Change Matters for Monetary Policy and Financial Stability. Speech at the Federal Reserve Bank of San Francisco at The Economics of Climate Change Conference. 8 November.

Commonwealth Scientific and Industrial Research Organisation (CSIRO). 2002. State of the Climate 2022 Report. Canberra. https://www.csiro.au/-/media/OnA/Files/SOTC22/22-00220_OA_REPORT_StateoftheClimate2022_WEB_221115.pdf.

European Central Bank (ECB). 2021a. ECB Presents Action Plan to Include Climate Change Considerations in its Monetary Policy Strategy. Press release. 8 July. https://www.ecb.europa.eu/press/pr/date/2021/html/ecb.pr210708_1-f104919225.en.html.

———. 2021b. *Climate Change and the Strategy Review*. Frankfurt. https://www.ecb.europa.eu/home/search/review/html/climate-change.en.html.

———. 2022a. *ECB Climate Agenda*. Frankfurt. https://www.ecb.europa.eu/press/pr/date/2022/html/ecb.pr220704_annex~cb39c2dcbb.en.pdf.

———. 2022b. ECB Takes Further Steps to Incorporate Climate Change into Its Monetary Policy Operations. Press release. 4 July. Frankfurt. https://www.ecb.europa.eu/press/pr/date/2022/html/ecb.pr220704~4f48a72462.en.html.

HM Treasury. 2021. Remit for the Monetary Policy Committee. Letter from the Chancellor of the Exchequer to the Bank of England. 3 March. London. https://www.bankofengland.co.uk/-/media/boe/files/letter/2021/march/2021-mpc-remit-letter.pdf?la=en&hash=C3A91905E1A58A3A98071B2DD41E65FAFD1CF03E.

Kearns, J. 2022. *Climate Change Risk in the Financial System*. Speech at Credit Law Conference "Managing Financial Services Risks in an Age of Uncertainty." 24 August. Sydney. https://www.rba.gov.au/speeches/2022/sp-so-2022-08-24.html.

Monetary Authority of Singapore (MAS). 2022. *MAS Sustainability Report*. Singapore. https://www.mas.gov.sg/-/media/MAS-Media-Library/publications/sustainability-report/2022/MAS-Sustainability-Report-2021_2022.pdf?la=en&hash=4B850000BE2CE8279A1913D29763C0370E3B8E70.

Network for Greening the Financial System. 2021. *Adapting Central Bank Operations to a Hotter World – Reviewing Some Options*. March. Paris. https://www.ngfs.net/sites/default/files/media/2021/06/17/ngfs_monetary_policy_operations_final.pdf.

Powell, J. 2023. *Central Bank Independence and the Mandate – Evolving Views*. Speech at the Sveriges Riksbank Symposium on Central Bank Independence. 10 January. Stockholm. https://www.federalreserve.gov/newsevents/speech/powell20230110a.htm.

Reserve Bank of New Zealand (RBNZ). 2022. *Our Climate Change Strategy*. Wellington. https://www.rbnz.govt.nz/about-us/how-we-work/our-climate-change-strategy#:~:text=The%20strategy%20 focuses%20on%20ways,for%20New%20Zealand%27s%20 financial%20system.&text=The%20Reserve%20Bank%20of%20 New,sustainable%2C%20productive%20and%20inclusive%20economy.

Sveriges Riksbank. 2021. *Climate Report – Climate Risks in Policy Work*. Stockholm. https://www.riksbank.se/globalassets/media/rapporter/ klimatrapport/2021/the-riksbanks-climate-report-december-2021.pdf.

Chapter 13

Climate Risk Disclosure and Green Technology Innovation—A Survey

Zijun Zhao

13.1 Introduction

Under the threat of climate risk, policymakers, standard-setters, and regulators need to be more active in efforts to combat climate change and stabilize the financial system, helping to lead the transition to a cleaner economy, including in the area of information transparency.

Motivated by threats of climate-related risk on the financial market, and recognizing the role of policy tools to combat such risk, this chapter surveys the literature in green finance, environmental accounting, management of climate risk disclosure, and green technology innovation to provide more clarity about the policy implications of enhancing information transparency and facilitating green innovation. In so doing, it can shed more light on the role that policymakers and regulators can play in these areas.

These factors have a pivotal function in mitigating the devastating impact of climate change and in achieving national decarbonization targets (e.g., Christensen, Hail, and Leuz 2021; Popp, Newell, and Jaffe 2010). Accurate and adequate information is critical for financial market efficiency, particularly in relation to climate risks.[1] Investors and stakeholders in recent times are increasingly demanding firm-level, climate-related information to assess whether a company is operating under a sustainable

---

[1] Attention in the chapter focuses on carbon transition risk, which is about uncertainty in policy or technological innovation aspects generated when reducing carbon dioxide (CO_2) emissions and transitioning to a cleaner economy, since the discussion here is closely related to policy and technology factors for revealing and reducing emissions.

model. For example, by focusing on the United States (US) and global markets, Bolton and Kacpercyk (2021a, 2021b) confirm that carbon emission risk (or so-called carbon transition risk)—as a systematic risk—is priced into the financial market. A follow-up paper by Bolton and Kacpercyk (2021c) further illustrates that carbon disclosure reduces uncertainty about emissions and thus leads to a lower cost of capital for individual firms.

Consistent with the importance of climate disclosure, debate is intense about "whether to stimulate voluntary disclosure or enforce mandatory requirements by the governments." Section 13.2 therefore analyzes the issue by considering the benefits of both disclosure regimes (section 13.2.1) and their potential costs and policy implications (section 13.2.2).

Governments and nongovernment organizations have recently been strongly encouraging green technology innovation, recognized as a pivotal instrument to reduce emissions and accelerate the speed of achieving national decarbonization goals. The United Nations Framework Convention on Climate Change (UNFCCC) Technology Executive Committee points out that technological innovation is a critical accelerator and enhancer of efforts to implement federal climate action and achieve Sustainable Development Goals.[2]

Section 13.3 therefore outlines the key features and role of green innovation in transitioning to cleaner energy (section 13.3.1). Moreover, as green technologies help curb carbon dioxide (CO_2) emissions and improve firms' environmental performance, it would be interesting to explore whether green innovation can be extended to affect corporate disclosure decisions (section 13.3.2), and what policy tools (such as regulation, taxation, and subsidies) could motivate green innovation (section 13.3.3).

Christensen, Hail, and Leuz (2021) conducted a comprehensive literature review of the determinants and potential consequences of voluntary and mandatory disclosure for corporate social responsibility topics. However, this chapter differs in its focus only on climate disclosure, a crucial component of corporate social responsibility reporting. More importantly, corporate social responsibility disclosure encompasses a broad range of environmental, social, and governance topics and thus has more complex incentives to disclose. For example, polluting firms might choose instead to reveal better human rights or social services behaviors to offset a negative social image rather

---

[2] See UNFCCC (2017).

than concentrating on reducing greenhouse gas (GHG) emissions. Grewal, Hauptmann, and Serafeim (2021) note for example that Exxon Mobil has high corporate social responsibility disclosure scores but poor environmental, social, and governance performance ratings in the same year. Therefore, a policy that motivates firms to report corporate social responsibility information might not lead to better environmental performance and transparency with key information about a firm's carbon risk. Consistent with this perspective, it would be necessary to analyze climate risk disclosure solely, and then consider the policy implications to identify which policies could lead to better disclosure and superior environmental performance.

The chapter extends the analysis to discuss the political determinants of green innovation and their effects on disclosure decisions, which are not covered in Christensen, Hail, and Leuz (2021).

13.2 Climate Risk Disclosure

Researchers, commentators, and governors suggest that information transparency promotes well-functioning capital markets (e.g., Ilhan et al. 2021; Ross 2021). The view is growing that climate risk is systematic with adverse impacts on the financial market (e.g., In, Park, and Monk 2019; Bolton and Kacpercyk 2021a). In this situation, robust disclosure of climate-related information is required for multidimensional audiences to assess firms' climate risk and to price the risk into capital markets. This section discusses the pros and cons of both voluntary and mandatory disclosure.

13.2.1 Benefits of Voluntary and Mandatory Climate Disclosure

Voluntary disclosure provides firms (the board and managers) to decide whether and what factors to disclose: disclosure decisions are a trade-off between their costs and benefits (Leuz 2010; Goldstein and Yang 2017; Christensen, Hail, and Leuz 2021). In other words, firms have incentives to disclose corporate information when it can benefit them. This section summarizes the primary benefits of voluntary climate disclosure in four areas.

First, disclosure improves information transparency and reduces uncertainty about emissions to help investors assess firm-level climate risks, reducing firms' cost of capital (Bolton and Kacpercyk 2021c; Matsumura, Prakash, and Vera-Muñoz 2022). Second, consistent with a signaling theory, voluntary disclosure conveys a positive signal that the company is engaging (or going to engage) in decarbonization, facilitating efficient allocation of capital to this type of firm best positioned to transition to low-carbon business models (Ross 2021). Third, a report on firm-level environmental performance, especially superior performance, could reduce the penalty for emissions on the capital market (Matsumura, Prakash, and Vera-Muñoz 2014), or mitigate unwelcome political attention (e.g., Innes and Sam 2008). For example, by focusing on S&P 500 firms, Matsumura, Prakash, and Vera-Muñoz (2014) find that CO_2 emissions are penalized by the capital market, but firms that voluntarily disclose such emissions are punished less than non-disclosers.[3] Finally, as a nonfinancial disclosure with multidimensional audiences, climate disclosure could be motivated by social responsibility (Bolton and Kacpercyk 2021c). In this situation, disclosing GHG emissions (especially positive news on emissions) enhances firms' reputation and social trust. It thus increases sales and long-term relationships with stakeholders (Flammer, Toffel, and Viswanathan 2021).

Despite the benefits of corporate climate disclosure, it is still insufficient to justify a mandate since corporates would have incentives to provide information voluntarily when benefits exceed costs (Leuz 2010; Leuz and Wysocki 2016; Christensen, Hail, and Leuz 2021). So why execute mandatory disclosure? To answer, Leuz (2010) and Christensen, Hail, and Leuz (2021) analyze financial and nonfinancial corporate social responsibility reporting.

First and most important, mandatory reporting creates externalities, which may not be sufficient under a voluntary condition. Existing studies suggest that voluntary climate risk disclosure is more prevalent among large firms (Hahn and Kühnen 2013; Li, Lu, and Nassar 2021). However, small firms could also cause excessive pollution and adverse impacts on the environment. Therefore, enforcing mandatory standards helps monitor and regulate corporate-polluting activities. Meanwhile, firms usually use disclosure as a tool to gain financial benefits (such as a lower cost of capital). They are thus not responsible for providing positive externalities to society under a voluntary regime.

In this case, government intervention is required to address externalities. One can infer from this perspective that a mandatory climate report is required when the social value of disclosed information exceeds its private value to firms, to increase positive externalities (i.e., lower GHG emissions). For instance, by exploiting a unique law in the United Kingdom that mandates GHG emissions

---

3   The empirical evidence in Matsumura, Prakash, and Vera-Munoz (2014) illustrates that the median value of firms that disclose CO_2 emissions is about $2.3 billion higher than nondisclosing firms.

disclosure, Jouvenot and Krueger (2021) and Downar et al. (2021) demonstrate that firms reduced emissions after the mandatory disclosure. Tomar (2021) focuses on the US GHG Reporting Program's impact, which mandates thousands of industrial facilities to measure and report their GHG emissions. The empirical evidence illustrates a 7.9% reduction in GHG emissions following the mandatory rule. Tomar's study also finds that peer benchmarking is the mechanism driving this result.

Second, mandates improve standardization and comparability of reported climate information. Bernow et al. (2019) argue that investors complain about a lack of comparable information. EY (2021) demonstrates that even increasing the number of companies disclosing under the Task Force on Climate-Related Financial Disclosures recommendations, the complement of disclosed elements is still insufficient. In this context, mandatory reports create a standardized corporate reporting regime, which enhances the audience's understanding and clarity about the disclosed information. Consistent with this insight, robust climate disclosure regulations and clear policies are required to improve the quality and comparability of disclosure.

Third, mandatory regulations are legislated and therefore have better investigation power to detect violations and a more potent force to impose penalties if their rules are violated. More robust fraud detection and user information protection preserve the financial system's stability and investors' confidence in the financial market, allowing firms to commit more credibly. It is therefore conjectured here that a mandatory standard is more necessary in countries where the disclosure quality is low under a voluntary regime, or with salient industries with high CO_2 emissions, since they have a high probability of fraud or violation issues.

13.2.2 Costs and Implications of Voluntary and Mandatory Climate Disclosure

However, the implication of voluntary or mandatory climate disclosure might not mean that a "one-size-fits-all" regime is suitable for all countries and all firms. In some cases, voluntary disclosure has more benefits than mandatory disclosure and vice versa. On the one hand, voluntary disclosure provides more discretion to firms, which could be cost-saving, as it enables managers to convey private information to markets at less cost (Leuz 2010). Discretion allows managers to fine-tune the needs of firms and investors, avoiding the problems of a one-size-fits-all approach. Conversely, regulators might not be as well informed as the managers of firms about specific cost–benefit trade-offs. Christensen, Liu, and Maffett (2020) point out that by increasing transparency beyond the value-maximizing level, greater financial reporting enforcement reduces the equity value of firms. However, discretion is not perfect as it can be used opportunistically to hide poor firm performance or related agency problems.

Next, the costs of disclosure make various companies reluctant to provide emissions information voluntarily, impeding market efficiency and reallocation of capital in financial markets. Generally, the direct costs involve measuring and reporting emissions (Bolton and Kacpercyk 2021c), which might be more affordable for large companies. Ilhan et al. (2021) state that institutional investors' demand for climate information is greater for large firms with relatively lower information production costs. The disclosure cost might cause a dramatic negative impact on firm value under a mandatory regime—if disclosure benefited firms, they would disclose before the mandate. Chen, Hung, and Wang (2018) examine the impact of mandatory corporate social responsibility disclosure requirements in the People's Republic of China and find a negative impact on firms' profitability. Besides, the indirect costs of the disclosure include revealing business secrets to competitors—proprietary costs (e.g., Verrecchia 1983; Breuer, Leuz, and Vanhaverbeke 2019), which could be a more severe concern under a mandatory regime, since all targeted firms are forced to disclose. The Financial Stability Board (2019) points out that in a Task Force on Climate-Related Financial Disclosures survey, almost half of respondents indicate that disclosing scenario analysis assumptions is difficult because of their inclusion of confidential business information.

Therefore, in some cases, even though mandatory climate disclosure could generate economic benefits and positive social externalities that exceed the benefits of voluntary disclosure, mandatory disclosure could still be politically expedient. This is true even though it might lead to far from innocuous unintended consequences (Christensen, Hail, and Leuz 2021). For instance, publicly listed firms are usually targeted for the adoption of mandatory reporting. However, firms could avoid being regulated and penalized by shifting to unregulated (private) firms (Leuz, Triantis, and Wang 2008; Kamar, Karaca-Mandic, and Talley 2009; DeFond and Lennox 2011). By now, the empirical evidence of the economic consequences of regulatory avoidance strategy is still sparse. However, one can conjecture that it could undermine national decarbonization targets or even have negative economic implications for capital markets.

To sum up, how firms use discretion in reporting should be a firm-specific issue, and firm-level characteristics, such as corporate governance, might shape it. In the big picture, policymakers and governors need to better understand and clarify which policy tool or tools may suit different circumstances and realities, including different scenario analyses based on national legal environments and national cultural backgrounds. For example, Djankov et al. (2003) suggest that regulation is particularly compelling when there is inequality in the distribution of resources or "weapons" among the private parties. Leuz (2010) suggests creating a "global player segment" in which member firms play by the same reporting rules and face the same enforcement.

13.3 Green Technology Innovation

Political attention to green innovation is growing and seeking renewable alternatives. The United Kingdom announced £16 million in new government funding in 2021 to promote green innovation as it continues efforts to help businesses reduce their carbon emissions.[4] Germany committed €2.5 billion for investment in electric vehicle infrastructure and a €9,000 subsidy per vehicle to encourage green initiatives.[5] This section reviews the potential impact of green innovation on climate disclosure decisions and the consequences of environmental policy tools on innovation activities.

13.3.1 Role of Green Technology Innovation

Green technology innovation has been recognized as a pivotal instrument to reduce emissions and accelerate the speed of achieving national decarbonization goals. For example, innovation in renewable solar and wind energy helps reduce energy-related emissions; improvement in new biofuel or vehicle efficiency helps decrease mobility-related emissions (Tobelmann and Wendler 2020). As a result, green inventors could successfully reduce CO_2 emissions, emissions intensity, or the rate of change in emissions. Recently, national and pan-national organizations are strongly encouraging green innovation activities as an effort to combat climate change and to fulfill "net neutral" commitments. OECD (2010) explains that the ability of firms to

---

[4]   See the UK Government at https://www.gov.uk/government/news/government-invests-over-116-million-to-drive-forward-green-innovation-in-the-uk.

[5]   See Six Ways that Governments Can Drive the Green Transition at EY. https://www.ey.com/en_gl/government-public-sector/six-ways-that-governments-can-drive-the-green-transition.

generate new technologies to reduce pollution and its effects —can drastically decrease the costs of future environmental policy. The UNFCCC Technology Executive Committee also points out that technological innovation is a critical accelerator and enhancer of efforts to implement national climate action and achieve global objectives.[6]

13.3.2 The Impact of Green Technologies on Disclosure

Green innovation that helps reduce CO_2 emissions and meet environmental targets might increase the benefits of climate disclosure—and incentivize firms to disclose voluntarily. If so, appropriate policies to motivate green innovation, would lead the transition to a cleaner energy and stabilize the financial market.

Some studies agree that superior environmental performance is a determinant of corporate disclosure. Clarkson et al. (2008) explain that firms with superior environmental activities will convey their "type" by demonstrating their compliance with objective standards, which are difficult to mimic by inferior firms. In other words, superior performers have stronger incentives to disclose their emissions and signal their type to attract investors and preserve their reputation. Conversely, inferior performers would reveal less and hide their disappointing capacity transfer to a cleaner economy.

Drawing on these studies, an argument is that green technologies drive firms' incentives to disclose through an improved environmental outcome, making firms more confident to demonstrate their type. For example, Clarkson et al. (2008, 2011) find a positive association between corporate environmental performance and the level of environmental disclosures. Li et al. (2018) suggest that green innovating firms have more propensity to disclose their emissions for their confidence, capability, and motivation.

However, legitimacy theory stands for an alternative assumption that better environmental performance is negatively related to environmental disclosure decisions. In particular, legitimacy theory argues that firms report environmental performance under social pressure in an attempt to legitimize their long-term operation (Solomon and Lewis 2002; Mobus 2005; Cho and Patten 2007). In this situation, firms with better environmental performance face less legitimacy pressure and, thus, lower incentives to

---

[6] See UNFCCC (2017).

disclose (Li et al. 2018). From the perspective of green innovation impact on the environment, an alternative conjecture is that new technologies reduce emissions and thus mitigate legitimacy concerns for corporations, which might reduce incentives to report their climate-related news voluntarily.

In addition, proprietary costs could impede corporate disclosure, as mentioned in section 13.2.2; this might be particularly true for innovative firms since technological innovation usually involves professional knowledge or business secrets. In this context, green innovation would weaken firms' incentive to disclose, due to concern about divulging technical information to competitors.

13.3.3   What Are the Determinants of Green Innovation

In keeping with their pivotal capacity in reducing emissions, policymakers and standard-setters need to understand what determines green innovation and develop granular policies as tools to stimulate innovation and decarbonization. Based on the discussion in section 13.3.2, if green innovation is a determinant of climate disclosure, then effective policies would be to motivate firms to seek and utilize renewable technologies, which in turn could enhance voluntary disclosure for corporates (i.e., two birds with one stone). On the other hand, if green innovation would undermine disclosure decisions, then more progressive policies are required to facilitate innovation without impeding corporate disclosure. For example, more appropriate protection for intellectual property might mitigate concerns about proprietary costs of disclosure, which in turn improve green innovation and climate disclosure. The rest of this chapter reviews and summarizes existing studies on the impact of laws and regulations on innovation, which might shed more light on this area and assist policymakers and standard-setters in their decision-making.

The OECD (2010) report highlights the importance of utilizing environmental policy tools to promote green innovation. The report emphasizes that without pricing in the cost of pollution, companies may lack motivation to pursue sustainable and environmentally responsible practices. In order to address this issue, governments can apply a range of policy tools, including regulatory mechanisms such as carbon taxes, as well as market-based tools like tradable permits. Furthermore, governments can offer subsidies to support research and development in the field of cleaner technologies, providing an additional boost to green innovation.

First, OECD (2010) highlighted the effectiveness of market-based tools, such as carbon taxes, in providing incentives for innovation.[7] It is because the costs of emissions motivate polluters to seek and utilize cleaner alternatives. Moreover, Deloitte's (2015) research delves into the impact of the US Federal solar investment tax credits, which provide a 30% tax credit for solar energy systems installed on residential or commercial properties. Their findings reveal that since the solar investment tax credit was passed in 2006, $66 billion has been invested in solar installations nationwide. However, the increase in corporate taxation might lead to opposite results. Mukherjee, Singh, and Žaldokas (2017) find that an increase in state-level corporate tax in the US leads to fewer patents and less investment in research and development (R&D), indicating that higher corporate taxes reduce innovation incentives. The authors also find that innovation increases less following tax cuts.

Second, tests of the impact of regulatory tools have mixed results. Lerner (2009) uses global data and finds that policies on patent protection are positively related to the innovation rate. However, Mezzanotti (2021) illustrates that strict patent law raises patent litigation risks and impedes innovation activities for firms in the US.

Third, Howell (2017) investigates the impact of US government R&D subsidies on innovation and finds a positive result, indicating that early-stage grants mitigate financial constraints firms face and enable firms to invest in reducing technological uncertainty. However, Kong (2020) illustrates that government spending reduces corporate innovation due to resource diversion.

To sum up, the mixed results identified in prior studies suggest that this area is also less likely to have a "one-size-fits-all" approach that positively affects green innovation in all situations and all countries. This supports the need for a more comprehensive analysis by policymakers. For example, policies should be more granular to suit different circumstances by using various scenario analyses based on national legal environments, national cultural backgrounds, differences between geographic regions, and levels of national financial wealth.

---

[7] The case studies examining the innovation impacts of the United Kingdom's Climate Change Levy on fossil fuels and electricity found that firms subject to the full rate of the levy patented more than firms subject to a reduced rate, only one-fifth of the full rate.

13.4 Conclusions

To mitigate the adverse impacts of climate risk on the financial market and facilitate the transfer to a more environmentally sustainable economy, governments can play a critical role in increasing information transparency in relation to the firm-level, climate-related performance and actions and incentivize firms to seek and use cleaner technologies. Drawing on existing literature, this chapter discusses the relative merits of incentivizing voluntary climate disclosure or enforcing mandatory regulations.

To sum up, the implications of voluntary and mandatory climate disclosure suggest that a "one-size-fits-all regime" is not suitable for all countries and all firms. For example, in some cases, discretion allows managers to fine-tune the needs of their firms. However, standardized information provided under a mandatory regime helps investors compare and assess firms' sustainable models. In addition, mandatory enforcement helps promote social externalities, which might be inadequate under a voluntary regime, but the costs of mandatory disclosure might erode firm value.

Because green technology innovation can enhance and accelerate efforts to fulfil "net-neutral" commitments, the chapter also discusses whether green innovation could affect climate disclosure decisions. One argument is that cleaner technologies reduce emissions and thus increase firms' incentives to disclose positive news to the public. Another is that there might be concerns that better environmental performance reduces firms' legitimacy pressure and, thus, their incentives to disclose.

Finally, the chapter considers different environmental policy tools (such as regulation, tax, and subsidies) to motivate corporate green innovation. Again, the mixed results in prior research imply that there is no perfect policy tool to fit all situations. In all, these mixed results are part of an initial attempt to shed more light on this area to assist policymakers and standard-setters in decision-making.

Further work to enhance understanding and clarity about which policy tool or tools may suit different circumstances and realities could include different scenario analyses based on national legal environments, national cultural backgrounds, differences between geographic regions, and levels of national financial wealth.

References

Bernow, S., J. Godsall, B. Klempner, and C. Merten. 2019. More than Values: The Value-Based Sustainability Reporting that Investors Want. *McKinsey and Company*. 7 August.

Bolton, P. and M. Kacperczyk. 2021a. Do Investors Care about Carbon Risk? *Journal of Financial Economics*. 142 (2). pp. 517–549.

_____. 2021b. Global Pricing of Carbon-Transition Risk. *NBER Working Paper Series*. No. 28510. Cambridge, MA: National Bureau of Economic Research.

_____. 2021c. Carbon Disclosure and the Cost of Capital. https://ssrn.com/abstract=3755613.

Breuer, M., C. Leuz, and S. Vanhaverbeke. 2019. Reporting Regulation and Corporate Innovation. *NBER Working Paper Series*. No. 26291. Cambridge, MA: National Bureau of Economic Research.

Chen, Y. C., M. Hung, and Y. Wang. 2018. The Effect of Mandatory Corporate Social Responsibility Disclosure on Firm Profitability and Social Externalities: Evidence from China. *Journal of Accounting and Economics*. 65 (1). pp. 169–190.

Cho, C. H. and D. M. Patten. 2007. The Role of Environmental Disclosures as Tools of Legitimacy: A Research Note. *Accounting, Organizations and Society*. 32 (7–8). pp. 639–647.

Christensen, H. B., L. L. Hail, and C. Leuz. 2021. Mandatory Corporate Social Responsibility and Sustainability Reporting: Economic Analysis and Literature Review. *Review of Accounting Studies*. 26 (3). pp. 1176–1248.

Christensen, H. B., L. Y. Liu, and M. Maffett. 2020. Proactive Financial Reporting Enforcement and Shareholder Wealth. *Journal of Accounting and Economics*. 69 (2). 101267.

Clarkson, P. M., Y. Li, G. D. Richardson, and F. P. Vasvari. 2008. Revisiting the Relation between Environmental Performance and Environmental Disclosure: An Empirical Analysis. *Accounting, Organizations and Society*. 33 (4–5). pp. 303–327.

———. 2011. Does It Really Pay to Be Green? Determinants and Consequences of Proactive Environmental Strategies. *Journal of Accounting and Public Policy*. 30 (2). pp. 122–144.

DeFond, M. L. and C. S. Lennox. 2011. The Effect of SOX on Small Auditor Exits and Audit Quality. *Journal of Accounting and Economics*. 52 (1). pp. 21–40.

Deloitte. 2015. Credits and Incentives Provide Green for Going Green. https://www2.deloitte.com/us/en/pages/tax/articles/credits-and-incentives-provide-green-for-going-green.html.

Djankov, S., E. Glaeser, R. La Porta, F. Lopez-de-Silanes, and A. Shleifer. 2003. The New Comparative Economics. *Journal of Comparative Economics*. 31 (4). pp. 595–619.

Downar, B., J. Ernstberger, S. Reichelstein, S. Schwenen, and A. Zaklan. 2021. The Impact of Carbon Disclosure Mandates on Emissions and Financial Operating Performance. *Review of Accounting Studies*. 26 (3).

EY. 2021. If Climate Disclosures Are Improving, Why Isn't Decarbonization Accelerating? https://assets.ey.com/content/dam/ey-sites/ey-com/en_gl/topics/assurance/ey-if-the-climate-disclosures-are-improving-why-isnt-decarbonization-accerlerating.pdf.

Financial Stability Board. 2019. Task Force on Climate-Related Financial Disclosures: Status Report. https://www.fsb.org/wp-content/uploads/P050619.pdf.

Flammer, C., M. W. Toffel, and K. Viswanathan. 2021. Shareholder Activism and Firms' Voluntary Disclosure of Climate Change Risks. *Strategic Management Journal*. 42 (10). pp. 1850–1879.

Goldstein, I. and L. Yang. 2017. Information Disclosure in Financial Markets. *Annual Review of Financial Economics*. 9. pp. 101–125.

Grewal, J., C. Hauptmann, and G. Serafeim. 2021. Material Sustainability Information and Stock Price Informativeness. *Journal of Business Ethics*. 171. pp. 513–544. https://doi.org/10.1007/s10551-020-04451-2.

Grougiou, V., E. Dedoulis, and S. Leventis. 2016. Corporate Social Responsibility Reporting and Organizational Stigma: The Case of "Sin" Industries. *Journal of Business Research*. 69 (2). pp. 905–914.

Hahn, R. and M. Kühnen. 2013. Determinants of Sustainability Reporting: A Review of Results, Trends, Theory, and Opportunities in an Expanding Field of Research. *Journal of Cleaner Production*. 59. pp. 5–21.

Howell, S. T. 2017. Financing Innovation: Evidence from R&D Grants. *American Economic Review*. 107 (4). pp. 1136–64.

Ilhan, E., P. Krueger, Z. Sautner, and L. T. Starks. 2021. Climate Risk Disclosure and Institutional Investors. *Swiss Finance Institute Research Paper*. No. 19–66 / *European Corporate Governance Institute—Finance Working Paper*. No. 661/2020.

In, S. Y., K. Y. Park, and A. Monk. 2019. Is "Being Green" Rewarded in the Market? An Empirical Investigation of Decarbonization Risk and Stock Returns. Unpublished working paper. Stanford Global Project Center. https://papers.ssrn.com/sol3/papers.cfm?abstract_id=3020304.

Innes, R. and A. G. Sam. 2008. Voluntary Pollution Reductions and the Enforcement of Environmental Law: An Empirical Study of the 33/50 Program. *The Journal of Law and Economics*. 51 (2). pp. 271–296.

Jouvenot, V. and P. Krueger. 2021. Mandatory Corporate Carbon Disclosure: Evidence from a Natural Experiment. https://ssrn.com/abstract=3434490.

Kamar, E., P. Karaca-Mandic, and E. Talley. 2009. Going-Private Decisions and the Sarbanes-Oxley Act of 2002: A Cross-Country Analysis. *Journal of Law, Economics, and Organization*. 25 (1). pp. 107–133.

Kong, L. 2020. Government Spending and Corporate Innovation. *Management Science*. 66 (4). pp. 1584–1604.

Lerner, J. 2009. The Empirical Impact of Intellectual Property Rights on Innovation: Puzzles and Clues. *American Economic Review*. 99 (2). pp. 343–348.

Leuz, C. 2010. Different Approaches to Corporate Reporting Regulation: How Jurisdictions Differ and Why. *Accounting and Business Research*. 40 (3). pp. 229–256.

Leuz, C., A. Triantis, and T. Y. Wang. 2008. Why Do Firms Go dark? Causes and Economic Consequences of Voluntary SEC Deregistrations. *Journal of Accounting and Economics*. 45 (2). pp. 181–208.

Leuz, C. and P. D. Wysocki. 2016. The Economics of Disclosure and Financial Reporting Regulation: Evidence and Suggestions for Future Research. *Journal of Accounting Research*. 54 (2). pp. 525–622.

Li, D., M. Huang, S. Ren, X. Chen, and L. Ning. 2018. Environmental Legitimacy, Green Innovation, and Corporate Carbon Disclosure: Evidence from CDP China 100. *Journal of Business Ethics*. 150 (4). pp. 1089–1104.

Li, J. M., S. Lu, and S. Nassar. 2021. *Corporate Social Responsibility Metrics in S&P 500 Firms' 2017 Sustainability Reports*. Rustandy Center for Social Sector Innovation: The University of Chicago.

Matsumura, E. M., R. Prakash, and S. C. Vera-Munoz. 2014. Firm-Value Effects of Carbon Emissions and Carbon Disclosures. *The Accounting Review*. 89 (2). pp. 695–724.

———. 2022. Climate Risk Materiality and Firm Risk. https://ssrn.com/abstract=2983977.

Mezzanotti, F. 2021. Roadblock to Innovation: The Role of Patent Litigation in Corporate R&D. *Management Science*. 67 (12). pp. 7362–7390.

Mobus, J. L. 2005. Mandatory Environmental Disclosures in a Legitimacy Theory Context. *Accounting, Auditing and Accountability Journal*. 18 (4). pp. 492–517.

Mukherjee, A., M. Singh, and A. Žaldokas. 2017. Do Corporate Taxes Hinder Innovation? *Journal of Financial Economics*. 124 (1). pp. 195–221.

Organisation for Economic Co-operation and Development (OECD). 2010. *Taxation, Innovation and the Environment*. Paris: OECD Publishing.

Popp, D., R. G. Newell, and A. B. Jaffe. 2010. Energy, the Environment, and Technological Change. *Handbook of the Economics of Innovation*. Vol. 2. Elsevier. pp. 873–937.

Ross, S. 2021. The Role of Accounting and Auditing in Addressing Climate Change. *Center for American Progress*. 1 March. https://www.americanprogress.org/article/role-accounting-auditing-addressing-climate-change/.

Solomon, A. and L. Lewis. 2002. Incentives and Disincentives for Corporate Environmental Disclosure. *Business Strategy and the Environment*. 11 (3). pp. 154–169.

Toebelmann, D. and T. Wendler. 2020. The Impact of Environmental Innovation on Carbon Dioxide Emissions. *Journal of Cleaner Production*. 244. 118787.

Tomar, S. 2021. Greenhouse Gas Disclosure and Emissions Benchmarking. Working paper. https://ssrn.com/abstract=3448904.

United Nations Framework Convention on Climate Change (UNFCCC). 2017. *Technological Innovation for the Paris Agreement*. Bonn, Germany. https://unfccc.int/ttclear/misc_/StaticFiles/gnwoerk_static/brief10/8c3ce94c20144fd5a8b0c06fefff6633/57440a5fa1244fd8b8cd13eb4413b4f6.pdf.

Verrecchia, R. E. 1983. Discretionary Disclosure. *Journal of Accounting and Economics*. 5 (1). pp. 179–194.